CRISTINE DAHL, CTC
Foreword by Jean Donaldson

Good
Dog
101

EASY LESSONS TO TRAIN YOUR DOG THE HAPPY, HEALTHY WAY

SASQUATCH BOOKS
SEATTLE

For Anders, without whom this book would still be a dream. Now it is a dream come true. You are my husband, my best friend, my inspiration, my sounding board, my security—my all. And for Maddison, Oliver, and Tippens whose divine patience, endless humor, and purity have allowed me years of wonder and learning, and have provided the spark for the fire that drives me every day. To David and Susan, who not only allowed my exploration into animals of all kinds, but encouraged it with the patience of saints and the never-ending support a kid needed to follow her dream.

Printed in the United States of America
Published by Sasquatch Books
Distributed by PGW/Perseus
15 14 13 12 11 10 09 08 07   9 8 7 6 5 4 3 2 1

Book design & composition: Kate Basart/Union Pageworks
Cover design: Kate Basart/Union Pageworks
Cover photographs:
Top image: © Don Hammond/ Design pics/ Corbis
Bottom image: Animal Attractions/ Photodisc Photography/ © 2005 Getty Images

Library of Congress Cataloging-in-Publication Data

Dahl, Cristine.
    Good dog 101 : easy lessons to train your dog the happy, healthy way / Cristine Dahl ; foreword by Jean Donaldson.
       p. cm.
    Includes index.
    ISBN-13: 978-1-57061-517-7
    ISBN-10: 1-57061-517-9
    1. Dogs—Behavior. 2. Dogs—Training. I. Title. II. Title: Good dog one hundred and one.

SF433.D34 2007
636.7'0887—dc22
                         2007030241

Sasquatch Books
119 South Main Street, Suite 400
Seattle, WA 98104
(206) 467-4300
www.sasquatchbooks.com
custserv@sasquatchbooks.com

Contents

Foreword

A confession: I am a bona fide dog training book snob. I like what I like, which collectively turns out to be an incredibly tiny percentage—a handful really—of actual available books and products. Of course I am in no way unique in my snobbery. There are wine snobs, literary snobs and word-usage-o-philes, foodies, movie plot device nose-wrinklers, and fitness superiority snobs.

I know other dog training book snobs. We flock together. My preferred strategy to training manuals is avoidance. But because this is my field I dutifully trudge through a fair amount of the offerings. Some of them I'd judge as "not terrible" and some, well let's just say that some have decent bits here and there (even saying that much for some books though sure is a stretch). Most training manuals I just don't like. Techie terms are woefully misused; "behaviorists" spend pages and pages wading us through their imaginings of what the dog is thinking, knowing, and planning; the method is Marquis de Sade; the dog's "rank" is solemnly discussed ad nauseum; or the writing is just painful. Usually I find a combination of three or four out of these five peeves. It makes me Eeyore but sometimes I feel like if I have to read one more treatise on preceding dogs through doorways, written by someone—we're talking adults, mind you, with credit cards, a mortgage, the power of speech, and the right to bear arms, members of the most technologically advanced species that has ever walked the planet—who feels insecure about whether they are "dominant" over their dog or, amazingly, feels desperately control-freaky about the *dog's* opinion about who's dominant, I will have to jump off a cliff.

Cristine Dahl, though, was rather a breath of fresh air from the first time I met her. Smart, clear-headed, and a talented trainer. Compassionate, a dog's advocate. Conferred not a single more gift, she would be marvelous. But there's more. As a former student of mine, she was a spongy learner and natural critical thinker, someone who could communicate. As a trainer, Cristine is unsurpassed as a medium to translate the tangles of animal learning science to people with ever more compressed time and assaulted by wrong information from all sides. She likes her clients, fiercely in fact, no small feat in our profession. She has the patience for people that the rest of us have mainly for dogs. And her communication style is clean and clear. The greatest virtue of *Good Dog 101* is the crispness and complete absence of impenetrable gibberish. It is fully user-friendly. The next greatest, and related, virtue is that none of it is made up. The arguments, management pointers, and training techniques are grounded in sound behavioral science.

I am so glad Cristine took the time to write this book. Seattle's lucky secret is now available to all.

—Jean Donaldson,
Founder and Director
San Francisco SPCA Academy for Dog Trainers
May 21, 2007

Acknowledgments

Thank you to Jean Donaldson, Janis Bradley, and Dr. James Ha, for your generous support and involvement in this process. I am grateful to Sasquatch Books for this opportunity and their continued hard work and support, and I owe a special debt of gratitude to Terence Maikels for his unmitigated patience and willingness to make this project real. And for thanks beyond words I acknowledge my clients and their furry companions. You are the reason I fight for smart, humane training and get up in the face of defeat to fight again. And for furry coats, velvety paws, wagging tails, and warm breath, I acknowledge Lucy, Coby, Puff, Bijou, Stevie, Aster, Scooter, Lucky, Sophie, Charlotte, Henry, Samson, Winston, Dude, Louie, Rufus, Spencer, Mr. Sparky, Mr. Dudley, Logan, Senta, Rocco, Yankee, Torrey, Sydney, Red, Frodo, Saffron, Polly, Whidbey, Birdie, Otis, Marco, Hugo, Missy, Cuddles, Chopper, Archie, Rosie, Kiley, Luna, Molly, Stella, Anabelle, Bailey, Huckleberry, Lily, Dahlia, Porter, James, Marina, Taylor, Sucia, Taco, Lola, Junah, Max, Comet, Roxie, Roo, Rufus, Martha, Helo, Bacci, Sylph, Royal, Alki, Brock, Grace, Marie Claire, Dexter, Marble, Finney, Hazel, Brodie, Finley, Dash, Hailey, Rooney, Poncho, Tippy, Riley, Tahoe, Klaus, Angus, Bo, Painter, Tulip, Nelson, Shasta, Sophie, Manny, Anna, Elle, Zeus, Apollo, Jack, Scarlett, Barclay, Toby, Dutch, Dakota, Troy, Daisy, Marley, Tommy, Millie, and Woody.

PART I

An Introduction to My Training Philosophy

Few things will divide a room of current day dog trainers faster than a discussion about methods, philosophies, and credentials. Unfortunately, because of the highly unregulated landscape of the professional canine field in the United States, today's companion dog owner must solely navigate through the rough terrain of theories, opinion, and hype to piece together a useful way to cultivate a well-behaved dog.

The two most popular camps consist of those who hold firmly to the traditional/military model of training and those who have abandoned those methods in search of a kinder, more scientific approach.

While the former of these styles is rooted in rich history and is the most prevalent method of training currently used in the United States, it is popularly criticized by modern animal welfare authorities such as the Society for the Prevention of Cruelty to Animals (SPCA) and the American Humane Association (AHA) as being too heavy handed, unscientific, and outdated.

The latter camp, most commonly known as "positive trainers," are criticized by trainers in the traditional/military camp as being too theoretical and practically soft, and using technical methods that are too complicated for most owners to use.

The method I present in this book borrows from each of these camps, but sifts through the hype and technical challenges plaguing both styles. It's meant to give owners a user-friendly, practical, efficient, and kind way of training their dogs using techniques that fit with today's lifestyle—one that is often time-starved, hectic, and busy. The style itself is borne of one hundred years of evolution of the field, but with special consideration of the sophisticated dog/human relationship of today. By retaining time-proven methods and abandoning those known to be ineffective or unkind, this new method is revolutionary.

While my approach adheres to AHA guidelines for humane training, I have not abandoned the traditional approach entirely and still employ some traditional techniques that I find useful on a practical level.

In the first section of the book, I set out to explain the basics of my teachings and how they were developed. To help you understand the current state of training, I begin with a brief history of dog training in the United States followed by an introductory and balanced look at both the traditional/military model and popular alternative methods. I have also included a chapter dedicated strictly to an in-depth analysis of the traditional/military model. While it remains the most recognizable style to dog owners, this model is loaded with defects, the severity of which is seldom recognized.

CHAPTER 1

A Brief History of Dog Training

While today's companion dog enjoys a life that is richer than it has been for companion dogs at any other time in history, his behavioral health faces a crisis of epic proportions. The same dog who beds down on a plush mattress, eats from a designer bowl, and is considered a part of the family as much as any other member is regularly subjected to highly popular training and behavioral techniques considered severely outdated, uncivilized, and even inhumane.

Unwitting but well-meaning owners routinely employ behavioral approaches based on little more than anecdote, or worse, consider them acceptable simply because highly marketable TV personalities, celebrities, and/or best-selling authors have touted them. While the field of canine behavior does include highly qualified professionals worthy of imparting behavioral coaching, the vast majority of current practitioners have little to no formal education in animal behavior, and consider a "love of dogs," "years of experience," "breed knowledge," and an "innate understanding of canine psychology" actual credentials.

There is a current movement among the top credible professionals in the field to educate both owners and professionals so that they have a cutting-edge, scientifically based understanding of canine behavior. This will help owners ensure a smart training and behavioral approach that will benefit their families for years to come.

The Creation of the Traditional/Military Model

The history of dog training in the United States is really very young. Still the most accepted and prevalent method used in our country is called the *traditional/military model*. To understand how training in our country arrived at its current state, we need only to trace its history back a few decades.

While the birth of current training methods on U.S. soil took place in the mid-twentieth century, the seeds of these methods were being cultivated on German ground in the early 1900s.

Born in 1878, Colonel Konrad Most can be credited with the conception of the companion animal training movement. Most's methods are firmly rooted in strict obedience, focus on physical correction, stern voice and techniques, and defense and guarding. At the age of 28, Colonel Most was appointed police commissioner at the Royal Prussian Police Headquarters in Saarbrücken, Germany. Here, he began training service dogs and instructed the constabulary on all training and management of police dogs from 1906 to 1914. In 1912, Most was appointed principal of the State Breeding and Training Establishment at Berlin, where the focus of his training shifted to service personnel needs and criminal tracking.

In 1914, World War I erupted and Colonel Most was assigned the task of training German Army dogs on the Eastern Front one short year before being granted control of all Army canine efforts on both the Eastern and Western Fronts.

When WWI ended, Colonel Most acted as both head of the Canine Research Department of the Army High Command and as head authority on canine training to the Finnish Government for Finnish Canine Services.

In 1931, both the Canine Research Society and the German Society for Animal Psychology were founded, and both credited Colonel Most with their creation. By the late 1940s, Colonel Most headed the Experimental Department of the Tutorial and Experimental Institute for Armed Forces' Dogs and acted as Technical Principal of a massive training center called the North German Dog Farm.[1]

By the time of Colonel Most's death in 1954, his methods had been applied to tens, if not hundreds, of thousands of dogs in Germany.

Colonel Most's own manual, *Abrichtung Des Hundes* (Training of the Dog), states his methods evolved of his own accord. One can say, then, that Colonel Most was the first in a long line of self-taught dog trainers. While admitting he consulted a number of training texts during his early years, Colonel Most largely discarded these references and established his own techniques based on experience and observation.

While dogs were regularly used in military action by many countries during WWI, including Germany, England, and France, the United States did not formally acknowledge the usefulness of dogs in war until World War II. It is worth mentioning that while many accounts of dogs being used in military action before WWII by the U.S. Army do exist and can be validated, the U.S. military did not recognize canine efforts officially for the first time until 1942.[2]

One of the most noteworthy efforts by civilians took place shortly after the bombing of Pearl Harbor. Unsolicited by the military, Alene Erlanger, a well-known and respected breeder, took on the project of proposing and organizing a nationwide civilian effort to coordinate and train dogs for the military. Until this time, only one book on dogs, a field manual on canine care and transport in the Arctic, existed in the U.S. Army library.[3]

Erlanger's efforts, paired with those of other influential individuals of the time, including Leonard Brumbly of the Professional Handlers Association, obedience authority Dorothy Long, banker and director of the American Kennel Club Harry Caesar, and *New*

York Sun columnist Arthur Kilbon, engaged in preliminary discussions on the topic of recruiting civilian dogs for military use. A key contributor to this effort was Felician Philippe, an Italian authority on the military dog efforts in Europe.

Still unsupported by the military, this small group of individuals established the Dogs for Defense (DFD) program in 1942. In short order, the DFD used its highly connected network of leaders to organize kennel clubs, trainers, and volunteers across the United States in hopes of presenting an irresistible package to the military that would satisfy the needs of the nation while acknowledging the importance of the American dog in war efforts.[4]

At the same time, the American Theater Wing was also searching for a feasible program to help the U.S. military effort. After a series of private meetings, Quartermaster General Major General Edmund Gregory approved a trial program of 200 sentry dogs as depot defense.

Approved by General Gregory, the DFD was appointed the agency in charge of canine recruitment and training in March 1942. This date is considered the official recognition of dogs being accepted into the U.S. military.

A tremendously successful recruitment effort headed by Harry Ceasar enlisted the help of 402 U.S. kennel clubs. As these clubs operated privately and independent of one another, the training effort lacked consistency and standardization and, therefore, was seen as useless to the Army. To redeem the program, Alene Erlanger authored the technical training manual *TM 10-396—War Dogs*, and produced a series of training films. This effort was rewarded by General Gregory's order for 125,000 dogs for use by the Navy, Army, Marines, and Coast Guard.[5]

This marks the inception of the movement to establish training and reception facilities across the United States for the purpose of taking in, screening, and training civilian dogs for military use.

With the aid of propaganda, the companion animal training movement continued to progress. Unlike today's country of divided opinions of war, the citizens enjoyed an unrivaled sense of patriotism in the WWII era and civilians took their role in helping the military succeed very seriously. During these few short years,

tremendous propaganda efforts—photographs, newspaper articles, special articles, flyers, posters, popular personalities, films,
and even presidential support—communicated the dog's role in
war. Numerous photos of civilians, even children, honorably handing over the family dog to the local processing facility circulated
throughout the general population and can be seen in historical
documents today.

The next prominent and lasting influence on today's behavioral
and training climate is William Koehler. Koehler was officially recognized as a trainer in 1942 at the Pomona Ordnance Base in California, a processing facility for the Japanese. Shortly thereafter, he
was transferred and appointed as Principal Trainer at the War Dog
Reception and Training Center in San Carlos, California.[6]

Because of the classified status of operations at these military
establishments, we can only speculate about the exact nature of his
training approach while working for the military. However, much
is known about the methods he employed after the end of the war.

It is widely accepted that Koehler's methods were based very
heavily on obedience. Beginning in 1946 as chief trainer for the
largest open membership dog club in the United States, the Orange
Empire Dog Club, Koehler was responsible for leading an obedience training effort of unrivaled magnitude. From this date forward, Koehler's resume lists significant involvement in numerous
breed clubs, field dog classes, specialized and general obedience
instruction, and Hollywood dog training enterprises.

While Koehler's resume is impressive, it does not include a formal education in animal behavior or credentials in dog training
any different than those of Colonel Most. Koehler evolved his own
style of training, never indicating it was based on anything other
than his personal style, biases, observations, and experience.

After the war era, Koehler took his dog training philosophy
to Hollywood. He is credited with work in the movies *The Ugly
Dachshund* (1966), *That Darn Cat!* (1965), *Those Calloways*
(1965), *Disneyland* (1964), *The Incredible Journey* (1963), *Big Red*
(1962), *The Shaggy Dog* (1959), and *Around the World in Eighty
Days* (1956).

The great number of training facilities today, including obedience and kennel clubs, show circuits, and even franchises, were
founded by people who were a part of the efforts I describe in
the previous paragraphs. The majority of professional trainers in
the United States today have credentials that exclude any formal,
proven, academic, and/or scientifically based training. Most will
list their experience with dogs, observations, work with a mentor,
familiarity with a few books (although ones written by authors
who also lack formal education), completion of a certification
program, genuine love and appreciation for the dog, and "understanding of how a dog thinks" as qualifications.

Development of Alternative Training Methods

Because of early but widespread influences, the landscape of today's
training field is packaged differently than it was a few years ago.
The term "military" has been abandoned, and friendlier-looking
personalities have replaced stern, heavy-handed military-type
trainers. But the methods used by Colonel Most, Koehler, and their
followers are still predominant in the United States. Beneath this
mammoth movement of the traditional/military model of training
has sprung a smaller, grassroots type of effort geared toward alter-
natives to these styles.

The beginning of this movement, known as the *positive* or
clicker training movement, can greatly be credited to trainer Karen
Pryor. While Pryor enlisted alternative behavior modification techniques as early as the 1960s, her very different style using a noisemaker called a "clicker" only became popularized in dog training
in the late 1980s. Holding an impressive resume of formal education in animal behavior and behavioral psychology, Pryor has been
a tremendously influential force in the effort to abolish archaic
and unfounded training methods in favor of kinder, smarter, more
effective, and relevant ones. Nonetheless, her influence remains
dwarfed by the massive influences of military and traditional
training.

As the positive movement began to gain popularity, animal welfare organizations and a small number of training facilities and individual trainers embraced its focus on kind methods and modified their training techniques to treat dogs more humanely. In more recent years, many larger breed clubs, training facilities, and pet supply chains offering training have attempted to gear their training programs to a more positive approach as well.

While new celebrity dog trainers have come onto the scene in recent years, none can be credited with having a revolutionary impact on the field. The two methods introduced here, the traditional/military model and the alternative positive approach, remain the two pillars of theory structuring today's behavior modification landscape. Understanding their historical roots enables you to fully explore each model independently.

1. Konrad Most, *Training Dogs, A Manual* (Great Britain: The Anchor Press Ltd, 1954).

2. Michael G. Lemish, *War Dogs: A History of Loyalty and Heroism* (Washington, DC: Brassey's, 1996).

3. Ibid.

4. Ibid.

5. Ibid.

6. William R. Koehler, *The Koehler Method of Dog Training* (New York: Howell Book House, 1962).

CHAPTER 2

The Military/Traditional Model of Training

The predominant method of training used today, the military/traditional model, is still heavily rooted in the history from which it arose. Though it's often confusingly packaged using terms such as "pack theory," "alpha method," "dog psychology," "leadership," "natural," "energy," "obedience," and even, on rare occasion, "positive," the underlying approach is still considered traditional, as it rises from the traditional, aka military, model of training I introduced in the previous chapter. Despite its vast and varied lingo and somewhat varying applications, the underlying theory of the traditional model is based on leadership—establishing the humans in the family as the heads of the pack and the canines as submissive to the humans, with the most harmonious relationship being one in which roles are clearly defined and rank is static.

The foundation for the model is simple: Dogs (as descendants of wolves) originally lived in packs in the wild and, therefore, naturally are accustomed to living in a pack setting. In the 1940s, a very limited series of small studies was conducted to better understand the social hierarchies and structures by which wolves live. These studies were conducted with no intention of applying the findings to domesticated dog training. However, because the timing of the published study results coincided with the end of World War II, and as the public's new interest in better understanding dog psychology had piqued, the findings were readily packaged with the other aspects of companion animal behavioral care. Given genetic similarities between dogs and wolves, the very catchy idea of training a dog by his "natural" method of living was accepted with tremendous ease.

According to the military/traditional model, a number of guidelines must be established for the in-home pack. The most common guidelines are:

- Dog must eat after human.
- Dog must walk behind human and pass through doors after human.
- Dog must never be allowed to have his head above human's head.
- Dog must never sleep on human bed.
- Dog must never be allowed on human furniture.
- Dog must not pull on leash.
- Dog must never initiate and break eye contact first.
- Dog must never show any level of aggression, including growling, snarling, or snapping.
- Dog must never jump on human.
- Dog may never be allowed to win at games such as Tug and fetch.
- Dog must never squirm in human's hold.

The list goes on, but the general idea is that any possible display of canine dominance over human family members must be thwarted immediately.

According to the military/traditional model, the fallout of a lax pack structure is aggression. It is clear that dogs are predators; they have a big snoot, sharp teeth, powerful jaws, and even a belly filled with special enzymes to digest not only kibble but also bone, raw meat, and putrid flesh. As part of the military/traditional model, the primary goal is to set up a strong enough pack environment to derail aggression in dogs.

Inserting yourself into the established pack mindset of the dog is easy to do and understand. Once the general idea is established ("human be dominant, dog be submissive"), you can apply the system to almost any situation, from play to rest to ignoring cues to acts of aggression.

When you combine the deep natural need for humans to circumvent aggression in dogs out of fear for potential injuries with the very user-friendly idea of becoming part of the pack, it's easy to see how this model of training has remained so popular over the past eighty or so years.

Practical Application of the Traditional Model

The military/traditional model of training (which, for the sake of simplicity, will be referred to as the traditional model from here on) focuses very heavily on the symptom of a behavior rather than its cause. For example, if a dog is barking, the traditional model concentrates on eliminating barking regardless of its purpose or cause. If a dog is chewing on something he's not supposed to chew on, the traditional model punishes chewing. If a dog is aggressing on a leash at other dogs, the traditional model focuses on banishing the symptom(s) of aggressing: growling, barking, lunging, pulling, or showing teeth.

To modify behavior, the traditional model uses *positive punishment* and *negative reinforcement* to modify behavior. Please note, in the science of behavior, "positive" does *not* mean lovely, wonderful, and kind, as it does in the general human vernacular. Likewise, "negative" does *not* mean horrible, painful, and not so lovely. These terms are used in a mathematical way. So "positive" simply means the addition of something. Likewise, "negative" refers to the removal of something.

Also, a "punishment" is something done to bring down a behavior in frequency and/or intensity. "Reinforcement" is something done to support or increase a behavior in frequency and/or intensity.

To illustrate traditional methods, I've listed a couple of examples to demonstrate both positive punishment and negative reinforcement techniques.

Example: Barking

Methods of *positive punishment* include yelling at the dog, squirting him with a water bottle, hitting him over the snoot, and grabbing hold of his nose. The positive here is the addition of a thing: yelling, squirting, hitting, holding. This is considered punishment because the behavior being modified (barking) decreases in frequency and intensity.

On the other hand, methods of *negative reinforcement* include pinching his ear until he's quiet and then releasing, and holding a choke chain tight until he stops barking, then releasing. The negative here is the removal of the thing causing discomfort: ear pinch, choke chain hold. This is considered reinforcement because the desired behavior (to be quiet) increases in frequency and intensity.

Example: Pulling on Leash

Methods of *positive punishment* include applying a pinch/prong collar and leash popping (giving a stern, firm jerk on a choke chain). The positive here is the addition of a thing: pressure and discomfort from collar or jerk of chain. This is considered punishment because the behavior being modified (pulling on leash) decreases in frequency and intensity.

On the other hand, methods of *negative reinforcement* include releasing the pinch/prong collar when he stops pulling, and stopping leash pops when the leash is loose. The negative here is the removal of the thing causing discomfort: holding on pinch/prong collar, or popping of choke chain. This is considered reinforcement because the desired behavior, to stop pulling and walk on a loose leash, increases in frequency and intensity.

The Traditional Model and Obedience

Because of its focus on behavioral symptoms and pack behavior, the traditional model is very, very deeply anchored by obedience and, to this day, the main focus of the method is to create an obedient dog: one who listens to commands and responds in a timely and correct fashion. This objective fits beautifully with the hierarchy of the home: dog listens to commands and order is maintained, thereby thwarting any possible dissonance or serious behavioral problems.

Common obedience cues are sit, stay, down, come, stand, lie down, wait, and heel. They also may encompass more creative commands such as go-to, settle, don't jump, and do tricks. The popularity of obedience training has persisted since the 1950s, when originally it was borne out of military calls and then later was adopted by U.S. breed clubs and the American Kennel Club (AKC). These clubs have tremendous presence in the United States today, much as they did in the mid-twentieth century. The majority of today's largest obedience schools and even private training and behavior facilities are run by people directly hailing from the traditional movement or by staff that has been trained by its original pioneers.

Famous Practitioners of the Traditional Method

There are several lasting strains of the traditional model of training being distributed throughout the United States today, the most accepted of which can be found written in popular books and shown on widely broadcast television networks.

Cesar Millan: The Dog Whisperer

Cesar Millan is popularly known as "The Dog Whisperer" and is featured on a regular broadcast of the same name on the National

Geographic network. He has authored two books and has numerous training and behavior modification videos.

Millan is perhaps the most widely publicized traditional trainer of the current day. His philosophy is based in establishing dog owner as pack leader and never allowing dogs to shift rank from submissive to dominant. He also emphasizes the human impact on today's dysfunctional human/canine relationship—that humans have spoiled the companion dog to such a degree that the dog's natural state has been so far removed that he can't help but misbehave.

Millan also argues for the need for dogs to get back to their dog roots. In other words, as they are not humans and have certain dog needs, they should be treated as dogs. One of these needs is exercise, and another is balance in the pack. According to his philosophy, dogs both emit and sense energy before anything else; thus, it is a basis for their behavior and is imperative that owners assert dominance over their dogs using only the appropriate energy.

It's important to note that like most traditional trainers, Millan has no formal education in any discipline of animal behavior or learning. Millan attributes his early interest in dog training to his grandfather, Teodoro Millan Angulo. While managing cattle on a farm in Mexico, Teodoro used dogs to manage the herds and to protect land and property. As a young boy, Cesar would regularly visit the farm and observe these interactions. Later, as a young adult, Cesar observed dogs in a veterinary hospital and grooming salon and while employed as a kennel boy at a training facility in California. He credits much of his theoretical knowledge to the two books he read at the beginning of his career: Dr. Bruce Fogle's *The Dog's Mind* and Dr. Leon Whitney's *Dog Psychology*.[1] Millan states his own credentials as intuition, a gift, a passion, experience, and observation.

The two key elements of Millan's approach are discipline and physical exercise. The beginning of his best-selling book *Cesar's Way* outlines how he has cared for his own dogs and those dogs who visited his Dog Psychology Center, stressing their enjoyment of four hours of "vigorous exercise alternat[ed] with moderate exercise and rest" followed by several more hours of the pack following him.[2] He is very keen on establishing and maintaining his role as the Alpha wolf in his pack and describes the interactions of each of these dogs in terms of his role in the pack and dominance and submission.

While Millan packages and labels his methods as psychology, his techniques are consistent with the traditional model: he utilizes positive punishment and negative reinforcement, but couches these terms with dominance and pack theory, applying them to behavioral symptom and trigger rather than cause. For example, Millan deems the barking dog as one who has lost his rank in the pack. The owner has become complacent in his role of establishing and maintaining dominance and, therefore, the dog is acting out in an attempt to reestablish his rank.

While the vast majority of his philosophies jive with the traditional model flawlessly, his approach also includes some elements that are not consistent with mainstream traditional training; for example, the need for dogs to work for their food. He also observes dog/dog interactions with alarming detail and departs from the traditional model by attempting to diminish the breed biases owners can perpetuate. Millan also emphasizes the importance of preparing a dog for a stressful situation, such as moving or going to the vet, and avoiding discipline out of anger.

The reoccurring concept throughout Millan's book and television episodes is the idea of energy. He emphasizes the importance of understanding a dog's energy, an owner understanding his own energy, and the energy shared between them. Millan also uses phrases in his behavioral approach to explain the dog's feelings such as jealous, insecure, terrified, dominant, and submissive.

As an example of Millan's teaching, in an episode of the TV show *The Dog Whisperer* called "Dog Park Duke," Duke, a male adult Doberman, started a scuffle with another dog at the dog park. To positively punish Duke, Cesar took hold of Duke's prong collar, jerked his head into a Sit, then forced him into the ground in a Down, and then onto his side, and held him in place. As negative reinforcement, during the same interaction, Cesar held Duke in the position on the ground in front of and next to the dog with whom he was scrapping until Duke exhibited submission behavior. Then Duke was allowed up.

Another example of Millan's use of positive punishment and negative reinforcement can be demonstrated in another episode of *The Dog Whisperer* called "Walking Opie." In that episode, Opie, a male mixed-breed adult, strained to meet passing dogs whenever he was on leash. As positive punishment, Millan used both leash jerks and holds in conjunction with knee bumps to correct Opie from attempting to interact with another dog as it walked by. In the same interaction, Millan negatively reinforced Opie by releasing his leash, and stopped kneeing him when he refused to acknowledge the dog.

In both examples, Millan explained that the owner's inability to correct his or her dog's behavior stemmed from his inability to assert dominant energy. In each case, the focus of the behavior modification was the behavioral symptom: scrapping and attempting to greet another dog, respectively.

Another procedure that Millan regularly employs is *flooding*. Flooding is a technique of immersing a dog in an environment that will cause him fear, anxiety, or aggression until he reaches a breaking point. This is identical to flooding therapy used with humans, such as having a person overcome her fear of heights by skydiving or a fear of spiders by allowing them to crawl all over her body. In flooding, the goal is to effectively push the dog over his reactivity threshold for a period intense and long enough to override his response.

The Monks of New Skete

Another very popular traditional presence in the current training and behavior modification landscape are the Monks of New Skete. Collectively, they have written three books, two of which are very popular among dog owners: *The Art of Raising a Puppy* and *How to Be Your Dog's Best Friend: The Classic Training Manual for Dog Owners*.

Like Cesar Millan and most traditional trainers, the Monks do not claim any formal education in any discipline of animal behavior or learning. Instead, their approach is a derivative of spiritual and cultural studies, paired with a history of their German Shepherd breeding program at the New Skete monastery dating back to circa 1973. They state their qualifications as experience, a natural knowledge, intuition, and listening to and reading dog reactions. These traditions were passed on through the years to new monks at the monastery by oral account.

Like Millan's approach, the Monks' philosophy is also based on establishing the dog owner as pack leader, and never allowing dogs to shift rank from submissive to dominant. Living their lives among a group of German Shepherds, the Monks also emphasize the need for a highly structured, disciplined, clearly defined relationship between canine and human based in obedience and respect.

While the Monks do acknowledge the need for training in the traditional sense, they also state the importance of not only training but also "educating" a dog holistically. This approach relies on establishing human dominance by asserting Alpha status as well as using direct eye contact, appropriately limited praise, and swift and adequate punishment.

The Monks also use phrases in their behavioral approach to explain the dog's inner thoughts and feelings such as "he knows," "he understands," "he recognizes," and "he feels."

Interestingly, the Monks also use terminology similar to Millan's such as "natural training" and "leadership." Though they claim to have manufactured a unique method of their own, drawing from the techniques of other schools of training methodology, their general approach can easily be distilled down, and separated from the lingo, to reveal purely traditional elements. They adhere consistently to the positive punishment and negative reinforcement model with the symptom focus of the traditional method.

Like Millan, the Monks also deviate from the traditional mainstream approach in some ways: they acknowledge the valuable benefits of using food to train, and they teach the importance of socializing a dog as a puppy to ensure a sound adult. Also unique to the Monks' method is their detailed attention to nutrition as it affects behavior and the benefits of building the human/canine relationship by employing massage.

The Monks' training toolbox includes a training slip collar, a prong or pinch collar, and a lead. Popular punishers are verbal corrections, leash pops, and other more forceful techniques. For common behaviors such as barking, growling, house soiling, stealing, destruction, and poor dog/dog manners, the Monks suggest both verbal and physical corrections.

The most popular of the Monks' discipline techniques is the "shakedown."[3] For the offenses listed previously, the appropriate approach is to grab the dog with both hands near his neck/jowl area and lift his front feet off the ground while making sure to make direct and unbroken eye contact. While in this position, the dog is vigorously shaken back and forth while being verbally scolded. After a good scolding, the dog may be lowered back on the ground. The shakedown is modified for puppies by grabbing the scruff instead of the neck/jowl area.

Should the shakedown not elicit the proper response from the dog, the next level of discipline is the "cuff under the chin." To correctly receive this penalty, the dog must be grabbed tightly by the back of the collar and forced into a Sit. Once there, his head is pulled up, facilitated by the hold, and the handler's free hand comes around in an upward motion to hit the dog under the chin, while maintaining direct eye contact. To ensure the strike is hard enough, the Monks write, "A good general rule is that if you did not get a response, a yelp or other sign, after the first hit, it wasn't hard enough."[4] Both the shakedown and the cuff under the chin should be followed by thirty minutes of ignoring the dog.

In the original edition of their book *How to Be Your Dog's Best Friend*, the Monks recommend the alpha-wolf rollover (forcing a dog onto his side or his back and holding him there while reprimanding him) as the third level of physical punishment. Because of injury to dog owners, the most current edition of the same book no longer recommends this technique.

Millan and the Monks of New Skete are by no means the only practitioners of the traditional model today. However, they are two prominent forces perpetuating the method and their influence should not be underestimated.

1. Cesar Millan and Melissa Jo Peltier, *Cesar's Way: The Natural, Everyday Guide to Understanding and Correcting Common Dog Problems* (New York: Harmony Books, 2006).

2. Ibid.

3. The Monks of New Skete, *How to Be Your Dog's Best Friend: The Classic Training Manual for Dog Owners* (New York: Little, Brown, and Company, 2002).

4. Ibid.

 Problems with the
Traditional Model

While the traditional model remains the most popular technique used in the United States today and is readily accepted by most owners and the majority of present-day trainers, it has serious drawbacks that profoundly affect both dogs and humans. These defects range from the mundane and rather innocuous to those that are serious enough to cause both physical and emotional harm.

Perhaps the most glaring disconnect between today's human/ dog relationship and the traditional model of training is that it doesn't address the sophistication of the relationship most current owners have with their dog. Today's dog is a more integral part of the human family than at any other time in American history. The traditional model admonishes owners who think of their dog as part of the family, especially if that dog is allowed to indulge in shared joys such as snuggling on the furniture, sleeping with his owner in the bed, and eating designer foods. Rather than embrace this wonderful evolution, the model vehemently refuses to evolve along with it, instead continuing to preach division by way of establishing leader and follower, squelch canine independence and personality, and focus on obedience rather than real-life training.

Sadly, the model doesn't acknowledge that discipline can be part of today's relationship without it succumbing to the old-fashioned way of doing things. Instead, the traditional model criticizes this new heightened relationship as being unruly, lacking respect for the owner, indulgent, and ultimately, dangerous. Further, it views any attempt at a kind and/or alternative approach to dog training as weakness on the owner's part. It attributes the out-of-control dog of today to the cushy lifestyle and weak backbone of today's owner. Rather than accept that discipline can be established in a sophisticated, kind, and effective way, most practitioners of the traditional model dismiss this possibility in favor of an all-or-nothing position.

It can be successfully argued that today's owner is simply looking for a smarter, gentler, more effective and mature method of training without having to succumb to the old methods of yesteryear. There is no reason an owner should ever be forced to feel inadequate for his or her discomfort with the idea of delivering a leash pop or shakedown, or even with the idea of establishing himself as the dominant head of the household. The dog owner of the twenty-first century recognizes that these ideas, while not always abusive or barbaric, are often vulgar and primitive. He likes having a close relationship with his dog and doesn't want to have to give up the rituals that define this bond between them.

Problem #1: The Model Has a Limited Scope

By definition, the traditional model is based in obedience. It focuses on the dog's responsiveness to behavioral orders such as sit, down, stay, heel, and come. This all-important obedience ensures that a dog will remain controllable in any situation.

In the traditional model, the vast majority of a companion dog's life with his human hinges on his ability to sit, lie down, stay, heel, or come. While these are nice-to-haves, a more useful approach addresses not jumping up on people when they visit, not stealing trash or laundry, not bursting through the door the moment it is opened, not clearing the table of its main entrée, riding calmly in the car, and avoiding scuffles at the dog park.

The traditional model does attempt to address these very common behavioral challenges, but with the same old bag of tricks: sit, stay, down, heel, and come. The result is a misalignment of irrelevant behavior fixes to common behavior problems.

Problem #2: The Model Lacks Lasting Power

Another drawback of the traditional model is that it doesn't stick. By its own design, this training method only addresses the symptom of a behavior rather than its root cause. In doing so, it perpetuates, not eliminates, poor behavior.

To be clear, positive punishers used in traditional training *do work* to modify behavior, but only in the moment and only with cues that a dog will learn to discriminate.

For example, the traditional model says to punish the barking dog by squirting him with a spray bottle of water. Except for the dog who finds this rewarding (some do), he will cease barking for the moment. However, the second the water bottle is out of sight, the dog will seize his opportunity to bark without having to endure the squirt. Imagine the uselessness of this technique if your dog begins to bark and the water bottle is nowhere to be found.

Jumping is another great example. Traditional trainers approach jumping with a series of positive punishers: yell at the dog, tell him "no," swat him on the nose, knee him in the chest, and step on his rear toes. However, the model is only concerned with the behavioral symptom, jumping, not why the dog is jumping.

A dog who jumps is seeking attention. Without exception, every one of the previously listed traditional techniques actually reinforces jumping. Yes, the dog will get down in each and every instance when the punisher is applied, but this dog has already been reinforced for jumping in the first place. This dog will still jump for years to come as long as this technique is used because he is willing to endure the subsequent punishment for just a sweet, albeit brief, taste of the attention he is seeking, regardless of its intent.

Problem #3: For the Model to Continue to Work, Punishers Need to Escalate

Another unfavorable element of traditional training is the need for punishers to escalate in order to continue to be effective.

By this method, a punisher for chewing an inappropriate item, for example, may start out as a fairly innocuous firm verbal scolding such as "no." Few people would argue that this could ever be considered abusive, even when said emphatically.

When a dog no longer responds to "no," the traditional model says the punishment was not intense enough. The next level of punishment may be simply grabbing the dog by the collar and pushing him in another direction or it may be grabbing hold of his collar or snout, making eye contact, all while issuing the verbal scolding.

When that is not effective and the dog insists on returning to the illegal chew item yet again, the owner is instructed to deliver a swat either on the rear end, under the chin, or over the nose. He may also be told to deliver an ear pinch, and the other element of the traditional model, negative reinforcement, is introduced. Without further detail about the way this path will unfold, you can see how punishers must continue to escalate in order to remain effective.

Problem #4: The Model Only Offers Half the Answer

Animal behavior expert Karen Pryor is credited with saying, "Giving a dog a hard jerk on the collar is like rapping a child's hand in school when she gets the wrong answer. It may make the child afraid of making a mistake, but it doesn't teach her the right answer."

While the traditional model has hundreds of schemes in place to teach a dog what not to do, rarely does it tell a dog what to do instead. Dogs are regularly and repeatedly punished for chewing, pulling on a leash, digging, barking, house soiling, stealing, and getting on furniture. However, the traditional model almost never teaches the clear lesson of what the dog is to do instead of what he's not supposed to do.

It's safe to assume that if a dog is not dead or unconscious, he's behaving. By leaving him hanging after a punishment, not directing him to a more appropriate and desirable behavior, he's left to his own devices to deduce the intended lesson of the punishment he just endured and to find a behavior in which to engage that is less likely to get him punished. After a traditional punishment, the dog is usually clear on what not to do but because of the infinite possibilities of what to do instead, he will repeatedly choose behaviors that will continue to get him in trouble. Only by trial and error will a dog finally settle into a behavior that is acceptable to his human, but not until he has endured the prolonged anxiety that is a symptom of desperately seeking to avoid a seemingly random schedule of punishment.

Learning to walk nicely on leash is a great example. A leash pop, giving a quick jerk on the leash with a training collar such as a choke chain or prong/pinch collar, is the most popular technique used in traditional training when teaching a dog to heel. By this method, when the dog falls out of line, the handler issues a leash pop and the dog falls back into position. As long as the dog continues to step out of position while walking, the owner will continue to issue leash corrections of this type.

While this may seem at first to have taught the dog to walk nicely by his owner's side, it's actually accomplished the opposite; it has taught the dog he's punished for something and the punishments are timed with those moments he's at the end of the leash. Again, this might seem like the technique has accomplished the intended lesson, until you consider how many other things the dog is doing at the same time he's being punished for being away from his owner's side. He may be sniffing something in the air or on the ground, he may be hopping over a crack in the sidewalk, he may have just broken into a trot from a walk, he may have blinked or opened his mouth to pant. This is just a small pool of possible behaviors happening at the exact same time the correction was delivered. While the dog is learning something in this department has gotten him in trouble, he has no idea what he's supposed to do instead. Only by numerous walks and hundreds of corrections will the dog, by default, learn to avoid all behaviors other than walking by his owner's side. Remember, he has not learned that this pays off with rewards, but only that it's the only thing he does that doesn't get him punished. If the intended message, walking next to owner is good while walking away from owner is not as good, could be taught in the first few lessons, the result would be infinitely better.

Problem #5: The Model Depends on Unrealistic Interpretations and Assumptions

The traditional model readily explains behavior in terms of what's going on inside a dog's head. It uses terms when describing dog behavior such as what a dog is thinking, feeling, wanting, trying to do, and insisting on. Further complicating things, it applies a dog's intentions to a behavioral scenario by using terms such as "he's intimidated," "he's jealous," "he resents you," "he lacks will power," "he feels insecure," and "he's getting revenge."

Because of the relationship between human and dog, it can be endearing to imagine what's going on in a dog's head. Clearly, every dog has his own personality, and humans love indulging their curiosity by speculating about what it is this captivating animal spends his time thinking about. This wonderment should never be considered wrong or weak as it's part of what makes the dog so charming, but it should never be taken out of context and be applied to anything that can potentially modify behavior.

While it is perfectly reasonable for anyone to attempt to analyze a dog's behavior based on these things, it is unsound for a person to then take that interpretation as reality and use it to apply a behavior modification technique. There are a number of problems with doing so.

Most obviously, humans cannot read each other's minds, let alone cross the species gap to read dog minds. While it can be fun to guess at what our human companions are thinking, it's useless for anything beyond entertainment.

By modifying behavior or forming an opinion of a dog based on what's going on in his head, we run the risk of applying morals, ethics, standards, boundaries, and other human-specific traits to a dog. While our furry companions often exhibit very human-like behavior, there is a more effective, kinder approach when it comes to changing the way he acts.

Problem #6: The Model Is Just a Theory, Not a Fact

Training a dog by establishing a pack dynamic with a human as an Alpha and a canine as always submissive is a very attractive idea. However, this approach has vast and serious drawbacks.

The pack-theory model itself relies on the fact that a dog has mistaken a human as another dog. This basic assumption must be accepted in order for the pack theory to work. Based on this oversight, a dog sees his human family as others in his pack and he must vie with them in everything he does to make sure he becomes and remains Alpha. The model also assumes that being Alpha is his ultimate goal and his whole life is spent trying to dominate humans to obtain that status.

The truth of the matter is that the dog is smart enough to recognize humans as non-dogs just as he recognizes cats, tables, and cars as non-dogs. If he mistook humans for dogs and this was an acceptable condition, there would be hundreds of thousands of canine-human hybrids roaming the face of our planet. Using this simple example, you can see that the domesticated dog can tell the difference between his kind and all others.

The other fiction-based assumption of the pack model is that the dog's ultimate life goal is to dominate the human species to achieve the ultimate Alpha status. This is just simply not true, and thank goodness for that.

The introduction of this idea came together in the mid-twentieth century, born of a few strong but simple components: the 1940s wolf social structure studies I mention in CHAPTER 2, THE MILITARY/ TRADITIONAL MODEL OF TRAINING; the American desire to better understand the dog and how to train him, along with William Koehler's national presence; and the American Kennel Club's new dedication to obedience training. These ingredients gave rise to the pack-theory model that has prevailed in the United States for decades.

At no time has this element of the traditional model been scientifically proven or legitimized in use for modifying behavior in the domesticated dog. Rather the method has been immortalized by anecdotal accounts of its benefits and usefulness. To the contrary, recent studies have proven the uselessness and damaging effects to both humans and canines when using the pack-theory model to modify dog behavior.

This is not to say that wolves and dogs do not live by a social hierarchy based on rank. Quite certainly we can say that they do. But they do this among their own species only, and the social web of interactions and communications within these hierarchies is extremely complicated. When researchers observe a pack of wolves who have lived together for a long time, they find the assumed social ranking system at a given time can change without notice and for reasons that are greatly unknown.

A wolf, for example, may appear to lead the pack one day by eating first, but the next day may hang back from the carcass, allowing another to eat first. The supposed head of the pack at a given moment may be female or male, of any age or size. This wolf may or may not scold other dogs, groom them, be groomed by them, walk in front of them, walk behind them, share resources, or not share resources. The important message in these studies is that hierarchies, while they do exist, are extremely complicated and are not static.

The idea, then, of inserting a human into that social system with beneficial impacts on behavior modification and training can actually do serious harm.

Problem #7: The Model Can Cause Harm

In most cases where an owner attempts to assert his dominance by passive methods, such as walking before his dog, passing through a door before him, and keeping his head higher than his dog's, the dog truly just doesn't notice or care. The only harm done is to the human, who must now maintain this approach.

However, there are two areas in which using the dominance model for delivering punishment are very dangerous and are considered inhumane:

- When a dog is positively punished for a normal behavior without being told what to do instead
- When a dog is punished aversively for an emotional behavior

While it's a concept greatly denied by the traditional model of training, dogs exhibit a number of behaviors resulting from an emotional cause. Just like humans, dogs do experience fear, anxiety, terror, aggression, and other emotional behaviors. While you cannot get into a dog's head to telepathically analyze these "feelings," you can observe behavior and learn to identify behaviors based in these emotional roots. Once you've identified the roots, you can implement a proper behavioral modification plan.

However, because of its lack of academic and scientific foundation, the traditional model of training applies the same positive punishment and negative reinforcement techniques to *all* behaviors, regardless of their emotional or non-emotional basis.

While there are exceptions to these examples, in most cases, non-emotional behaviors include but are not limited to: jumping up, house soiling, chewing, digging, stealing, and destroying things. The traditional model of training attributes each of these infractions to a dog who is being defiant, asserting his displeasure with his position in the family rank.

The positive punishment in these cases is often disconnected and seemingly arbitrary, but it is all meant to put the dog back in his place, submissive to the dominant humans in the family. The dog being punished almost never learns an appropriate way to conduct himself as a result of the positive punisher and is sentenced to a daily life of being fearful of his owner's actions and being left to guess what to do to avoid being punished.

The most serious situations are ones where an owner applies a positive punisher to a dog exhibiting a behavior arising from an emotional cause. The most common displays of behaviors in this category are: squirming during a nail trim or trip to the vet, displaying aggression at people or other dogs, and destroying the house in owner absence. Each of these behaviors is based in a serious emotional state—fear or anxiety, or in very rare cases, actual aggression. In any event, imagine the dog who is positively punished for showing signs of discomfort associated with an emotional cause.

Nail trimming is an excellent example. Many dogs who take a trip to the vet or groomer to have their nails trimmed struggle when the handler grabs a foot. At this struggle, the handler following the rules of the traditional model interprets the dog's behavior as defiance and an attempt to obtain Alpha status.

To counter this attempt, the handler asserts his or her strength in the struggle until the dog cannot move. If the dog then growls or wiggles loose, this is seen as an escalated and potentially dangerous attempt at dominance on the dog's part and the handler may choose to administer an alpha rollover, shakedown, or other positive punishment technique. Tragically, an alarming number of dogs who react this way in this situation are deemed aggressive simply from this one interaction.

In actuality, the dog attempting to pull his paw from the person trying to trim his nails is just uncomfortable with the situation. Paws have incredible adaptive significance and dogs are highly sensitive to them. The traditional model insists that dogs should accept having their toenails trimmed without the slightest protest, regardless that they have never been desensitized to the chore; they should pop from the womb accepting all human handling, no matter how foreign or uncomfortable it is.

When a dog in a position in which he shows signs of discomfort is then punished for these behavioral symptoms, he doesn't become less fearful about the situation. He simply learns to hide the outward signals he uses to communicate it. In addition, he's learned to dislike the vet or groomer, the smell of the facility, the ride in the car to this place, and any other thing he associates with the experience, which unfortunately may include his owner.

While the subdued dog may seem at first to have overcome his fear or to have readily accepted submission, a very serious side effect has just been born: this dog has become a behavioral time bomb.

Dogs have a limit to how much of something they can tolerate before becoming upset about it. For example, many dogs don't mind the usual sounds of the world they live in. But, when a thunderstorm or the Fourth of July rolls around, the sound stimulation is too much and their reactivity threshold may be exceeded. Likewise, many dogs don't mind being held and touched. But, if they're held strongly, touched, manipulated, and then forced to have their nails trimmed (an uncomfortable experience for any dog, and a particularly agonizing one if the quick is nicked), they will quickly escalate over their reactivity threshold and a non-emotional event turns emotional.

Punishing a dog who is over his reactivity threshold is like striking a child for crying because he is scared of the dark. Doing so will not suddenly make the child more comfortable with being in the dark, but it will make him less likely to show his discomfort to whoever it was who punished him. It may also have a secondary effect: it may actually escalate the child's fear and anxiety, extending past a breaking point. This is identical to the effect positive punishment can have on a dog in an emotional fit.

The dog who has been sufficiently punished to suppress the symptoms of his emotional discomfort is a dangerous and unhealthy soul. This dog will not show behavioral discomfort to a certain degree, but he will react when the fearful stimulus is great enough to elicit a response. If this dog has been repeatedly punished for the same behavior again and again, the punishments have given the false impression of fixing the problem. However, only the symptoms have been fixed; the underlying problem still exists. Given the right set of triggers, the dog will display his discomfort.

While it seems logical that the triggers would have to be excessive, this is not the case. The circumstances simply have to be right. The emotional release by the dog who has suppressed his behavior due to repeated punishments is extreme, out of control, dangerous, and highly emotionally damaging. Whereas the traditional model interprets this delayed explosion as hard-core aggression, the truth is that a history of events leading to the final blowup can be identified in almost every single case.

Problem #8: The Model Doesn't Address Individual Needs

One of the other oversights of the traditional model is that dogs are individuals and each has his own set of favorite and not-so-favorite things.

Just like people, some dogs like sweets, some like meat. Some dogs enjoy a rub behind the ears while it bothers others. Some dogs love to fetch and will level anything between themselves and a tennis ball just to satisfy their urge. Some dogs prefer to watch other dogs play fetch and wouldn't be caught dead actually chasing after a ball. Some dogs like to be squirted with water, some don't. Some dogs like people, some don't. The list goes on and on.

The traditional model does attempt to explain significant behavioral differences by breed, but that idea was abandoned by the elite in the dog behavior field over a decade ago. It can be said that certain traits are bred heavily into a certain breed, but except for the very high-drive breeds, defined as those still actively working in the field (such as Malinois, Shetland Sheepdogs, Australian Shepherds, and Border Collies), only weak and anecdotal arguments can be made for segmentation in the companion dog.

Particularly among the most popular companion breeds, today's purebred lines are very, very diluted when you consider the standard for each breed. These lines are not only diluted, but they are also now polluted with genetic deviations, the effects of inbreeding, contamination from the puppy mill phenomenon (in which dogs are mass produced with little regard for health, comfort, or genetic purity), and the variance that comes with breeding multiple generations of anything in great number over a relatively long period of time.

It's strikingly common for a Labrador owner, for example, to complain that his dog is afraid of water. A tragic number of Golden Retriever owners have dogs who can't stand people. Even the English Bulldog, bred in fairly small numbers because of their inability to give birth without human intervention, varies tremendously in each individual specimen.

It's important for today's owner to acknowledge and accept the current breeding landscape in the United States when addressing behavior modification. It is taboo to discuss the potential contamination of a "purebred's" line, but the joyous truth is that any "contaminations" have made for a great number of intriguing individuals, who may or may not adhere to their breed standard, but are endearing nonetheless. Rather than shy away from this diversity, the progressive owner must embrace it to make sure his or her dog gets the best behavioral care possible.

This said, it is reasonable to believe that many dogs will retain and exhibit any number of behavior and temperament traits associated with their breed. While it is perfectly acceptable to acknowledge this, it's no longer useful to structure dog behavior modification based on these assumptions.

The traditional model looks at a symptom behavior such as barking and applies a technique to end it. Typical techniques are yelling, squirting with water, and using a shaker or "startle" can filled with coins or pebbles. Regardless of an individual's particular association with these things, the same punisher is applied in every case.

But take, for example, the dog who is barking to alert his owner of a potential intruder. Remember, there are literally dozens of reasons he could be barking, but this example focuses on alert or "watchdog" barking.

For this dog, all of the previous "solutions" may be productive or counterproductive, depending on what the individual dog is like. If the dog is an obsessive retriever, for example, having a shaker can thrown at him may actually be exciting and wonderful. The attempt to end his behavior may increase it instead. A dog who is sound-sensitive, however, will find this punishment extremely aversive and his behavior will likely end for the moment. The "bulletproof" dog, one who seems to repel all punishers regardless of their severity, will simply ignore the correction.

The dog who is squirted for barking may or may not enjoy the experience. While most dogs dislike the squirt at first, some either learn to enjoy it or always have. It is not unusual for a dog who was first squirted for alert barking to develop request barking to actually be squirted with water for the sheer fun of it!

The same goes for rewarding behaviors. If a dog enjoys socializing with a great number of other dogs, then the dog park may be highly rewarding. However, if he follows his owner around at the park growling, snarling, or barking at other dogs, it's safe to assume this "great for all dogs" experience may not be for him. If he jumps up and down when the leash comes out, walks are clearly exciting. If he runs and hides or doesn't so much as open an eye when it comes out, it's not a good reward.

It's equally important to recognize that not only does each and every dog have his own set of rewards and punishers, but the set can fluctuate from day to day. Just because a dog loves pigs ears now doesn't mean that he'll be equally enthusiastic for one next month. The dog who loves a walk through the neighborhood in the sunshine may cower in the mudroom when the wind blows. A dog who loves to play with other dogs may be highly rewarded by doing so unless his other option is fetch.

Dogs not only have likes and dislikes, but they also have a hierarchy of rewards and punishers just as humans do. A dog who likes to eat (some are very finicky) may love meat, may like potatoes, may tolerate kibble, and may despise vegetables. Each of these things has its value. While a dog may always eat meat if given the choice between kibble and prime rib, he still likes kibble and it has a place in his individual reward hierarchy.

When contemplating a punisher or a reinforcer for a particular behavior, it's imperative that the dog's particular reward and punishment system be considered. Applying a blanket fix to every dog for a given behavior is a recipe for frustration and unsuccessful behavior modification plans.

Problem #9: The Model Doesn't Always Allow the Dog to Learn Efficiently

Learning is defined as a change in behavior based on experience. This simple definition allows for a highly analytical approach to measuring learning.

As first proven by animal behavior pioneers B. F. Skinner and Ivan Pavlov, dogs learn in two ways: by consequence and by association. While very good arguments can be made for other methods of learning, such as learning through observation, only these two types of learning can be proofed, tested, and proven again and again.

While the traditional model does claim to impart learning, it explains it in terms of the dominance model, pack hierarchies, rank, what's going on inside a dog's head, and feelings, and there is a gross disconnect between the traditional interpretation of what a dog has learned versus what he's actually learned. It has been successfully argued that learning does take place when this method is used, but the timeline for learning is immense, and the actual lessons learned are far from what they were first intended to be.

By the traditional model, a dog who is corrected with leash pops learns to walk next to his owner as a result of these pops. However, two very interesting components of this technique negate this claim when they're analyzed scientifically: when a dog and his owner are observed over a thirty-day period, and the number of leash pops delivered are tallied during each training session, the number in the fourth week is usually the same or more than that number delivered in the first week and the dog is still walking all over the place.

If learning is a change in behavior based on experience, by definition, this month-long observation indicates that no learning whatsoever has taken place. In order for learning to have taken place, the number of pops would have needed to increase or decrease and/or the dog would have to be walking worse or better than he did thirty days prior.

Eventually, literally after months of this technique, a dog will learn not to do anything else other than walk next to his owner, given that his owner's leash pops continue to be punishing. The more likely scenario is that the dog will continue to pull, the owner will enlist a more aversive collar such as a choke chain or prong/pinch collar, and the cycle of unintended, drawn-out, escalated lessons continues.

Squirting a dog with a squirt bottle is another great example. The intended lesson when using a squirt bottle is to teach a dog not to bark. However, when the bottle is gone, the dog will bark much more readily until the bottle is brought back out. The traditional model claims that using the bottle has taught the dog not to bark; the dog has learned not to bark because of the behavior modification used: squirting him. However, many adult dogs have endured the squirt for years of their lives and the only behavior that has changed is barking in the presence of the bottle. Learning has happened, yes, but the intended lesson has not been imparted.

Problem #10: Some of the Model's Methods Are Inhumane

Perhaps the most taboo of topics is the humanity or inhumanity of dog training in any form. It can be very upsetting for a caring owner to learn that the methods he has employed at the suggestion of someone in the canine professional arena are actually inhumane or damaging to the relationship with his dog.

Because of the controversy, many owners choose to ignore the data available that supports findings that even the most commonly used tools and techniques, such as prong and pinch collars, swats, and alpha rolls, are inhumane.

Unless a person has specialized training or an education in behavior, you should assume that she is no more qualified to give behavioral or training advice than the average dog owner.

To clarify, a pet shop clerk is an expert in products only. A veterinarian, unless he has gone through specialized training, is an expert in animal medicine only (currently, most veterinary schools offer little to no behavioral education as part of their curriculum, and those that do offer the course(s) as electives). A groomer is an expert in grooming only. A dog walker is an expert in picking up dogs and walking them only. The daycare worker is an expert in managing packs of dogs who get along during the day.

These designations are constantly changing as dog behavior techniques and approaches continue to change. Before choosing anyone to work with your dog, always research the credentials behind his or her name.

Armed with this knowledge, an owner can feel empowered to be an advocate for her dog and can consider current scientific data that supports claims that many of the techniques used in the traditional approach are inhumane.

Despite the pet shop worker stating that a prong collar doesn't hurt a dog, or a veterinarian claiming that an alpha roll is necessary, the Society for the Prevention of Cruelty to Animals (SPCA), Humane Society of the United States (HSUS), American Humane Association (AHA), and other leaders in the animal welfare and behavioral arena deem this tool and technique inhumane. The reason owners readily accept these instructions is not a great mystery. It's difficult for them to navigate the animal behavior landscape. Any person who works with dogs is considered an expert: the vet, vet tech, pet store clerk, dog walker, daycare owner or wrangler, self-proclaimed behaviorist, trainer, dog psychologist, or dog counselor.

To help empower owners with knowledge, here is a key to the various titles used in the canine behavior field:

- **VETERINARY BEHAVIORIST:** A veterinarian who has gone through advanced training and is certified by the American College of Veterinary Behaviorists (ACVB).

- **CERTIFIED APPLIED ANIMAL BEHAVIORIST (CAAB):** A professional certified by the Animal Behavior Society (ABS); some CAABs are also Doctors of Veterinary Medicine (DVMs). At this time, there are forty-seven CAABs in the United States; that's less than one official behaviorist per state. However, a striking number of people use this designation without actually being behaviorists.

- **TRAINER:** The person who works hands-on with a dog, and implements a plan to change a dog's behavior. Many dog trainers are also qualified as behavior specialists, counselors, and the like, or a trainer may operate solely as a trainer. At this time, no formal education or training is necessary to become a trainer.

- **CERTIFICATE IN TRAINING AND COUNSELING (CTC):** A person with a CTC holds a certificate in training and behavior counseling from the San Francisco Society for the Prevention of Cruelty to Animals Academy directed by Jean Donaldson. The CTC trainer has completed an academically rigorous course based in animal learning theory and humane methods and has passed an accompanying exam.

- **CERTIFIED PET DOG TRAINER (CPDT):** The CPDT has logged 300 hours of experience in dog training stretched over five years, and has passed a certification exam issued by the Certification Council of Pet Dog Trainers. The methods used by CPDTs vary widely.

- **BEHAVIOR SPECIALIST:** This is a somewhat arbitrary designation, and the title alone does not qualify or disqualify a person to professionally work with dogs; not to be mistaken for a Veterinary Behavior Specialist.

- **BEHAVIOR THERAPIST:** This is a somewhat arbitrary designation, and the title alone does not qualify or disqualify a person to professionally work with dogs.

Following is a list of props and techniques specific to the traditional model that are damaging and/or inhumane. Some are very commonly used while others are seen less often but are still recognized and warrant mentioning:

- **PROPS:** Prong/pinch collars, choke chains, citronella collars, electric collars, bark collars, radio collars, shaker cans, air horns.

- **TECHNIQUES:** Knee bumps, nose swats, holding a dog's muzzle shut, stepping on his back toes, yelling at a dog, squirting him with a squirt bottle, leash pops and jerks, spanking a dog, holding him up by the front paws, ear pinches, helicopters (swinging a dog around by the leash), shakedowns, alpha rolls, flooding (a technique commonly used by Cesar Millan that consists of subjecting a dog to extreme levels of stimuli to "break" him of a behavior problem), holding a dog off the ground by his scruff, jowls, or other body part or collar.

Alternatively, I discuss friendly props and methods in detail in **CHAPTER 5, THE CRISTINE DAHL METHOD.**

CHAPTER 4

Animal Learning Theory and Positive Training

The most common term used to explain alternative methods to the traditional model is *positive training*. Karen Pryor is credited with having pioneered the positive training movement (also known as the clicker training movement) in the United States. Pryor is highly educated in zoology, biology, and biological psychology, and her academic and experiential resume includes extensive involvement in both public and private animal behavior arenas. She holds a number of esteemed recognitions and titles, not the least of which is co-founder of Hawaii's Sea Life Park and Oceanic Institute.

In the 1960s, Pryor worked with dolphins in Sea Life Park developing a force-free, operant conditioning–based method for training them. *Operant conditioning*, perhaps best associated with psychologist B. F. Skinner, is a type of training in which the animal being trained acts as the operator on his environment. He is not upset in any way and has learned that certain actions pay off with

predictable consequences. These behaviors are voluntary and pro-
duce an effect. They are not reflexive or reactive. For example, he
may have learned that bumping a wand with his nose will open a
gate, or that responding to a particular cue by his trainer will earn
him a reward.

This method is anchored very firmly in animal learning theory
and uses positive reinforcement to modify behavior. Animal learning theory is the discipline that is used to explain how animals
learn. Learning in this context is described as a change in behavior
based on experience.

Pryor paired her understanding of animal learning and behavior
modification with the theories of Skinner and became a crusader
for using a "marker" in positive training for companion animals.

This marker, known as the clicker, is the most recognized tool
associated with Pryor and the positive training movement. Pryor
identified the need to establish a powerful communication system
with the animals she trained and knew it needed to be universal. Building her methods on the theories set forth by pioneers in
behaviorism, she found that if she could sound a whistle or other
noise to signal to an animal that the behavior he just did was "correct," she could then use the same marker and reward system for
other behaviors that were part of his usual behavioral repertoire.

Conditioning

The principle used for clicker training is known as operant conditioning. It is not to be confused with classical conditioning, otherwise known as Pavlovian conditioning, in which an emotion or
reflexive response is modified using associative techniques. Classical conditioning focuses very heavily on instinctive, involuntary,
and reflexive response, whereas operant conditioning focuses on
learning by consequence.

When an animal learns by consequence, he is the operator on his
environment. Thus, the dog being trained by operant methods is
not emotionally upset in any way; he's neither fearful, aggressive,
frustrated, nor otherwise disturbed. In this approach, consequences

are used to modify voluntary behavior. An operantly conditioned behavior may be seen in an active training situation where the trainer asks for a behavior, the dog gives it, and then the dog is rewarded, or it may be seen in a behavioral situation in which the dog has learned that his actions have a desired reaction.

For example, if a dog sits, he gets a treat. If he waits, he can pass through a door. If he barks for attention, he'll get it. If he paws at the door, he'll be let in. If he nudges a hand, he'll be scratched. The list is limitless. In each of these examples, a dog has intentionally performed a behavior in order to trigger a consequence.

As I discussed in CHAPTER 2, THE MILITARY/TRADITIONAL MODEL OF TRAINING, the two approaches to modifying behavior using traditional methods are positive punishment and negative reinforcement. The positive training movement uses the inverse of each: positive reinforcement and negative punishment.

As stated earlier, in the science of behavior, "positive" does *not* mean lovely, wonderful, and kind, as it does in the general human vernacular. Likewise, "negative" does *not* mean horrible, painful, and not-so-lovely. These terms are used mathematically. *Positive* simply means the addition of something; *negative* means the removal of something. A *punishment* is something done to bring down a behavior in frequency and/or intensity. *Reinforcement* is something done to increase a behavior in frequency and/or intensity.

In Chapter 2, I gave a couple examples of how certain problematic behaviors would be treated using the traditional/military method. For comparison, here are the same example behaviors, only they're treated by using positive training.

Example: Barking for Attention

One methods of *positive reinforcement* would be choosing an alternative behavior for the dog instead of barking, such as fetching a toy or settling in with a chew item, while rewarding him with pets and praise. The *positive* here is the addition of a thing: a treat, a pat, praise, the toy or chew thing, or even the chance for the dog to stay in the presence of his family. This is considered *reinforcement* because the desired behavior (being quiet) goes up in frequency and intensity.

Negative punishment could include removing the dog from the room if he refuses to be quiet. The *negative* here is the removal of his opportunity to be around his family. This is considered *punishment* because barking goes down in frequency and intensity.

Example: Pulling on Leash

Positive reinforcement could include rewarding the dog for walking in the correct position. The *positive* here is the addition of a thing: a treat, a pat, verbal praise, moving forward. This is considered *reinforcement* because the desired behavior (walking nicely next to the owner) goes up in frequency and intensity.

A *negative punishment* would be to stop moving forward when the dog is at the end of the leash and to not reward him for being out of position. The *negative* here is the removal of his opportunity to move forward when he's pulling, and the removal of rewards when he's out of position. This is considered *punishment* because pulling goes down in frequency and intensity.

Marker Training

In clicker training, the clicker is used as a marker. The word "marker" here has only one meaning: that behavior, whatever it is, just earned you something good. The clicker has been the tool of choice for dogs because of its structure; it's portable and sturdy, but it's also extremely salient to dogs. The click itself is clear, succinct, travels well over a distance, and is unlike most other sounds a dog is likely to have already tuned out.

The clicker is not used as a cue or command such as come, sit, stay, down, and so on. Instead, by avoiding any one meaning, it becomes an invaluable universal tool that can be used in training not only with a number of single movement behaviors but also with long, complicated behavioral chains. Examples include learning to switch off or on a light switch, fetching a newspaper, or even opening, passing through, and then shutting a door.

Benefits of Clicker Training

One of the greatest benefits of clicker training is it's fun. Not only can a dog be taught a joyous number of interesting behaviors, but it can also be exhilarating to watch a dog learning by clicker training. The technique also encourages both mental and physical activity for the owner and dog.

While the fun of clicker training is undeniable, the overwhelming benefit of this method is to the mental and behavioral health of a dog. First and foremost, the method approaches training from the completely opposite direction as traditional training: it teaches a dog what *to do* instead of what *not to do*. It acknowledges the fact that dogs are behaving every moment they're conscious, and that the healthiest way to approach their behavior is by channeling their efforts into appropriate, safe, and beneficial outlets.

Whereas a traditionally trained dog is always trying to find ways not to be punished, the positively trained dog is always trying to find ways to be rewarded. Clicker training does not use fear, discomfort, or startle methods such as choke, prong, or pinch collars; shaker cans; squirt bottles; ear pinches; loud voices; strikes; kicks; electronic collars; alpha rolls; shakedowns; and other aversive techniques to modify behavior. Not only is this approach civilized and humane, but it also encourages a dog to be comfortable and happy and actually look forward to training. Never is he left to fear what his next punishment will be. Instead, he becomes a fountain of behavior, allowing his individuality to flow.

This element of positive training does wonders for the human/ dog relationship. The bond between a positively trained dog and his owner is infinitely greater and healthier than the bond between a traditionally trained canine and his owner.

Another innate benefit of clicker training is that it requires a handler to be calm, to observe behavior, and to really learn to watch his or her dog. Any amount of physical or verbal prompting, use of force, or manual encouragement is not part of clicker training; thus, the clicker-trained relationship is inherently more sophisticated than more hands-on methods. The traditionally trained dog who is taught to suppress behavior rather than redirect it cannot help but develop behavioral problems. One of the unfortunate side effects of this way of learning is generalized anxiety.

Take jumping up on people, for example. For the jumping dog, the traditional model of behavior modification says to punish him with a "No!", knee bump, swat on the nose, squirt bottle, shakedown, and the like. However, right out of the gate the positive training approach teaches a dog what to do instead of jumping so he is never left guessing about how he is to behave. The alternative behaviors commonly used to counteract poor manners are called Differential Reinforcement of Incompatible Behavior (DRIs).

The positive method encourages owners to abandon the phrase, "I want my dog to *stop* X" in exchange for "I want my dog to do X *instead.*" So if your dog is barking, rather than adopting the mindset of "I want my dog to stop barking," the mindset is "I want my dog to be quiet on cue." Instead of "I want my dog to stop jumping on people," the mindset is "I want my dog to keep all four feet on the ground when he meets people."

Pure positive training abandons any training that attempts to analyze what's going on in a dog's head. Instead, it approaches behavior modification by analyzing a behavior, applying a technique meant to change it, and then measuring and analyzing it again. Without complicating the formula with mind reading, the technique is simple, kind, and efficient.

Misconceptions About Positive Training

Perhaps the most unfortunate misconception about the positive training movement is that it doesn't use discipline or punishment. Quite the contrary is true.

The positively trained dog, if trained properly, has learned the rules that govern his environment. He's learned that he will be allowed to engage in the activities he likes as long as he's polite and well behaved. For example, he can pass through the door if he first waits. He can go to the dog park if he first sits for his release. The ball will be thrown for him if he delivers it into his owner's hand during a game of fetch.

He has also learned that he will be punished by losing those opportunities for poor behavior. For example, until he settles and waits, the door will not be opened. If he pulls on his leash through the parking lot to the dog park, he will not be let off leash until he settles and is released. If he insists on dropping the ball ten feet from his owner, it will not be thrown for him.

The rules and regulations of this training model scream discipline. However, because the discipline doesn't use the overt methods found in the traditional model, the discipline component of the model is greatly overlooked by the mass public.

Elicitation versus Emission

A great debate exists among positive trainers: to elicit a behavior or to wait for its emission. In fundamentalist clicker training, the trainer sits quietly with his clicker waiting for behavior to happen. Depending on his goal, he clicks and rewards the behavior he wants to see. This is considered training by *emission*.

The benefits of emission are that it encourages a dog to think without being inhibited by outside influences. This makes for a very clever dog and extreme owner relevance. It also requires an owner to keep his hands off his dog and develop a keen sense of observing dog behavior. The drawbacks of this method are that it can be slow, frustrating, and less than desirable for the impatient trainer.

Elicitation involves some sort of encouragement from the trainer such as prompting, luring, or environmental rearrangement. For example, if a dog is being taught to walk to the mat, tossing the mat onto the ground may be a trigger to the dog to walk over to it, whereas if the mat was where it normally is placed, it would be less likely to draw attention. Fanfare is a common elicitor: bending over, slapping knees, whistling, and the like is considered elicitation.

The benefits of elicitation are that it gets faster results and impatient trainers enjoy the quick payoff. The drawbacks are that the props and actions used to elicit behavior must be faded and removed from the training equation before the behavior is considered fluent. This dog is also less likely to develop the degree of behavioral freedom seen by dogs enjoying purely emission-based training.

Drawbacks and Common Grievances of Positive Training

Positive training in its purest form requires basic handler skills, the most important of which is clicker timing. The correct way to click is at the very moment the dog exhibits the desired behavior. If you click too early or too late, you run the risk of rewarding a non-target behavior.

These non-target behaviors, also known as *superstitious behaviors*, can be as tiny and unnoticeable as a blink or lip lick, or can be as obvious as a bark, a head turn, kicking a leg out, or an altogether different behavior than was desired. Mistiming is more an annoyance than a serious problem, but it can be frustrating for some people attempting to use clicker training.

The technique also requires the use of a clicker and bait. Many owners feel overwhelmed by having to use props when training and when it entails being armed with bait pouch, bait, clicker, leash, and dog. While practice makes handling these tools easy, it can be technically challenging to keep track of all the paraphernalia required for clicker training, and handlers, especially those new to the method, often prefer to be prop light.

Certain types of clicker training, such as capturing and shaping, can be technically challenging and slow. *Capturing* is a term used for the type of clicker training used to click and reward behaviors a dog gives in his normal environment without being prompted or urged to give the behavior. For example, a dog who shakes each time before he comes inside from the rain will do so more often if he's clicked and treated each time he does so. After the behavior has been rewarded many times, the dog will begin to give the behavior in generalized settings; not just when coming inside from the rain. This technique is great fun for many people, but for the impatient owner, it is tedious and slow because a behavior can only be captured when the dog just happens to give it. The owner must be ready with clicker and treats when the dog gives the target behavior and this level of attention can simply be too much for many owners.

Shaping is the term used for the type of clicker training in which a series of behaviors approximating a final behavior are strung together into a chain. Common examples are walking over to a mat and settling on it; jumping up to turn on a light switch; and opening a door, passing through it, and then shutting it.

Before a behavior can be shaped, the trainer must devise a parameter plan, built of small and digestible criterion. In other words, if a dog is being taught to head for the mat to lie down on it, he may first look at the mat. Next, he may take one step towards it. Then, he may take two steps towards it, and so on. Training this requires some skill as each level must be rewarded efficiently. The dog who has been punished for behavior in the past, or who has never been positively reinforced for throwing behaviors (giving behaviors previously or not previously rewarded, often in rapid succession with enthusiasm), may warm up to the technique slowly and the trainer may become frustrated and discouraged.

Another drawback of clicker training is that it's "training." Many owners complain of tight schedules and hectic lifestyles, and they are searching for a type of dog training that doesn't require much work. They not only feel they don't have a few uninterrupted minutes a day to train, but also they actually find the time-consuming activity to be a chore instead of fun.

Clicker training does require some planning, education in the technique, physical skill, and practice. And many harried owners are looking for a type of behavior modification approach they can use *now*. They're often stuck in the world of training obedience and feel pressured to teach their dog sit, stand, down, and other obedience cues when they truly need to know how to manage a dog in everyday real-life situations specific to their individual lifestyle. Sit and stay are nice-to-haves, but these owners really want to know how to quickly fix the door-dasher, the humper, the table surfer, the beggar, the jumper, and any other less-than-savory poor manners their dog has developed.

Positive Training Today

Today's training landscape is littered with people using the term "positive" to explain the method of training they use. However, though the term is the same, the underlying philosophy used by these trainers varies greatly.

The great separation between the two groups who use the term "positive" is in the two interpretations of the word itself.

The current majority of positive trainers use the word to mean good, nice, soft, kind, and gentle. These are tremendously subjective terms that leave a great deal of room for variation. "Nice" to some positive trainers means they use verbal praise while others insist on using food to reward dogs. Some call themselves positive trainers because they use these things but then they also employ aversive techniques such as prong collars and shaker cans. This is the style of training used by PETCO and PetSmart, the two main pet supply chains in the national U.S. market.

Trainers claiming to use only unadulterated positive methods can be excessively laid back in their approach, not only when it comes to using food and praise but in their vehement refusal to use any amount of discipline or punishment. This excludes even the most inoffensive punisher, the no-reward marker (NRM): a quick "ah-ah" statement used by many trainers to communicate to a dog that what he just did didn't earn him a reward.

Traditional trainers and the mass public familiar with more mainstream methods such as the alpha and pack theories often ridicule and dismiss these ultra-soft trainers as being too "warm and fuzzy," "woo-woo," and "out there." Sadly, clicker training gets thrown into this dismissal.

While trainers teaching solely by animal learning theory's kind and humane methods are part of today's landscape, they are the extreme minority. The vast majority of trainers claiming to use "positive" methods still employ aversive techniques that are not consistent with Karen Pryor's movement. Because it is unnecessary for dog trainers to have any amount of formal training, the terrain is unregulated and owners must look past the clever lingo a canine professional uses to see her actual credentials.

Given the dilution of the word "positive" and the method's current applications in the canine behavior field, another movement among some community members, who use science to kindly and humanely modify behavior, is under way to abandon the phrase "positive training" completely in favor of yet another designation.

 # The Cristine Dahl Method

My approach to dog training borrows bits and pieces from the traditional and positive training models, but it also adds elements from my own years of experience, the requests and struggles of my students and clients, and my formal and informal education in animal behavior, biology, and the animal mind and brain. It is meant to address today's evolved relationship between dogs and their humans in a way that's smart, candid, relevant, kind, and scientific.

It is also meant to teach you how to have a very close relationship with your dog without having to give up all the amazing benefits and indulgences a dog offers. The method provides a way to achieve good-dog status by acknowledging and tackling the challenges faced in today's real-life setting—very often a busy, hectic, time-starved lifestyle.

I aim to arm you with the tools necessary to quickly and kindly fix urgent and relevant problem behaviors such as poor manners so that harmony can be restored in the home and the benefits of the human/canine relationship can be realized. While my method does have a component of obedience, it primarily addresses everyday issues in the home such as jumping up, bolting out the door, destroying furniture and other home fixtures, surfing the counters, and so on. I also address common socially challenging situations such as on-leash aggression, poor dog park manners, aggressive behavior toward visitors to the home, nuisance barking, poor public greeting behaviors, and the like.

I recognize that today's owner lives a real life. While training by obedience is reasonable for those competing in the field of obedience, and sit, stay, and down are helpful and nice-to-have behaviors, I believe they are significantly less important than making sure a dog lives peacefully among his humans. It's not unusual to hear me say, "I don't care if my dog can sit if he eats my turkey off the table!" Today's family simply doesn't benefit from a program built solely on obedience; this evolved relationship needs a training method as sophisticated and real as it is.

My method focuses on manners, behavioral soundness, and gentle guidance. It is meant to address the companion dog—one who lives in today's cities among families with adults and children, who needs to be a good citizen in every situation in which he is placed.

The Dog/Human Relationship

A great complaint of the popular personalities currently touting traditional models admonishes owners for spoiling their dogs, or not recognizing that a dog is a dog and a human is a human. While some of these arguments can be substantiated, I disagree with the general rule.

I am fully aware that my own dogs are not humans, yet I allow them to share my bed, the family furniture, to accompany my family on family outings, and to exhibit the endearing, charming, and even humorous personality traits that make them so wonderful. My dogs enjoy designer foods and leashes and collars and toys, they sleep on orthopedic beds, and they even wear tailored coats in the winter. (This is not to say that you must give your dog these things; it's simply meant to say you don't have to deny them.)

However, my dogs have impeccable manners. They do not rush through the door when it's opened, and they only jump up to snuggle on the furniture when invited. They come when called and do not put their feet on the countertop. They sit politely when guests arrive and are model citizens on leash.

They do know how to follow basic obedience cues such as sit, down, and stay, but my family and I rarely find the need to use these cues. Instead, we find our lifestyle with our dogs consists of very few, if any, actual training sessions; rather, it is a lifestyle of checks and balances. I dislike the idea of a training task very much, and will avoid having to set aside a few uninterrupted minutes to train my dogs unless I am teaching a class or preparing them for an advanced lesson.

This is not to say that my dogs always behaved this way. My older one had relatively pronounced dog aggression for the first seven years of her life, and was one of the most assertive attention seekers I have seen to this day. She would not respond to "come" or any other basic obedience cue with any amount of regularity and her human greeting manners were an embarrassment.

My other dog, whom I acquired as an adult, came with serious cases of on-leash aggression, barrier frustration, stranger aggression, and uncontrolled prey drive.

Although I had trained my older dog by the traditional method for seven years, we were still at odds daily. No amount of positive punishment or negative reinforcement could curb her more serious aggression issues, and her attention-seeking behaviors were absurd. I was frustrated by the uncivilized struggle I fell prey to each day while striving for even just a little behavioral control.

Not until retraining and educating myself in alternative methods and becoming dedicated to the techniques I've outlined in this book did I help my dog the amazing citizen she is today and did I finally feel like my approach to training her was modern and civilized. My younger male dog, too, has overcome all aspects of the very serious behavior problems he came with and both dogs are a joy to live with.

Are Today's Dogs Too Spoiled?

Explaining away the problems of today's human/canine relationship in terms of dogs being treated as little humans is greatly overstated. I refuse to acknowledge that any person actually mistakes his or her dog for a human being. Just as dogs know the difference between their species and ours, humans, too, know a dog is an animal.

A more likely explanation for this criticism is that today's owner has very different needs for a dog in his life than he did fifty years ago. This has nothing to do with him thinking his dog is a human child and losing all sense of drawing a line between himself and his canine. However, there is a basis for this belief.

According to the American Pet Products Manufacturers Association (APPMA), 43.5 million American households have a dog. This number has grown 7 percent since 1988, and the trend continues. The APPMA reports the annual household expenditure on basic canine needs averages $1,571. The amount of money spent across the nation in the pet category increased from $17 billion to $29 billion from 1994 to 2002. The number of dollars spent on goods, medicines, and services is predicted to grow between 5 percent and 8 percent each year as the trend pushes on.[1]

In the last century, the majority of dog/human households were comprised of children and married parents. According to Mediamark Research, Inc., only one third of today's pet owners are married with children, and one of the biggest growing segments of dog owner is the empty-nest baby boomer.[2]

Of those families who do have kids, a greater number of them had a dog first and waited until a later age to have kids than did their own parents. While the direct cause cannot be proven, there is a strong argument for the elevated role a dog plays in today's world versus his role of the past. Because couples postpone having kids, dogs often becomes stand-ins for newly married couples or unmarried couples who choose to cohabitate. For those baby boomers suffering the void resulting from adult children leaving the family, a dog can be just the answer to bring life and focus back into the home.

The pet industry has reacted to this changing terrain by providing goods and services with items that cater to this setting. Specialty toys and supplies, designer foods, brand name clothing, pet insurance, advanced medical care, daycare, and other industry segments are new to the category. They are a direct measure of the central role today's dog plays in his family.

In this way, it's easy to explain why some people attribute today's behavioral crisis to spoiled dogs. However, the availability of material items and specialty services is completely unrelated to the behavioral health of a dog. Simply because he can live more comfortably now than ever does not mean he is a spoiled brat and is misbehaving because of it.

It seems more likely that what is being mistaken for spoiling a dog is actually the result of the struggle to find and implement reasonable behavioral discipline and guidelines while still enjoying all that is *dog*. The choices facing today's owner, to have a spoiled dog or a well-behaved one, aren't mutually exclusive. It is perfectly reasonable to treat a dog to the new and wonderful services and items available to him while still requiring him to behave like a gentleman.

The area of dog behavior and modification is not the enigma it's been presented as for so many decades, and dog owners are not the obedient drones they've been pegged as by the traditional dog training community for so many years. It doesn't take a mind reader, an obedience expert, a breeder, or even a veterinarian to understand or "communicate" with a dog. All it takes to achieve a harmonious relationship between human and dog is a general understanding of canine behavior and the system of rewards and punishments that govern this lifestyle.

The Theoretical Foundation of the Dahl Method

My training approach is based on animal learning theory—the study of how animals learn. *Learning* is defined as a change in behavior based on experience. Because of this clear definition, it's easy to look at a behavior, decide what you want a dog to do instead, apply a behavior modification technique, and see if anything has changed.

The science of this approach simplifies training and behavior modification. No amount of mind reading or guessing is needed. This also completely discards the idea of training by the pack model. Because dominance theory and establishing humans as Alpha is so subjective, it's too complicated. I see it as an unnecessary and often inhumane component of companion animal training.

My model employs positive reinforcement, the addition of something to increase the frequency and/or intensity of a behavior, and negative punishment, the removal of something to decrease the frequency and/or intensity of a behavior. This means the use of food, praise, pets, games, and opportunities to engage in high-probability behaviors such as dog play and scavenging as rewards. I utilize no-reward markers (NRMs); interruptions and redirections as positive punishments; the removal of reinforcers such as play, pets, treats, and attention; and timeouts as negative punishments.

As I discussed earlier, dogs learn in two ways: by consequence and by association. The former accounts for about 1 percent of a dog's learning; the latter accounts for the remainder of his learning experiences.

When a dog is learning by consequence, he's learning that an action on his part will be followed by a consequence. For example, if he jumps up, he will get attention. If he's asked to sit and he does, he'll get a cookie. He has also learned that if he barks, he'll get yelled at, or if he steals something, he'll be chased.

When a dog is learning by association, he is not an active part of his environment; he's learning that no matter what he does, things around him happen. Rather then being able to do something and have something happen, he's learned that certain things have innate meaning.

For example, he may have learned that when a thunder storm rolls in, his coat collects static electricity and he feels uncomfortable. He may have learned that when presented with dogs while he's on leash, he goes through an anxiety response. In every learning-by-association event, the dog has no control over his environment; he is an inactive bystander.

Along with recognizing that dogs learn by consequence and by association, my method recognizes that dog behavior can be modified using two types of conditioning: operant and classical.

Operant conditioning, otherwise known as Skinnerian conditioning, focuses on learning by consequence. In an operant conditioning situation, a dog is not upset. He is not fearful, or aggressive, or suffering from any anxiety. Popular operant conditioned behaviors are teaching a dog to sit, stay, come, and lay down.

Classical conditioning, otherwise known as Pavlovian conditioning, focuses on learning by association. In a classical conditioning situation, a dog may or may not be upset. The classical conditioning approach simply changes an association a dog has with something to something different.

Popular classically conditioned behaviors are teaching a dog to enjoy tail trims, teaching him to accept trips to the vet, teaching him not to fear strangers, and teaching him not to fear storms. In each of these cases, there is an emotional element present that must be classically conditioned. No amount of operant conditioning will achieve a change in associative learning.

Incorporating the two types of learning, consequence and association, with the two types of behavioral modification, operant and classical, creates a balanced and informed yet simple approach to any behavioral problem facing today's companion dog owner.

The approach also targets behavior from the teach-a-dog-what-to-do direction instead of the what-not-to-do direction. It is unfair and unkind to punish a dog for doing something wrong before he really learns what he's supposed to do instead.

This method also recognizes the need for emotional soundness by way of drive outlets and adequate stimulation. Before it is reasonable to expect a dog to learn anything, it is only fair to set him up to succeed. Finally, we're equipped with information about dog drives and now we can actually use that information to help achieve mental soundness. Rather than suppressing dog behavior, which then results in generalized anxiety and behavior problems, we can help a dog learn to exercise his drives in acceptable ways so that he is happy and healthy and it becomes reasonable to expect him to behave well.

How It Compares to the Traditional Model

The main concept retained from my experience as a traditional trainer is the need for discipline and structure in a dog's life. I also employ no-reward markers (NRMs) such as "ah-ah" or "too bad" to signal to a dog that a particular behavior of his didn't earn him a reward. There is a good argument that the NRM is actually positive punishment because it is an application of a thing (voice) to drop the frequency and intensity of a behavior (the thing a dog is doing wrong). This is consistent with the traditional model of training.

Most of the other elements of a traditional training model have been abandoned in my style: training by pack theory or dominance, establishing a human as Alpha, using positive punishers including squirt bottles; verbal scolding; physical force; pinch, prong, and choke collars; alpha rolls; shakedowns; other dominance moves; and any sort of electric or chemical physical suppressant such as a radio or citronella collar. I consider these punishers inhumane and plenty of documentation is available to support this claim, despite the number of canine professionals touting them as kind.[3–6] Interestingly, while the United States has not implemented restrictions on some of these tools, there are various legal restrictions on electric and prong/pinch collars in Australia because they are deemed inhumane.

I also abandon mind reading and projecting elements of traditional training in my method. It's useless to complicate training by reading a dog's behavior in terms of what's going on in his head. When a training approach begins to use phrases such as "he thinks, feels, worries, is resentful or angry, is getting back at you," or the like, the complexity and subjectivity of training escalates at an alarming rate. This overcomplicates training and quickly reverts back to an uncivilized approach.

My approach operates solely on observable behavior. While I, like most dog owners, do indulge in what I can imagine is going on in my dogs' heads, I never approach their behavior based on these intangible elements. Their personalities make them irresistibly endearing, but despite my desperate wish to understand what's going on in their heads, I admit I cannot.

Recognizing dog drives and necessary outlets for them is also inconsistent with the traditional model, as is the teach-a-dog-what-to-do-first approach.

How It Compares to the Fundamental Positive Model

My method shares more in common with the positive model than the traditional model, but it also deviates from it.

I employ the same positive reinforcement and negative punishment techniques used by fundamentalist positive trainers such as food, praise, and fun. I also insist on using a marker to communicate to a dog that he has done something right. However, I do not always enlist the clicker.

I deviate from the purely positive model in that I use prompting and luring to modify behavior. This means I use voice, physical gestures, food lures, and environmental props to encourage the behavior I'm seeking (I do not mold a dog by positioning his body manually). Fundamentalist positive trainers generally criticize these techniques, as they hinder a dog's willingness to give behavior on their own.

However, I find that luring, prompting, and using other techniques to encourage behavior from dogs is a great way to see results in training quickly and I believe that these methods are all very kind. While the benefits of clicker training cannot ever be overstated, the truth of today's companion animal setting is that the needs of most owners typically don't jive with an approach consisting entirely of clicker training. The owner needs a fix *now* just to install or regain harmony in the home.

The Practical Foundation of the Dahl Method

Humans have various pastimes and rituals in which they regularly engage to help lower the daily stresses and anxieties associated with living. Some exercise, some meditate, some relax in a bath, while others like a glass of wine, a game of computer solitaire, gardening, cleaning, or cooking.

No matter the chosen activity, the result is the same: a relaxed, calm, de-stressed feeling once the activity is underway or complete. When a person's favorite anxiety-lowering pastime is unavailable, he or she falls prey to the effects of increasing stress. The resulting manifestation of this bottled-up anxiety can be as innocuous as increased irritability or difficulty sleeping, or as serious as an anxiety disorder or severe aggression.

The urges to engage in these activities are very similar to the biological anxiety-lowering urges dogs possess.

Humans also live by a set of culturally acceptable guidelines. These standard codes of behavior are numerous, but common examples are greeting rituals (handshakes, nods, waves), manners (saying please and thank you, exhibiting proper table etiquette), and general politeness (quiet voices, kind language, decorum). Human behavior that deviates from these "normal" boundaries is seen as abnormal, uncivilized, and inappropriate.

For example, imagine that a person greets you by licking your face, thanks you by knocking you to the ground, or eats by scooping loads of food into his mouth with his bare hands. The person behaving this way could be seen as savage, inappropriate, rude, or otherwise socially handicapped. In reality, the person simply may never have been taught the preferred way to behave in these various situations.

These boundaries within which humans live are very similar to those that are missing in the lives of a great number of dogs. Often, a dog hasn't been taught the correct way to greet humans, the appropriate way to behave around the dinner table, or how to settle into the preferred routine and manner of behavior.

Today's dog misbehaves for two core reasons:

• His biological needs are not being met.
• He is not required to live by a set of boundaries.

From puppyhood, a dog inhabits the artificial human home environment, never setting foot into the wild dog environment he's biologically wired to live in. This environment, while warm, cozy, dry, and usually filled with love, doesn't automatically lend itself to his biological urges and needs. For example, while today's owner adoringly puts down a full bowl of food for his dog to eat from throughout the day whenever he's hungry, the act of doing so robs a dog of a natural outlet for his need to scavenge for his food.

This artificial environment also comes with its own set of boundaries not instinctively understood by a dog. For example, a dog in the home will not automatically know he is not to be on the furniture, as furniture does not exist in the wild dog world. Unless taught otherwise, he cannot know he is not to rush through an open door, as doors are absent in the wild.

Behavior Drives

Dogs are dogs, and as such, they each come with a set of species-specific behaviors known as *drives*. These drives are scavenging, chewing, digging, dissecting, barking, and hunting.

In the traditional approach, expressions of these drives are punished and dogs are forced to suppress the very urges that make them dogs. For example, if they show their scavenging drive by stealing laundry, they are punished for this behavior without being given an appropriate outlet. If they are caught chewing on something illegal, they are punished and never directed to a legal item. The fallout of this unfortunate condition is anxiety.

This is very similar to some of the urges people are born with, and we can compare these examples to our own favorite drive behaviors. A similar behavior in a human is anything in which you engage that decreases your anxiety. This may be yoga, running, reading a book, socializing, eating desert every night, watching a favorite television show, or playing a computer game. Every person has some favorite anxiety-lowering activity that can be compared to a drive in a dog.

If, say, your favorite anxiety-lowering activity is reading a book each night to wind down before falling asleep, then we can loosely compare this to a canine drive. Each evening, after a busy day of work, family, chores, errands, and so on, you settle in with a favorite novel. This seemingly simple act actually causes a drop in stress and generalized anxiety. Assuming this is a fairly strong urge, you must engage in the activity every night to keep sane.

But let's say, then, that you begin to share your bed with a light sleeper who cannot tolerate the light you need to read. Each time you settle in to read, your partner rolls over, gives a glare, and grouches at you. This experience is punishing and so you begin to avoid reading at bedtime.

The first few nights, you're slightly annoyed, but you're able to fall asleep eventually. After the third night or so, however, the little bit of anxiety you are unable to relieve each night with reading begins to mount. You are beginning to resent your partner for not allowing you this indulgence, you cannot shut off your brain from the busy day, and your nights are fitful. Each morning you wake up more irritable than you were the day before.

Simply because you've been punished for reading in bed likely doesn't mean you'll give up reading altogether unless the punishment is severe enough it curbs this strong urge. Instead, you are likely to find another way to read. You may read on the couch away from your spouse, or you may begin to sleep in another room altogether to get relief from your anxiety and wind down. Not a great relationship builder, of course, but the urge to relieve anxiety is strong enough that the switch in setting seems reasonable.

Now imagine if you, who found a way to read in places other than bed to avoid being bothered by your partner, continue to be punished for your natural urge to read no matter where you settle. After many sufficient punishments, you may decide to give up your favorite anxiety-lowering behavior, reading, altogether. Ah, but imagine the amount of anxiety you will suffer as a result. The stress and energy that could so easily be mollified by a few chapters a night now has nowhere to go and builds day after day, adding to your general stress and behavioral unsoundness.

This is one basis for today's deficiency in the behavioral care of our dogs: they simply lack appropriate daily outlets for their drive energies, and the accumulated anxieties that result from this deficiency lend themselves to an array of common problem behaviors.

Each drive behavior is detailed here:

- **CHEWING** is one of the strongest drive behaviors. A dog must chew in order to keep his teeth and jaws in great shape, as well as keep the muscles in his head in working order. Not only is chewing significant biologically, but also it is an exceedingly enjoyable activity. Simply by observing a dog settled in a fit of chewing, it's easy to see he's lost in the joy and soothing nature of the activity itself.

- **SCAVENGING** is also one of the strongest drive behaviors. Biologically, dogs, who are excellent scavengers, have an exceedingly better chance of survival among their species than those who do not come equipped with this skill. Scavenging behavior in pet dogs manifests most often as the dog stealing laundry, paper towels, toilet paper, dryer sheets, dinner off the counter or table, or any other item that he may then hoard or parade around the living room like some glorious hostage. Anyone who has ever witnessed the glee a dog engaged in illegal scavenging exhibits can attest to its reinforcing qualities.

- **DIGGING** is a drive that can be very strong in some dogs and almost nonexistent in others. Dogs who can dig to find food and other resources have excellent biological viability. As with chewing, if a dog is allowed to engage in digging, he will very often exhibit trancelike glee when in the middle of his messy masterpiece.

- **BARKING** can be a bit of a tricky drive behavior to use as an appropriate drive energy outlet, but it is worth mentioning. Dogs bark for countless reasons, but there are a limited number of types of barking in dogs exhibiting a drive urge. Drive barking can be seen particularly in herding and hunting breeds.

- **HUNTING** in domesticated dogs is a dumbed-down version of the predatory sequence seen in wolves. This ritualized predatory behavior, born into every dog no matter his size or deviance from normal wolf stature, can include any number of behaviors in the sequence, including searching, stalking, rushing, chasing, grabbing, killing/shaking, dissecting, and consuming. The very common tugging behavior seen in most dogs is a manifestation of this drive.

Happily, simply admitting your pup is a predator doesn't mean he loves to eat children or kill mailmen. It just means he's a dog. Depending on the individual, any portion of the predatory sequence may be present to different degrees. For example, retrievers are bred to have very strong search, stalk, chase, and grab instincts. Racing dogs are bred to have more of the sequence so they will chase the mechanical rabbit with extreme enthusiasm.

It is helpful to consider the breed specifics of your dog to understand his hunting drive needs, but it is not reasonable to count on this measure, as it can vary greatly in today's unregulated breeding landscape.

- **DISSECTING** is a specific portion of the predatory sequence, but it is often included in many of the steps seen in the entire sequence. If you've ever had a dissector, you know the behavior: you spend too much money on a lovely squeaky toy, usually something furry or plushy, and toss it to your dog. Often he freezes at first sight, and then rushes at the thing, lunging at it as if it's going to get away. Once his teeth have punctured the fuzzy's little body, your pup will shake the thing vigorously to kill it. After he's satisfied with his killing attempt, and he's deemed the thing dead, he will pin it to the ground with his forepaws, make a surgical incision in its gut, and disembowel it. Only when the plush body is empty does your pup lose interest entirely in the carcass, leaving it to adorn the living room floor for days to come unless somebody picks it up. He may also decide to tote it around, hoard it, or bury it. Although it's unusual, occasionally a dissector will consume the stuffing or outer body of a dissectible.

Socialization

Socialization is another biological need greatly overlooked in today's world of canine behavior.

It is no exaggeration to state that dogs are compulsively social by nature. They count on being able to assess situations up close in order to survive. Because of this deep biological urge, it's important to take their socialization seriously, and deficiencies in their social opportunities are common and potentially serious.

The biological root of this is plain: dogs who learn to avoid potentially dangerous and deadly situations when they are very young have a much greater likelihood of surviving into adulthood to pass their genes to another generation.

When they're born, puppies have a short period of time to gain the valuable life-preserving lessons their environment offers. While the window of opportunity varies somewhat, the general consensus is that the most beneficial socialization window closes when a pup is twelve weeks of age. Before this time, a puppy must encounter a mind-blowing number of experiences in his or her environment to ensure sound social health as an adult.

Socialization can be a widely misunderstood term. Whereas humans generally take it to mean socializing a dog to people and other dogs, the task is actually much greater. A dog must experience people and dogs—people of all ages, sizes, sexes; people wearing a variety of types of clothing such as hats and trench coats; people in wheelchairs and on crutches; people on skateboards, bikes, and rollerblades; garbage trucks and delivery personnel; the vet; various smells; visitors to the home; strangers on the street—as well as infinite permutations of their environment such as rain, sun, night, and day, and the list goes on and on. Because dogs are such brilliant discriminators, it's up to a pup's human to expose him to as much as possible when he's young to thwart behavioral problems when he's an adult.

Common adult problems stemming from undersocialization include barrier frustration, stranger aggression, on-leash aggression, poor social manners with other dogs, fighting, and fear. Because of the suburban setting in which many dogs live today, they are isolated much of the time but are also required to endure social outings to public places or in-home events for which they may not be adequately socialized.

A common argument is made by many breeders and veterinarians that a dog must remain in the home until his third round of vaccines has been administered; often long after the twelve-week marker. However, while this was appropriate decades ago because the vaccinated population was fairly unregulated, today's dog is much more at risk of being euthanized due to a behavioral problem than he is of dying from a communicable disease. While owners must exercise common sense when socializing a puppy by avoiding dog parks and other common dog areas, keeping a dog away from the world is a grave mistake. Documentation from some of the nation's top veterinary schools is now available to help owners make an educated decision about keeping their dogs biologically safe while making sure their social needs are met.[7-8]

Stimulation

The third biological need not being met in most dogs today is the need for stimulation. A shocking number of problem behaviors stem from a home environment void of any mental or physical enrichment. The most common result of a dog living in such a stark setting is generalized anxiety, which can lead to the problems discussed previously, but the lack of stimulation can also manifest in seemingly less-serious ways, such as boredom or nuisance barking; chewing on inappropriate items; stealing; surfing the counters; destroying household items such as furniture, clothing, and fixtures; and exhibiting an increased energy in general. More serious, the dog who goes a prolonged period of time without his environment being enriched often develops obsessive-compulsive-type behaviors such as spinning, pacing, or incessant licking and barking. These unhealthy manifestations directly result from a lack of proper stimulation.

A dog is brought home and expected to become a calm and harmonious member of the family although some of his most biological needs are not met. Many dogs today receive only a walk in the morning as an attempt at adequate stimulation and a great number of dogs don't even get that.

Satisfying Biological Needs

Satisfying all of the previously mentioned biological needs—drive outlets, socialization, and stimulation—ensures a dog who is not only mentally sound, but also a dog who is then prepared to learn. It is unfair to expect a dog who is experiencing anxiety for any of these reasons to behave in a controlled and calm manner or to learn at a reasonable rate. This is the same as expecting any human experiencing anxiety to learn a new foreign language in a calm, productive, and reasonable way; picture yourself attending a Latin class when you're already agitated from a week of poor sleep—impossible.

Satisfying a dog's biological needs is easier today than ever before. This doesn't mean he's going to be allowed to run wild through the house, but it does mean that his basic needs are going to be met in legal and appropriate ways.

SATISFYING DRIVES

One of the wonderful things about teaching a dog to exercise his drives in an appropriate way is that he is adequately punished simply by being interrupted when he gets it wrong. Before embarking on a plan to get a dog's drive behaviors under control, it is necessary to establish a setting of legal and appropriate outlets. Remember, before you can tell a dog what not to do, you have to teach him what to do instead.

- CHEWING: Begin by taking a trip to the pet supply store and stocking up on a plethora of novel and varied chew items. Sample items from each of the categories available, such as various hard natural bones, soft plush toys, ropes, Nylabones and other hard plastic items, rubber things, and dried animal parts. Novelty is irresistible to dogs and having a number of things on hand will ensure he'll like something you've bought him at least, if not more, than your furniture. For suggestions, see PART III, RECOMMENDED TOYS AND PRODUCTS, ON PAGE 265. For specific instructions on tackling common chewing problems, refer to CHAPTER 11, CHEWING, ON PAGE 183.

- **SCAVENGING:** Most dogs today are fed by bowl. While it seems a very nice and caring way to provide food for a dog, it turns out it actually robs him of an outlet for one of his strongest drives: scavenging. Dogs who are not given appropriate outlets for their scavenging drive are more likely to steal things around the house such as laundry, paper products, trash, and things off the counter.

  Before embarking on any of the behavior modification techniques suggested in **PART II, COMMON CANINE BEHAVIOR PROBLEMS AND HOW TO RESOLVE THEM,** first stock up with legal work-to-eat puzzles and props. These include but are not limited to the Tricky Treat Ball, Buster Cube, Kong, Talk-to-Me Treat Ball, and Busy Buddy Waggle. Instead of laying down a bowl of food, get rid of the bowl entirely and feed your dog using one of these fabulous tools. As a dog plays with each of these items, he's forced to get clever about emptying it of its contents. As he works to get his kibble out of the tool, he is exhausting his brain and satiating his scavenging drive. The result is a happy and less anxious dog, and an intact home.

- **HUNTING:** This drive manifests in several ways depending on the individual dog, the most common of which are seen in games of Tug, fetch, and chase. There are a number of great outlets for dogs who like to engage in these activities. For information on Tug, see **PAGE 99.** For props and great tools, see **PART III.**

- **DIGGING:** Digging is a strong drive in some dogs and a weak drive in others. If the setting allows, one of the best ways to satisfy a dog's drive to dig is by establishing a legal digging pit. This designated pit is an area about three feet by three feet. It is generally filled with the dog's favorite digging substrate such as dirt, pebbles, or sand. Without a legal digging pit, the avid digger left to his own devices in the backyard will choose multiple digging spots and the yard will begin to resemble a missile testing site. The pup who has learned to head to a digging pit when the urge hits him will do so each time to avoid being interrupted for illegal digging. For specific digging lessons, see **CHAPTER 14, DIGGING AND BURYING, ON PAGE 201.**

- **DISSECTING:** This is one of the most interesting drives. A subset of the hunting drive, dissecting is often seen independent of the rest of the behaviors associated with hunting. While it's not necessary to allow a dog to dissect, it is a great way to exercise his drive energy and allow him yet another way to lower anxiety—not to mention, it's fun to watch. Thankfully, it's also not necessary to buy retail "dissectibles" for him to get his jollies. Consider visiting the local Goodwill or secondhand store to stock up on stuffed toys that he can destroy. There are also a number of online stores selling actual plush dog toys for under a dollar.

Note: Always supervise your dog when he has a dissectible. Though it's unusual, some dogs will consume the material they dissect and are not good candidates for this drive activity. Always remove hard parts such as plastic eyes and beans from a dissectible before giving it to a dog.

SATISFYING THE SOCIALIZATION REQUIREMENT

The best way to socialize a dog is to start when he's a puppy and make sure he experiences a tremendous number of things when he's very young. While this is paramount, it's equally important to maintain socialization as a dog matures into and through adulthood.

The young puppy must be taken to social settings, public places, and bustling environments before the age of twelve weeks. It's not only necessary that he experience these things but that he has *good* experiences with these things. A bad experience will have as much impact if not more than a good experience and you must make every effort to gently overcome areas in which a puppy may be particularly sensitive.

When socializing a pup, it's wise to bolster experiences with jolly talk, praise, pets, and treats. Arming strangers with treats to give to a puppy is an incredibly effective way to socialize a dog to unfamiliar people, and gently chatting a pup through a loud situation can do wonders for his association with it. I cannot emphasize the importance of this task enough.

ACHIEVING ADEQUATE STIMULATION

There are two main categories of stimulation: mental and physical. Most dogs today suffer shortages in both categories. To achieve adequate stimulation, a dog must be given both physical and mental outlets for his energy.

Physical exercise is a necessity for every dog no matter his breed, age, or temperament. Unless he's recovering from an injury or he suffers from a medical condition that requires his activity to be limited, he must be exercised.

A morning and evening walk do *not* adequately satisfy this need. A general mark of good physical stimulation is an activity that raises a dog's heart rate for thirty minutes a day. If a dog is very small, this may be achieved with a very vigorous walk, but more likely the dog will need a run, a trip to the dog park, a visit to dog daycare, a half an hour or more of fetch or retrieve or even an activity such as agility (a popular activity in which a dog must complete a course of obstacles and actions), flyball, Tug, or another active game.

While this is my recommendation for adequate exercise, always consult your veterinarian before embarking on a plan of this nature to make sure your dog is old enough, physically developed enough, and otherwise capable of enduring this plan.

Simply adding work-to-eat strategies to a dog's life can do wonders because of the mental stimulation portion of this task. Other great mental activities include hide-and-seek, wall ball, fetch and retrieve, and other trained games. Great books and other resources are available with tons of these ideas and instructions on how to play the games.

The methods I recommend of achieving adquate physical and mental stimulation for a dog differ greatly from those that Caesar Millan uses. Millan's approach relies on exhaustion to achieve a subdued dog. In several episodes of his popular TV show, Millan discusses regularly using a treadmill to exercise the dogs with whom he works. Rather than running at will, they are tethered to the treadmill and are forced to run, often for hours at a time.

This popular technique found public attention in May 2006, when an adult Labrador Retriever, Gator, was rushed from Millan's Dog Psychology Center to the vet, bleeding from his mouth and nose, and suffering from severe bruising and trauma to his inner thighs. While the case is still pending, the dog was allegedly tethered and run on a treadmill as part of his training program until he could no longer hold his body up.[9]

While this is an extreme example of the potential damage that can result from the treadmill technique Millan employs, it is an excellent wake-up call.

The result of running a dog while tethered to a treadmill may be a subdued dog, but the appearance of a tired dog in these cases is deceptive. Rather than an indication that a dog is relaxed, he's literally fatigued to such a degree that he can hardly function. A kinder approach recognizes that exhaustion is not a measure of a healthy, relaxed dog; it's a measure of a dog who is exceedingly tired. Allowing a dog a balanced number of outlets, consisting of drive, physical, and mentally stimulating activities, is a far superior method, and one that is humane, scientific, and sound.

The treadmill can be used in a humane way, but a dog must never be tethered or otherwise strapped to it and he must never be punished for failing to run.

By understanding how your dog learns, giving him ample outlets for his biological drives, managing his environment for success, and teaching him what to do instead of what not to do, you can achieve a superior level of behavioral harmony and eliminate the daily struggle for good behavior common in so many American homes. This approach is not only easy and kind, but it also fosters a smarter and stronger relationship between your dog and everyone in his family.

1. PPMA, "Industry Statistics & Trends," http://www.appma.org/press_ industrytrends.asp, March 10, 2007.

2. Rebecca Gardyn, *American Demographics*, "Survey Results on Pet Ownership-Statistical Data Included," May 1, 2002.

3. E. Schalke, J. Stichnoth, S. Ott, and R. Jones-Baade, "Clinical Signs Caused by the Use of Electric Training Collars on Dogs in Everyday Life Situations," *Applied Animal Behaviour Science*, Available online 11 December 2006.

4. Matthijs B. H. Schilder and Joanne A. M. van der Borg, "Training Dogs with Help of the Shock Collar: Short and Long Term Behavioural Effects." *Applied Animal Behaviour Science*, Volume 85, Issues 3–4, 25 March 2004, Pages 319–334.

5. Advocates for Animals, "Why Electric Shock Collars For Dogs Should Be Banned," http://www.advocatesforanimals.org.uk/pdf/ electricshockcollars.pdf, March 17, 2007.

6. RSPCA, "Dog Training Collars—The Ones We Don't Like," http://blog1 .rspcasa.asn.au/2007/01/22/dog-training-collars-part-i-the-ones-we-dont-like, March 17, 2007.

7. Andrew Luescher and Steve Thompson, letter to author, May 10, 2004.

8. Robert K. Anderson, letter to the author, February 10, 2004.

9. Michael Linder, "Dog owner wants to bury Cesar?" (May 2006), http:// www.linder.com/archives/category/the-dog-whisperer.

PART II

Common Canine

Behavior Problems

and How to

Resolve Them

While most current schools of dog training focus on obedience such as sit, down, come, stay, and so on, this book focuses on real-life training for today's busy family. These lessons are meant to address the things facing companion animal owners in the home and neighborhood environment: basic manners and living harmoniously with their dog every day.

Filled with quick and lasting fixes that can be implemented in today's full lifestyle, this section tackles the most common behavior problems facing today's companion animal owner. Each lesson will help get relief quickly so that the full potential of the relationship between you and your dog can be realized.

Many lessons give easy, intermediate, and difficult training solutions. Difficult remedies are indicated as such because they are comprised of more steps than the easier solutions or require a slightly higher level of skill. However, all levels are easy to understand and are accessible to even the most novice home trainer. It is not necessary to complete more than one suggested remedy in order to fix a problem, but as individual dogs may respond better to different approaches it may be helpful to try more than one of the suggestions. Some lessons may also provide intermediate and difficult training options as a way to build on and practice a newly trained remedy. Each lesson is presented with information about the cause of a behavior (Why), followed by how to fix the behavior (Remedy). Tips are included in some sections. An introduction to some basic training vocabulary used throughout this section can be found starting on **PAGE 83**.

All of the methods used adhere to the American Humane Association guidelines for humane training and the lessons actually strengthen the human/canine bond. The result is a strong family bond between dogs and humans, a calm and harmonious environment, and a lifetime of peace and respect.

 **Basic Obedience**

While this book does not focus on obedience, parts of some lessons do include obedience elements. Because of this, a discussion of familiar obedience commands, behaviors, and lingo follows.

It is not necessary to teach your dog each of these behaviors in order to successfully complete most lessons in this book. Rather, this section is meant to act as reference, to help polish up on obedience cues your dog may already know, and to teach you how to train certain obedience cues that can be helpful in some lessons.

CUE: A cue is a signal you use to ask your dog to do something. You may say a word such as "Sit" or "Down," or you may use a hand signal or other visual sign.

CLICKER: The clicker is a noisemaker you use to communicate to a dog that he's completed a behavior correctly and has earned a reward. Commonly misunderstood, the clicker is not what you use to get a dog's attention, to ask him to come, or to mean any other command, such as sit, stand, down, and so on. The click only means, "Right! You get a reward!" The beauty of the clicker is that because it has only one general meaning, you can use it to teach limitless behaviors. Before the clicker is useful, it must be charged. See **CHARGING THE CLICKER OR MARKER WORD, BELOW.**

The noise of the clicker is preferable to voice and other oral cues as the sound it emits is salient, consistent, and clear. Be advised that some dogs may be sensitive to this sound. In this case, you can muffle it under your arm, use an i-click (a specially designed clicker with a quieter click) instead, or discarded it in favor of a *marker word*, explained next.

Examples:

- A click marks the completion of sit when the dog's butt hits the ground.
- A click marks the completion of a nose bump when the dog's nose bumps your hand.

MARKER WORD: A marker word is a verbal cue you use to communicate to your dog that he's gotten something right. You can use this word instead of a clicker and although it is not as salient or as consistent as the clicker itself, it can be a perfectly acceptable alternative. Common marker words are "Yes!" and "Right!" A marker may also be a tongue click or a smooch. Words such as "good" and "nice" do not work as well as markers as these words tend to better represent a reward instead of mark correct behavior. If you choose to use a verbal marker instead of the clicker, use a word you normally wouldn't use to communicate with your dog. You would use a marker word instead of a click in the examples under **CLICKER.** Before a marker word is useful, it must be charged.

CHARGING THE CLICKER OR MARKER WORD: When it's first introduced, the clicker and the marker word have no specific meaning. To make these tools useful, they must be given meaning, or "charged." In this case, the click must equal delivery of food. To do this, sit quietly with your clicker or the word you're prepared to use as your marker. In various places around you, set little piles of training bait: place some in your pocket, on the table, on the shelf, on the couch next to you, and so on. Then, remain silent and *regardless* *of what your dog's doing*, simply click or say your word and then toss a piece of food to him. Toss about ten to twenty pieces from various locations each time for about three days in a row. By delivering food from various locations and not requiring any specific behavior before doing so, you establish the clicker as a predictor of a reward. Soon, your dog will associate receiving reward treats with the sound of the clicker or marker word.

LURE: This term is used to describe the use of food to move a dog around. The lure itself is a small piece of training bait you pinch between thumb and forefinger. When using a lure, you make no other contact with the dog; you apply no leash pressure, no collar pressure, and no manual touching.

A *full lure* refers to the beginning and easiest step of lure training. In a full lure, the food actually touches the dog's nostrils.

FADING THE LURE: The goal of lure training is eventually to be able to ask a dog to do something by using a hand signal without having to use food to lure him. This hand signal, which you determine before the training begins, is a visual derivative of the full lure. Fading the lure is the process of moving the shape and position of your luring hand through a series of small changes that approximate the final hand signal. Because dogs learn visually much more readily than verbally, teaching a cue using a lure is an infinitely faster teaching process than using traditional obedience means.

Name Recognition

Puppies are not born with the natural desire to watch humans or to be interested in what we're doing or saying. It's important that we train them to be aware of their names as people are. Name recognition is not to be confused with "attention" as it cannot be measured by eye contact, an ear perk, or even a head turn. Instead, good name recognition just means that a dog has learned that his name precedes something of relevance to him, and he is more likely to respond to whatever is about to happen after his name is said.

If you have an adult dog who may have already learned to ignore his name in certain situations, not to worry. With patience and consistency, you can recover name recognition.

To begin, simply say your dog's name and toss him a treat. This exercise does not hinge on his response to a command; he's simply learning that something great follows the magic word (his name). In just a few days, start saying his name before handing him a favorite toy, taking out his leash, or giving him his dinner. He's learning that his name precedes good things and that it behooves him to listen up after you've said it.

After a few weeks of using this very purposeful association plan, begin using his name before issuing a command. Again, do not require your dog to make eye contact with you although you may begin to see him do so. Unlike people, dogs rarely make eye contact as proof of "attention." Just because he's not looking at you doesn't mean he's not listening.

Now that you've established good name recognition, remember to always follow these rules to make sure your hard work never goes to waste:

- Never use your dog's name just before punishing him. Doing so will not make it irrelevant; it will make it relevant but in a bad way.

- When trying to get your dog's attention, only say his name once. Saying it more than once will cause it to lose meaning and teach your dog to respond after his name has been said several times.

- Don't use your dog's name to call him for something unpleasant such as a bath, toenail trimming, and so on. While you never want to fool your dog into these activities, using his name without another cue specifically designed for these things will weaken his response and will result in a not-so-lovely association.

- Only say his name in a pleasant manner. Using it in a fit of anger or frustration will cause your dog to run and hide at the sound of his name.

Sit

Most dogs learn to sit very quickly as young puppies. Sitting pays off often with praise, treats, pets, toys, and so on. However, it's alarming how many dogs sit but have never really learned to respond to a verbal cue to do so. Instead, they sit in response to their owner's body posture, reacting to a common environmental cue such as the owner opening the kibble bag or treat box, or even just sitting to earn pets without ever having to have been asked to do so. While this behavior is endearing, it's not an indication that a dog has learned to respond to the verbal cue "sit."

If you're *sure* your dog *knows* Sit, try this test:

With a cookie in your hand, zip your mouth—be absolutely silent—and position your body towards him in the way you usually do when asking him to sit. Usually this is facing him, cookie in hand, elbow bent, perhaps slightly bent forward, eyes looking at him. Wait a few seconds. Did your pup sit? Likely, yes.

As the second half of the test, turn your back to him and stand upright. Do not allow him to walk around into a position in front of you. With your back to him, facing in the opposite direction, simply say "Sit" without making eye contact or turning around. If he moves to sit in front of you, keep moving so your back is to him. Did he sit? Most likely, he did not.

That clever canine of yours is very keen to your body language and he is a masterful discriminator of environmental cues. If your dog performed as outlined in the previous test, it's very likely he knows to sit in response to your body posture but has not learned that your verbal cue, "sit," has anything to do with it. Smart creature.

Though it may seem like a step back in training, it's essential he learns a pure Sit on your verbal cue.

For many obedience cues, it's most useful to teach the dog first to respond to a hand signal, then to a verbal cue. The technique used is called *luring*. These instructions teach a basic sit on a full lure, then *fade* the lure to a hand signal, and finally, teach the verbal cue.

SIT ON FULL LURE

A full lure just means you are moving the dog around by a piece of bait touching his nose. No leash or additional touching is allowed.

1. Hold a small piece of bait between your thumb and forefinger, and touch it to your dog's nostrils without letting him eat it.

2. Keeping contact between the piece of food and his nose; imagine a straight rod going through your dog's body from his nose to the base of his tail.

3. Gently moving your hand back and *slightly* up, push the tip of this rod as if you're threading the back end of it into a hole in the ground just behind your pup's rear end. Be sure not to lift your hand high enough to cause your dog to jump.

4. When his bottom hits the floor, mark that moment with a click or your marker word, and give him the treat.

5. Repeat this exercise several times until he sits quickly each time.

6. To make sure he learns to sit in front of you, next to you, behind you, and so on, train the move in many different directions by turning your body in various positions and moving your hand around to deliver the hand signal from various areas of your body. For example, have your back to your dog but give the signal over your shoulder. Bend at the knees with your side to your dog, delivering the signal in front of you while you stare straight forward.

FADING THE LURE AND ADDING THE HAND SIGNAL

The hand signal for Sit is a palm swept up near your belt. It's a small, tidy movement.

1. At the full lure position, tip your palm up and move your puppy into a Sit.

2. With your hand in the same position, do the same move with your hand six inches from his nose.

3. Continue to sweep your hand in this motion but further and further from your pup's nose. Increase the distance between your hand and his nose slowly so he doesn't lose you.

4. Remove the food from your hand when it's about eighteen inches from your dog's nose.

5. In the final step of this lesson, your hand will be in the final hand signal position at your waist, swept up in a small, neat movement, without food in it.

VERBAL CUE

When your dog will respond to your hand signal about 90 percent of the time you give it, no matter from which direction, you're ready install the verbal cue, "sit."

1. Start with your hand signal at your belt to refresh his memory and get him in the sitting mood.

2. Say "Sit" once, *wait four seconds*, give your hand signal, click or mark when his butt hits the ground and treat.

   Repeat this several times in a row for a few days, shortening the time you'll wait for a response from four seconds to three, and then to two.

3. With practice, your pup is learning to anticipate your hand signal and he's learned that the faster he sits, the faster he's rewarded.

4. At this step, your hand signal has become a "hint." In other words, when you say "Sit," if he doesn't respond right away, you can use your hand signal to remind him what he's being asked to do.

Tips: Only say your verbal cue once. Your dog heard you the first time; he's just learning and needs time to respond.

Make sure you don't give your verbal cue and hand signal at the same time. This is called *blocking*. Dogs cannot hear your cue and watch your cue at the same time. He will never learn a verbal cue with this complication.

Go slowly and keep training sessions short. It's common to expect a ton from your dog very quickly. Remember, he's just learning and a week or more to learn a hand cue is not unreasonable. Keeping sessions short will ensure they're fun for both owner and dog.

Stand

Before embarking on training, you must know the proper hand signal for Stand: fingers together and straight pointing away from you, palm swept to the side of your body. You teach Stand using a full lure, then fading it to a hand signal, and finally inserting a verbal cue.

STAND ON FULL LURE

A full lure just means you are moving the dog around by a piece of bait touching his nose. No leash or additional touching is allowed.

1. Begin with your dog in a Sit (see previous lesson). Hold a small piece of bait between your thumb and forefinger, and touch it to your dog's nostrils without letting him eat it.

2. Keeping contact between the piece of food and his nose, position yourself so that your dog has room to step forward to your side.

3. Gently draw the food in a *forward* motion to the side until his rear legs are straight. Click or mark this moment and give him the bait.

4. Be careful not to draw the food upwards as this will encourage him to jump. Whereas humans stand *up*, dogs stand *out*.

5. Repeat this exercise several times and in different directions until your dog stands quickly each time you draw the lure forward and to the side.

Note: As Sit is the first cue most dogs learn, they can be hesitant to lift their bodies up to stand. Be patient, go slow, and don't rush past a full lure until your dog is readily standing when lured.

FADING THE LURE AND ADDING THE HAND SIGNAL

The hand signal for Stand is a palm swept sideways near your belt. It's a small, tidy movement.

1. Complete the same move as at the full lure but with your hand two inches from your dog's nose.

2. Continue to sweep your hand in this motion but further and further from your pup's nose in small increments. Increase the distance between your hand and his nose slowly so he doesn't lose you.

3. Remove the food from your hand when it's about eighteen inches from your dog's nose.

4. In the final step of this lesson, your hand will be in the final hand signal position at waist level to your side, moved back in a small, neat movement, without food in it.

VERBAL CUE

When your dog will respond to your hand signal about 90 percent of the time you give it, no matter from which direction, you're ready install the verbal cue "stand."

1. Start with your hand signal at your side to refresh his memory and get him in the standing mood.

2. Say "Stand" once, *wait four seconds*, give your hand signal, click or mark when his back legs are fully straight, and treat.

Repeat this several times in a row for a few days, shortening the time you'll wait for a response from four seconds to three, and then to two.

With practice, your pup is learning to anticipate your hand signal and he's learned that the faster he stands, the faster he's rewarded.

At this step, your hand signal has become a "hint." In other words, when you say "Stand," if he doesn't respond right away, you can use your hand signal to remind him what he's being asked to do.

Lie Down

Before embarking on training, you must know the proper hand signal for Down: fingers together and straight pointing forward, palm swept down at your belt. You teach Down using a full lure, then fading it to a hand signal, and finally inserting a verbal cue.

DOWN ON FULL LURE

A full lure just means you are moving the dog around by a piece of bait touching his nose. No leash or additional touching is allowed.

1. Begin with your dog in a Sit. Hold a small piece of bait between your thumb and forefinger, and touch it to your dog's nostrils without letting him eat it.

2. Keeping contact between the piece of food and his nose, slowly draw your hand directly down to the ground.

3. The *moment* his elbows touch the ground, click or mark the behavior and give him the bait.

4. Repeat this exercise several times and in different directions until your dog goes down quickly each time you draw the lure down. This Sit, Down, Sit, Down series is known as "push-ups."

FADING THE LURE AND ADDING THE HAND SIGNAL

The hand signal for Down is a palm swept up near your belt. It's a small, tidy movement.

1. Complete the same move you do at the full lure but with your hand two inches from your dog's nose.

2. Continue to sweep your hand in this motion but further and further from your pup's nose in small increments, moving it up towards your waist. Increase the distance between your hand and his nose slowly so he doesn't lose you.

3. Remove the food from your hand when it's about eighteen inches from your dog's nose.

4. In the final step of this lesson, your hand will be in the final hand signal position at waist level in front of you, swept down in small, neat movement, without food in it.

VERBAL CUE

When your dog will respond to your hand signal about 90 percent of the time you give it, no matter from which direction, you're ready install the verbal cue "down."

1. Start with your hand signal at your waist to refresh his memory and get him in the mood to go down.

2. Say "Down" once, *wait four seconds*, give your hand signal, click or mark when his elbows hit the ground, and treat.

   Repeat this several times in a row for a few days, shortening the time you'll wait for a response from four seconds to three, and then to two.

3. With practice, your pup is learning to anticipate your hand signal and he's learned that the faster he drops down, the faster he's rewarded.

Leave-It

Unlike Drop, in which your dog already has something in his mouth, Leave-it teaches your dog to abandon his urge to go after something. Leave-it is handiest before your dog has something in his mouth or before he's decided to actively pursue something such as a squirrel, a buddy, or a moving toy. To ensure a solid and reliable Leave-it, you must practice it often and in a variety of places so that it is in place when you really need it.

1. Hold a yummy food treat in your hand, with your palm closed, and allow your dog to nudge it just as you say "Leave it." The *moment* he abandons his effort to pry the food out of your hand, open your hand, mark the behavior with your marker word and allow him to take the treat.

   Hold your hand absolutely still about three inches from his nose. Pulling your hand away from him during this exercise will not teach him to leave something on his own.

2. Hold your palm open with the food in it, say "Leave it," and present the food. Each time he heads for it, close your fingers over the food and only allow him to see it when he abandons it. When he actively abandons it for a second or two, praise him and allow him to take the food.

   Quick reflexes are the key to this step. Allow him to see the food and head for it, but close your hand quickly and reliably to make sure he's never rewarded by taking the food when he's been asked to leave it.

3. Hold your hand cupped over yummy food on the floor, say "Leave it" just as you did in step 1. However, this time when he abandons it, mark his correct behavior with your marker word and treat from the *other* hand.

4. Set yummy food on the floor with your hand next to it, poised and ready to cover it should your dog begin to head for it. Say "Leave it" just as you uncover the food, and the *moment* he abandons it, mark his correct behavior and, again, treat from the *other* hand.

   Just as in step 2, quick reflexes are key.

All of these steps teach your dog that when you say "Leave it," if he abandons whatever it is he's pursuing, you'll treat him from the other hand with something he can actually have.

To increase the difficulty of the Leave-it, use more and more valuable things as those your dog must leave. Be careful to build only on success as a quick leap from kibble to squirrels will ensure failure! Move as slowly through this progression as your dog requires.

Drop

Drop differs from Leave-it in that the dog is dropping an item he already has in his mouth rather than abandoning one he's not yet taken possession of. This is not only handy for something he may have scavenged off the street or from the laundry bin, but it is also a necessary precursor to the super-fun and useful game of Tug!

In the beginning, practice this exercise with low-value objects that your dog is likely to trade for a treat.

1. Sit quietly with your dog and encourage him to take hold of a favorite toy such as a tennis ball, tug toy, or plush animal.

2. When he takes the item in his mouth, *be silent* and place a treat directly on the front of his nose touching his nostrils.

3. The *moment* he drops the toy, mark the behavior with your marker word and treat. Allow him to retake the item and repeat steps 1 and 2 again.

   Do not pull the thing from his mouth. He must willingly relinquish the item for it to be considered a drop.

4. After your dog has dropped his toy several times in a row simply when you present your hand, it's time to insert the verbal cue "drop."

5. Now when your dog is holding a toy in his mouth, say "Drop" once. Wait up to three seconds. Then, bring your hand around with the treat or other toy.

   This series (say the cue, wait three seconds, present the hand) teaches your dog that the verbal cue "drop" always precedes you presenting your hand with the treat. The faster he drops, the faster he's rewarded.

6. Repeat the series until he drops his toy on your verbal cue only.

Note: Don't forget to wait after you've given your dog the "drop" cue. It's important to give him an opportunity to process what he's learning.

After your dog is reliably dropping his toy on your verbal cue only, begin upping the value of the things he must drop. Remember to increase this element slowly and on success so that eventually he'll drop high-value items such as his favorite toy or chew item the first time he's asked.

Go to Mat

Teaching your dog to settle on a mat is an incredibly useful behavior, which you can utilize in a variety of situations. You may wish to have your dog sit on the mat before your guests are allowed in, or you may like him to settle on his mat to stay out from underfoot during food preparation. Dogs can be taught to target a mat as their allowed area on a piece of furniture or the end of a bed, or even as their preferred position in a public place such as under a café table or in a community elevator.

To achieve Go to Mat quickly and efficiently, a technique combining shaping and prompting is best. Choose a mat made of something your dog is not likely to normally be drawn to such as a placemat, doormat, or towel.

Shaping is a technique used to teach dogs seemingly complicated chains of behaviors on command. In shaping, a series of behaviors approximating a final behavior are strung together as criteria and each level of performance is rewarded until the final behavior goal is achieved.

Prompting is a technique in which a signal or environmental cue encourages a behavior. For example, in this case you toss a piece of bait to encourage your dog to move his body to a certain spot.

When training any behavior pattern, it's important to picture what the final behavior will look like. For Go to Mat, your dog will *walk to the mat, walk onto it, and stay on it (either sitting or lying down) for up to five minutes when asked.*

Before beginning a training session, write down a list of the small steps (criterion) your dog must go through in order to accomplish the final behavior pattern. Breaking down the final chain from the previous example into tiny bits, this criterion plan looks like:

1. Dog touches mat with one foot
2. Dog touches mat with two feet
3. Dog touches mat with three feet
4. Dog touches mat with four feet
5. Dog touches mat with four feet for two seconds
6. Dog touches mat with four feet for four seconds

Until . . .

X. Dog touches mat with four feet, Sits or Downs, stays for five minutes.

Now that you've set the plan, you can begin hands-on training.

1. Start with level 1 as your criterion. Reward at this level ten times in a row over a period of two–three minutes.

   • Toss the mat to the floor just a few feet from your dog.

   • This usually prompts your dog to step onto it.

   • Click/mark the behavior in the chosen criteria step and deliver the treat on the mat.

   • Make sure your mark is timed with one foot touching the mat. This is your criterion.

   • Toss another treat off the mat to prompt the dog off of it.

   • Repeat.

2. After your dog is heading to the mat repeatedly at this level, up the criteria to level two: dog touches mat with two feet.

   • Repeat the steps in step 1.

   • Continue to up the criteria systematically moving through the steps of your training plan until you achieve the final behavioral chain: *walk to the mat, walk onto it, stay on it (either sitting or lying down) for up to five minutes when asked.*

3. After your dog is reliably completing the final behavior chain, it's time to install the verbal cue "go to mat." To do this, simply say "Go to mat" before tossing the mat on the floor.

   After a week or so of saying the verbal cue before tossing the mat, begin leaving the mat on the floor in an area in which you can casually supervise your dog.

   When he's not on the mat, say the verbal cue ("go to mat"), point to the mat, and when he goes to it and settles, pay off big!

Tips: Short, two to three minute training sessions are best.

In the first several days of training, keep the rate of reward high. This keeps your dog motivated. If more than a few seconds passes between times your dog gets a reward, drop the criteria to the previous step and work up again.

Until step 3, pick up the mat in between training sessions. This way you avoid any non-rewarded events.

To help lengthen the amount of time your dog stays on his mat, give him a favorite chew item. When he goes to the mat, hand him the item. If he leaves the mat at any time, ask him to drop the chew item and remove it from his reach.

Tug

For years, Tug has gotten a bad rap as an activity that "teaches a dog to be aggressive." The contrary is actually true. Tug is a game that most dogs and owners enjoy playing and it can be a great physical and mental energy burner, as well as a fun game to use for a reward. Rather than teaching your dog to be aggressive, it gives him a legal and controlled outlet for his drive energy, and it can actually be a very powerful behavior modification tool to help control dogs who chase prey, cars, joggers, and so on. In addition to teaching the very valuable skill of getting into and settling out of a drive (a very strong biological urge born into a dog), Tug also teaches a dog the all-important lesson: don't put teeth on people.

As with all games, in order to be effective, there are rules. These rules formalize the game and make sure that its benefits are achieved while keeping everyone safe and happy. Be sure to memorize these rules before ever attempting Tug with your dog.

TUG RULE SUMMARY

- **CHOOSE A DESIGNATED TUG TOY.** This should be something such as a rope or long piece of sturdy fabric that both a dog and a human can hold comfortably.

- **CHOOSE A START CUE.** A verbal phrase such as "tug time" or "get it" signifies the beginning of the formal game.

- **DOG MUST DROP ON COMMAND.** Before tugging, your dog must drop reliably on your verbal request. For instructions on teaching Drop, SEE PAGE 95.

- **NO UNINVITED TAKES OR RETAKES.** Only play Tug with your dog if you've initiated the game with your start cue. If he picks up the toy and encourages you to take it, don't.

- **TAKE FREQUENT OBEDIENCE BREAKS.** When he's engaged in the game, ask him to "drop," then ask him to "sit," "stand," "down," or say another obedience command. After one or a short series of these behaviors, restart the game as his reward. This key step teaches your dog to get into and settle out of a very high-excitement energy with impressive control.

- **NO TEETH ON HUMAN.** If your dog's teeth make even the most gentle contact with your skin, say "Ouch!" and immediately end the game by dropping your end of the toy.

If at any time he breaks any of the rules, immediately cease play, drop the toy, and return to play later. You may postpone the game a few minutes or return to it the next day.

Despite longstanding theories about making sure you end up with the tug toy, not letting your dog "win" the game, this is unfounded and unnecessary. The game itself is so highly rewarding that dropping the toy altogether regardless of who has possession is a punishment. Not only is it perfectly acceptable for your dog to growl and shake his head when playing Tug, but also he should be encouraged to do so as long as he's adhering to the rules listed previously.

Special Instructions for Kids

Today's family relationship with a dog is more intimate than it has been at any other time in history. Because of this, new dynamics involving children and dogs have become issues not seen in the past. To ensure a safe, respectful, and healthy relationship between child and dog, you'll need to consider a number of things:

- As a rule, it is never safe to leave a child under the age of six unsupervised with a dog. That said, children of any age over six can generally be allowed to interact with a dog for short unsupervised periods only when the child has learned to handle the dog correctly.
- Teach children that dogs are living, feeling things. As such, it's important that your child conduct himself calmly and respectfully around the dog. A child should never pull a dog's fur, hang on his neck, ride his back, or pull any part of a dog's body. The expectation that a dog will tolerate this behavior is unreasonable.
- Teach your child to ask before petting a strange dog. Doing so will keep your child safe.

- Only allow your child to engage with your dog once the dog has learned not to use his teeth on people. It is very, very normal for puppies, adolescent dogs, and even some adult dogs to use their mouths in play. By teaching your dog jaw prudence (see **TUG ON PAGE 99**), you can keep your child safe and your dog happy.
- Do not allow your child to walk the dog until he is physically capable of controlling the dog without yanking on his leash. It is not safe for either dog or child to go for walks until this is achieved.
- Teach your child the "be-a-tree" technique. This valuable move can be used to end scary chase and play that's become too rough.

To be a tree, your child must:

1. Abruptly stop and plant his feet in the ground.
2. Fold his arms (branches) across his body.
3. Be silent.

Until your child has mastered this technique, it is not safe for him to play with the dog.

- Teach your child to respect your dog's space and resources (such as water, food, and toys). Dogs cannot be expected to "reason" with a child over sharing resources. A child should never reach or take a resource when it's in a dog's possession. Likewise, when a dog is settled in his favorite area, instruct your child to leave the dog alone.
- Encourage your child to remain calm around dogs. Remaining calm and settled keeps potentially escalated situations under control and greatly improves the odds of a good relationship between dog and child.

CHAPTER 7

Potty Training

E ven the most skilled and attentive dog owners will admit frustration and aggravation when attempting to potty train a dog. Though a seemingly simple task, teaching a dog not to soil your home can seem tantamount to mastering a foreign language or doing brain surgery.

This common struggle is not a measure of an unintelligent or stubborn dog or even an incompetent owner. Rather, most owners simply don't have a good plan to tackle this task.

The recipe for successful potty training is finding a plan that works for your lifestyle and sticking to it. A good training plan is essential and consistency is absolutely necessary.

Starting Out Right: Adolescent and Adult Potty Management

After bringing a newly acquired adolescent or adult dog into a new home, excited owners show their new companion where to potty outside. While he's expected to signal his need to go out to the area thereafter, instead he almost immediately squats to relieve himself once inside with almost no warning at all.

Why

Simply showing a dog where to potty doesn't teach him where not to go and how to signal his need to go. Also, adult dogs often come with any combination of very common potty training challenges:

- During his time wherever it was he lived before meeting his new owner, he may have had little to no potty training at all. This can leave him physically stunted, making potty training for this dog even more difficult than it is for a puppy.

- He may also have been somewhat neglected, which, therefore, inadvertently reinforced his pottying anywhere and anytime he wanted.

- He may come with behavior resulting from being punished for inappropriate potty behavior in the past. You will need to re-teach these lessons.

Remedy

Regardless of the cause of the undesirable potty behavior, the plans to fix it are the same. The key for successful housetraining is 100 percent consistency. This approach will help avoid costly accidents that can hinder successful potty training.

1. Begin by setting up two types of confinement areas in your home:

   • **A SHORT-TERM CONFINEMENT AREA:** His crate, fitted with a snuggly blanket, some chewies, and a favorite toy. The crate may hold your dog for periods no longer than the amount of time he can physically hold his bladder. It may also be his nighttime sleeping area.

   • **A LONG-TERM CONFINEMENT AREA:** An area no bigger than ten by ten square feet; this area may be set up using an expen (a wire barrier described on **PAGE 276**) or a small room. In it, place your dog's crate, food and water, and, if your new dog will be required to be confined longer than he is capable of holding his bladder, an indoor bathroom substrate.* This confinement area will hold your dog for times you cannot be watching him 100 percent of the time. (It's analogous to a baby playpen.)

   Note: If your dog is not in his confinement area or his crate, he cannot be left alone to wander through the house unsupervised until he is fully housetrained. Doing so is a recipe for disaster and it will, without exception, end in potty accidents and failed potty training. Do not open your house to your new dog upon his arrival. Instead, systematically open your home to him upon potty training success.

2. Next, determine about how long is reasonable for your new dog to hold his bladder and bowels. If it's your first day with him, it's best to start this period at two hours. If you've had a few days to observe him and you have a good idea of how often he eliminates, choose the time that's been the shortest period of time he's been able to hold it.

---

* If you choose to leave your new dog for periods longer than he can physically hold his bladder and bowels and you wish not to use an indoor substrate, you must make arrangements for someone to allow him access to his potty area at various scheduled times throughout the day. This can be a neighbor, dog walker, or friend.

Note: This measurement is only valid during the day. Dogs can hold their bladders for a very long time overnight because of a hormone called ADH (antidiuretic hormone).

3. Write that amount of time here: _____.

After you've erected these confinement areas and determined your dog's starting point for the amount of time he can hold his potty, for adult dogs, proceed to the following lessons depending on your preferred method of training. For new puppies, proceed with the outlined puppy-specific housetraining methods on PAGES 241–247.

Adult Dog Potty Crate Training

Please review STARTING OUT RIGHT: ADOLESCENT AND ADULT POTTY MANAGEMENT ON PAGE 104 before proceeding with this lesson.

Why

Crate training is one of the easiest, most fail-safe methods of potty training available. Contrary to popular and lasting belief that the crate is cruel and robs your dog of the rights to freedom he so desires, most animal welfare organizations, including the Society for the Prevention of Cruelty to Animals (SPCA), consider crate training more humane than any other method as it avoids the training mistakes that can cause the dog to receive unnecessary punishments. It also helps to diminish the confusion that can accompany housetraining, thus strengthening the canine/human relationship. A dog can learn quickly to love the crate and it can become a safe place for him to retreat to when he needs security, and when he sleeps, travels, and relaxes.*

---

* Please refer to SEPARATION ANXIETY: BARKING INCESSANTLY IN OWNER ABSENCE ON PAGE 147 if your dog shows significant distress when being placed in a crate, including some or all of the following symptoms: extreme vocalization, self-mutilation, excessive drooling and panting, anorexia, and/or destruction of the crate door and door frame.

Remedy

It's best to start a crate training plan with your new dog first thing in the morning on a weekend (or some other time when you are off from work). Choose a small area that will be his potty area: a small patch of grass, a gravel potty pit, a dirt bed, and so on. You will need a kitchen timer for this lesson.

1. Begin by letting your dog out of his crate, avoiding any fanfare, and leading him outside on leash to a predetermined elimination area. *Bring treats.* Don't say a word or make any acknowledgement of him until he eliminates. Stand completely still for up to five minutes without saying a word or moving. When he pees, throw a huge party and feed treats, and shower him with loves, kisses, and the like.

   If he does not eliminate during this five-minute allowance, return him to the crate for ten minutes and then repeat step 1. Continue this pattern until he eliminates.

   Note: It's imperative that you remain still with him on leash so that he learns that his first order of business outside is to go potty. He will get bored with the small area to which he has access, leaving him little choice but to eliminate. Because of this, you will notice the amount of time you will need to wait for him to eliminate will get shorter with each day.

2. At this point, you may let him off the leash to play or lead him back inside to his long-term or short-term confinement area. Start your timer with the amount of time he can hold his bladder and bowels: _____.

3. Thirty minutes before the timer goes off, return your dog to his crate. When the timer goes off signaling the completion of the time he can reasonably hold his bladder and bowels, repeat step 1.

4. Repeat this sequence for seven days.

5. After seven days without accidents, slowly increase the amount of time you set your timer by thirty-minute increments every seven days.

With each successful week of training, you'll notice the amount of time between eliminations getting longer and longer!

Adult Dog Indoor Potty Area

Please review **STARTING OUT RIGHT: ADOLESCENT AND ADULT POTTY MANAGEMENT ON PAGE 104** before proceeding with this lesson.

Why

Many owners choose to have their dogs eliminate on indoor substrates. A great number of new products, including the Potty Park, PETaPOTTY, Wizdog, Pup-Head, and litter systems, are on the market, making this lifestyle much more pleasant than it used to be.

Remedy

Training your dog to use an indoor substrate is most effective when you're using a crate.

1. First thing in the morning, let your pup out of his crate, avoiding any fanfare, and lead him *on leash* to his indoor potty substrate. You may wish to encircle the substrate with an expen or gate while your puppy is learning to target it. Don't say a word or make any acknowledgement of him until he eliminates. Stand completely still for up to five minutes without saying a word or moving. When he pees, throw a huge party and feed treats, and shower him with loves, kisses, and the like.

   If he does not eliminate during this five minute allowance, return him to the crate for ten minutes and then repeat step 1. Continue this pattern until he eliminates.

Note: It's imperative that you remain still with him on leash so he learns that his first order of business when he leaves his crate is to go potty. He will get bored with the small area to which he has access, leaving him little choice but to eliminate. Because of this, you will notice the amount of time you will need to wait for him to eliminate will get shorter with each day.

2. At this point, you may let him off the leash to play or lead him back inside to his long-term or short-term confinement area. Start your timer with the amount of time he can hold his bladder and bowels: _____.

3. Thirty minutes before the timer goes off, return your dog to his crate. When the timer goes off, signaling the completion of the time he can reasonably hold his bladder and bowels, repeat step 1.

4. Repeat this sequence for seven days.

5. After seven days without accidents, slowly increase the amount of time you set the timer by fifteen-minute increments every seven days.

With each successful week of training, the amount of time between eliminations will get longer and longer. Before long, you'll be amazed at the progress you and your dog have made!

Adult Male Dog Urinating on Plants and Furniture

As adults, some dogs will develop a habit of lifting a leg on an indoor plant. This dog is sometimes caught in the act or evidence of his unmannerly behavior will appear as spattered traces of urine on a plant, pot, carpet, and, often, the wall. Dogs are also attracted to bed ruffles, lamps, counter corners, refrigerators, trash cans, and end tables. It's safe to assume that for the leg-lifter, any upright item in his home is fair game.

Why

Many male dogs develop the urge to urinate on upright fixtures and furniture. While there is significant evidence to suggest this is a manifestation of a need to mark, there is equally good evidence to suggest that it's simply more enjoyable and rewarding to urinate on something upright, especially if another dog has urinated on it in the past. The sheer physical anatomy of the male dog and leg-lifting behavior lends itself to this theory. Incidentally, marking is still greatly misunderstood and may be rooted in communication, competition for territory or other resources, or neither of these common beliefs.

Remedy

The wonderful thing about leg lifting is that you don't have to decode the cause of the behavior in order to fix it. Approaching this problem as a potty-training task readily produces excellent results.

1. First eliminate all access to the item your dog has chosen as a target either by erecting a barrier around it or by removing it from his environment altogether. Also keep an eye out for other items he may be likely to urinate on once his favorite item is removed.

2. Embark on a heavy management and supervision plan by establishing both a short-term and a long-term confinement area. Refer to **STARTING OUT RIGHT: ADOLESCENT AND ADULT POTTY MANAGEMENT ON PAGE 104** for instructions.

3. During the training period, when you catch him in the act of lifting his leg on an unapproved item, interrupt him firmly but gently with an "Ah-ah" and redirect him to his approved indoor or outdoor potty area. Pay off with *awesome* treats the moment he finishes his elimination on the appropriate potty area.

   It can be helpful to place an upright prop in his usual approved potty area to strengthen and reinforce the experience of urinating in the correct spot. The Doggy Loo

Fire Hydrant is a helpful tool for this task, but you can also use a small upright log or post of your own.

4. After several weeks of success, slowly reintroduce the items removed from his environment. But, beware! Only reintroduce these items when you are available to manage the environment 100 percent.

If, at this point, he heads for the newly reintroduced upright item, interrupt and redirect him to his approved potty substrate. This is very normal and is an opportunity for continued learning.

With consistency and airtight management, even the most persistent leg-lifter will learn to keep his urine to himself!

Note: For more housetraining tips, refer to HOUSETRAINING ON PAGE 241.

Adult Dog Elimination Under Furniture

Never does your heart sink deeper than when you're vacuuming under a table or couch only to discover an old pile of poop or a urine stain from lord-only-knows when. Under the bed and piano are particularly popular destinations for these ill-placed deposits, and even more alarming is that you thought the resident dog was potty trained.

Why

Adult dogs, whether they're acquired as puppies or as adults, who urinate and/or defecate under furniture almost always have a history of positive (not-so-lovely) punishment for eliminating in the wrong place. Unfortunately, because positive punishment, where *not* to go, is almost never accompanied by positive reinforcement, where *to* go, this dog is left to his own devices when choosing an appropriate toilet. Because he's likely never been caught for absconding behind the couch or under the bed, he has found this to be a perfectly acceptable place to go.

The truth of the matter is that if your dog is making mistakes in the house, he's not 100 percent potty trained.

Incidentally, owners interpret sheepish, skulking, cowering behavior after a potty discovery as the dog "knowing he's done something wrong." To the contrary, dogs are masters at reading body language. He knows that the subtle behaviors you're exhibiting generally lead to him getting in trouble, but he has absolutely no idea why.

Remedy

The goal in this lesson is to end the reinforcing cycle of eliminating under and behind furniture while reinforcing pottying in the appropriate area.

1. First eliminate all access to the area your dog has chosen as his unapproved toilet. You may need to erect an expen around the piano, stack boxes or hampers around or under the bed, or remove a piece of furniture altogether. He must not be allowed to make one more error without feedback.

   It is particularly important that you block access to the area in your absence as this is the time your dog is most likely to make a mistake.

2. Embark on a heavy management and supervision plan by establishing both short-term and long-term confinement areas. Refer to **STARTING OUT RIGHT: ADOLESCENT AND ADULT POTTY MANAGEMENT ON PAGE 104** for instructions. If you cannot keep your dog supervised during the training period, he should be in one of these areas.

3. Once you're back on the short-term and long-term confinement program, give your dog frequent opportunities to potty in his approved area, making sure to bring *great* treats to reward him with when he gets it right. This essential step increases the value of him eliminating in the area you want him to use instead of under your furniture.

4. After a few weeks of 100 percent success limiting his access to his old potty spots and reinforcing him for correct eliminations, slowly begin to reintroduce the areas from which he was banned.

   Be very careful at this point to stick to 100 percent supervision. If he disappears from your sight, it's safe to assume he's heading back to the area he used as a toilet in the past. This is very normal and is an opportunity for continued learning.

5. If, at this point, you do catch him in the act of disappearing to eliminate, interrupt him firmly but gently with an "Ah-ah" and redirect him to his approved indoor or outdoor potty area. Pay off with *awesome* treats the moment he finishes his elimination on the appropriate potty area.

Note: For more housetraining tips, refer to **HOUSETRAINING ON PAGE 241.**

Adult Dog Elimination on Carpets and Rugs

Indoor carpets and rugs are by far the most common targets for potty accidents. The plusher they are, the better, and they're out-ranked as a popular potty spot only by the antique or handmade family heirloom tapestry. Even the dog who seems potty trained in all other areas of the home and in public will relieve himself on these irresistible fixtures.

Why

Contrary to the belief that dogs learn where to go to the bathroom and where not to go based on inside versus outside, they actually learn by what's under their toes: the substrate. Most dogs prefer a soft, plush, substrate closely resembling grass, but occasionally they may prefer hardwood or slate. The truth of the matter is that if your dog is making mistakes in the house, he's not 100 percent potty trained.

Incidentally, owners interpret sheepish, skulking, cowering behavior after a potty discovery as the dog "knowing he's done something wrong." To the contrary, dogs are masters at reading body language. He knows that the subtle behaviors you're exhibiting generally lead to him getting in trouble, but he has absolutely no idea why.

Remedy

The goal in this lesson is to end the reinforcing cycle of pottying on indoor rugs while reinforcing pottying in the appropriate area.

1. First eliminate all access to the area your dog has chosen as his unapproved toilet. If the carpet is wall to wall or very large, you may need to erect an expen around his favorite spot or cover it with a piece of furniture. If the rug is portable, simply roll it up and tuck it away for later.

2. Embark on a heavy management and supervision plan by establishing both short-term and long-term confinement areas. Refer to **STARTING OUT RIGHT: ADOLESCENT AND ADULT POTTY MANAGEMENT ON PAGE 104** for instructions. If you cannot keep your dog supervised during the training period, he should be in one of these areas.

    Dogs who urinate and defecate on rugs as adults often choose multiple favorite spots. Because of this, managing it is especially important.

3. Once back on the short-term and long-term confinement program, give your dog frequent opportunities to potty in his approved area, making sure to bring *great* treats to reward him with when he gets it right. This essential step increases the value of him eliminating in the area you want him to use instead of on the rugs.

4. After a few weeks of 100 percent success limiting his access to his old potty spots, and reinforcing him for correct eliminations, slowly begin to reintroduce the areas from which he was banned or roll the rugs back out one at a time.

Be very careful at this point to stick to 100 percent supervision. If he disappears from your sight, it's safe to assume he's heading back to the area he used as a toilet in the past. This is very normal and is an opportunity for continued learning.

5. If, at this stage, you do catch him in the act of eliminating on a carpet or rug, interrupt him firmly but gently with an "Ah-ah" and redirect him to his approved indoor or outdoor potty area. Pay off with *awesome* treats the moment he finishes eliminating on the appropriate potty area.

Note: For more housetraining tips, refer to **HOUSETRAINING ON PAGE 241.**

Adult Dog Elimination on Non-Carpeted Floors

While most dogs who have potty accidents indoors prefer a soft rug or carpet under their feet, a portion of dogs prefer a non-carpeted floor. While this dog may choose more than one spot as an unapproved indoor toilet, it's likely he has his favorite substrate and will stick to it, be it hardwood, tile, slate, or linoleum.

Why

Contrary to the belief that dogs learn where to go to the bathroom and where not to go based on inside versus outside, they actually learn by what's under their toes: the substrate. Most dogs prefer a soft, plush substrate closely resembling grass, but occasionally they may prefer hardwood or slate. The truth of the matter is that if your dog is making mistakes in the house, he's not quite 100 percent potty trained.

Incidentally, owners interpret sheepish, skulking, cowering behavior after a potty discovery as the dog "knowing he's done something wrong." To the contrary, dogs are masters at reading body language. He knows that the subtle behaviors you're exhibiting generally lead to him getting in trouble, but he has absolutely no idea why.

Remedy

The goal in this lesson is to end the reinforcing cycle of pottying on indoor floors while reinforcing pottying in the appropriate area.

1. First eliminate all access to the area your dog has chosen as his unapproved toilet by erecting an expen or blocking access with a baby gate.

2. Embark on a heavy management and supervision plan by establishing both short-term and long-term confinement areas. Refer to **STARTING OUT RIGHT: ADOLESCENT AND ADULT POTTY MANAGEMENT ON PAGE 104** for instructions. If you cannot keep your dog supervised during the training period, he should be in one of these areas.

3. Once you're back on the short-term and long-term confinement program, give your dog frequent opportunities to potty in his approved area, making sure to bring *great* treats to reward him with when he gets it right. This essential step increases the value of him eliminating in the area you want him to use instead of on the floor.

4. After a few weeks of 100 percent success limiting his access to his old potty spots, and reinforcing him for correct eliminations, slowly begin to reintroduce the areas from which he was banned.

   Be very careful at this point to stick to a 100 percent supervision plan. If he disappears from your sight, it's safe to assume he's heading back to the area he used as a toilet in the past. This is very normal and is an opportunity for continued learning.

5. If, at this stage, you do catch him in the act of eliminating on a carpet or rug, interrupt him firmly but gently with an "Ah-ah" and redirect him to his approved indoor or outdoor potty area. Pay off with *awesome* treats the moment he finishes his elimination on the appropriate potty area.

Note: For more housetraining tips, refer to HOUSETRAINING ON PAGE 241.

Adult Dog Teaching Bell Signal to Go Potty

After a dog is fully housetrained, it's a toss-up whether or not he will develop his own signal to tell his owner when he needs to go outside to go to the bathroom. While a small handful of dogs do develop a woof or a scratch at the door to communicate their wish, the vast majority of dogs simply never develop any kind of signal, which results in the occasional potty accident by the door and owner frustration.

Why

It's unreasonable to task a dog with initiating communication about his needs to potty. While he likely comes with pre-elimination behaviors such as circling and sniffing, those behaviors are greatly innate and the leap from casually suggesting to actively signaling simply isn't in the canine behavior repertoire.

Remedy

One of the handiest skills a dog can learn is how to use a bell to signal his need to go outside to potty. You can hang this bell from the doorknob or by a hook by the door, and can even position a small radio doorbell near the door to remotely signal a ring in another room. Please note that your dog must be fully housetrained in order to successfully complete this lesson.

1. To begin, train your dog to bump the bell with his nose or paw out of context. To do this, simply sit quietly with him and a pile of bait, holding the bell very still in front of him. When he bumps the bell, mark the bump with a "Yes!" and give him a piece of bait.

2. After he's slightly bumping the bell regularly (after about three training sessions), up the criteria; instead of just touching the bell to get a treat, he must make the bell ring. If you are patient, you will watch him go through an *extinction burst* to get the bell ringing. An extinction burst is a spike in behavior as a last ditch effort to get a response. In this case, he will bump the bell harder or with another body part to earn a reward.

3. For your next few training sessions, still hold the bell, but move it closer to the door through which you'd like him to pass to go to the bathroom. After he bumps the bell, toss the treat on the floor, no longer treating from your hand.

4. After a few sessions, you'll reach the door. Keep the bell in front of you as you have in the previous steps, but this time when he rings it, open the door and *toss the treat outside* so he's forced to pass through the doorway to get his reward.

   This is the step in which generalization happens. This is also where the plan tends to stall just a bit, so be patient. Require him to return inside before you ask him to ring the bell again. Repeat this step a few days in a row.

5. Now, fix the bell to the doorway where he can reach it. At this step, he has not yet made the connection between eliminations and the bell—he only knows that when he rings the bell, he gets to go outside for a treat. Continue this for a couple of days: the bell is in its final location, and you simply open the door and toss a treat outside.

   If during this step he does go out and potty, pay him off with a *massively wonderful* treat.

6. In the final step, you'll only be treating for the complete behavior string: *dog rings bell, you open door, dog goes outside and eliminates, you treat.*

   Be clever: Because your dog is already housetrained, capitalize on the times he is likely to eliminate. Remember, only treat for elimination in this final step, so random bell-ringing behavior loses its reinforcing value and extinguishes.

 **Recall**

Perhaps the most common grievance expressed by dog owners is the lack of response they get from their dog when it is asked to come. Whether from the dog park, the backyard, or even inside the house, few things are more frustrating than issuing an urgent "Come" followed by your dog's best deaf impression.

Not only does this problem make for kinks in schedules, angry owners, and humiliating pursuits at the dog park, but it can also be very dangerous. The dog who has not learned to come when called may be at risk of running away, dashing into traffic, or bolting into some other type of trouble.

The key to building a strong and reliable recall is to train one consistently and soundly. The skills necessary for training a reliable recall are not difficult; the challenge comes with knowing how to train it and subsequently make training more and more advanced to ensure a beautiful, dependable recall.

Starting Out Right: The Formal Recall

A reliable recall, or Come is one of the trickiest behaviors for a dog to learn. Because of this, you'll need to distinguish between a formal and an informal recall for training purposes.

FORMAL RECALL: A formal recall is the cue you use when your *dog's life depends on it*. In other words, if your dog ignores your formal recall, he or someone else will endure bodily harm or even death. This includes running into the street, towards a dog who may be threatening him, and so on. The response percentage goal for a formal recall is 100 percent.

INFORMAL RECALL: An informal recall is the cue you use when your *dog's life does not depend on it*; it's a nice-to-have cue. In other words, if he ignores your informal recall, he or someone else won't be harmed. It's inconvenient, but you can afford to have an informal recall that may only be reliable 50 to 80 percent of the time, whereas it's imperative that your dog respond to the formal recall every single time you give it. The informal recall is useful for telling your dog it's time to leave the dog park, asking your dog to join you for a walk or a car trip, and so on.

Please note that with the exception of **DOG WON'T COME WHEN CALLED IN EMERGENCY SITUATION ON PAGE127**, the lessons here focus on practicing the formal recall in informal, non–life-threatening situations. These lessons should only be used as a way to build a very strong formal recall through practice in various environments.

Should you need to call your dog to you in a non–life-threatening situation and you are not actively training a formal recall, choose a phrase such as "Let's go" or "It's time." Say the phrase, then slap your knees, whistle, jolly talk, and otherwise encourage your dog to come to you without saying your informal recall phrase again. When he arrives, pay off with a favorite toy or yummy treat. With the informal recall, it is acceptable to follow the call with a less-pleasant event such as leaving the dog park or heading into the crate. A formal recall must *always* be followed by something good and must adhere to the five following rules so that the time it's needed in a life or death situation, it works.

At first, your dog may not respond to the informal recall cue. If this happens, simply walk up to him (don't get into a game of chase), gently grab his collar, and lead him to where you need him. With time, he will learn that you'll follow through each time you call and if he comes, he quickly gets a treat.

Before you train a formal recall, you must memorize the following five rules:

1. **ONLY SAY "COME" ONCE.** Your voice becomes irrelevant to your dog very quickly, especially when you repeat cues. If you have overused the word "come" in the past, choose another word such as "here," "aquí," or "now." Saying "come" only once will ensure that your dog won't wait until the second or third time you say it to come.

2. **ONLY CALL YOUR DOG IF YOU THINK YOU CAN MAKE IT HAPPEN.** This rule acknowledges that recall is a skill and as such you need to train it. Only use your recall phrase for the level of difficulty to which you've trained. In other words, if you've only worked on recall once, don't expect your dog to come out of dog play or abandon a fleeing squirrel.

3. **IF YOUR DOG DOESN'T COME, GO GET HIM.** If you called him and he didn't come, rule number 2 failed. No serious harm done, but you must not call him again. Instead, get comfy and relaxed. Follow him around until you catch him, making sure not to use any punishing voice or physical cues. Take a step back in the difficulty of your recall training and begin again.

4. **DON'T CALL YOUR DOG FOR SOMETHING UNPLEASANT.** This is as obvious as something such as nail trims or baths, but it can also be as subtle as leaving the dog park or coming inside to be left alone all day.

5. **OFFER BIG, BIG, BIG REWARDS.** Novelty is highly rewarding to dogs. You must use a food item for a formal recall and you may only use it for a formal recall. Great recall foods are salty, stinky cheeses; liver; squeeze cheese; and meat and gravy baby foods.

These five rules together establish a contract between you and your dog: If he comes when you say "Dog name, come," he'll not only *not* be punished for it, but also he'll be rewarded with something better than what he's currently being rewarded with. Remember, this is a formal recall that's very different than an informal nice-to-have recall, so train and use it wisely.

Dog Won't Come from the Yard or Inside the House When Called

Very early in life your dog may develop selective hearing to your recall cue. There are few things more frustrating than waiting in an open doorway flailing about, screaming your dog's name, waving a box of cookies, only to be met with a blank stare and perhaps even a casual retreat.

Why

As young pups, dogs learn the value of things in their lives, and coming when they're called is no different than any of the other lessons they learn. Typically owners dole out praise when a dog comes, no matter what he was just summoned from or what it is he is being called to do. Other times "Come!" is followed by "You bad dog," or nothing at all. In some cases, an owner may pony up some food, but typically the food is a dry cookie and the value is always the same.

As your dog's system of favorite and not-so-favorite things develops, he learns the value of your predictable reward for coming when called and fits it into his reward system. Because of this, sometimes the reward for coming trumps whatever it is he's doing and sometimes it doesn't.

Incidentally, an owner often equates a dog's failure to respond to "come" as ill feelings toward the owner. Unless a history of severe and long-lasting punishment exists, this is very unlikely. The dog is a very clever discriminator, indeed, and he's simply learned the rewarding and punishing nuances of his environment just as humans have learned theirs.

Remedy

Before beginning this lesson, please refer to STARTING OUT RIGHT: THE FORMAL RECALL ON PAGE 120. While coming in from the backyard does not necessarily indicate a life-or-death situation, it is the perfect opportunity to practice a formal recall.

EASY

Each of these exercises will help lay the foundation for a good formal recall. Practice a few times a week and you'll notice your dog responding more and more quickly to the recall phrase alone.

Round-Robin Recall

1. At home, inside, enlist the help of a family member or friend.

2. Say your recall phrase ("Dog name, come!") and then bend down, spank your knees, clap your hands, and whistle until your dog reaches you. This display is called *fanfare* and it's highly intoxicating to dogs. The higher your voice and the more animated you become, the more interested he will be.

   If your dog is upset by fanfare as a small handful of dogs will be, simply tone it down to tailor it to your dog's needs.

3. When your dog arrives to you, pay off with the recall bait and praise him for thirty seconds.

4. As your reward party is winding down, ask your friend to do the same thing from across the room.

5. Repeat back and forth.

   If your dog starts to come to you or your friend without being called, stop for a bit and return to training later. Your cue must signal your request to come.

Runaway Recall

1. At home, inside, say your recall phrase ("Dog's name, come!").
2. Quickly turn on your heels and run away from your dog enthusiastically into another room or just around the corner. Dogs love a good game of chase.
3. When he reaches you, turn around for your fanfare party and pay off with the recall bait.
4. Repeat.

DIFFICULT

You will notice that with a little bit of time your dog will begin to respond to the previous exercises every single time and his rate of response will get better and better. You will find that fanfare no longer becomes necessary because he is responding to the verbal cue alone. When that happens, up the difficulty by manipulating *one* of these criteria:

At home:

• Increase the distance over which he must come.
• Call him from each room in your home.
• Call him when he's engaged in a fun activity such as chewing.

After you've mastered the indoor recall, move out to the backyard using a long line to keep your dog secure if the yard is not fenced. Manipulate small elements of the training environment *one at a time*, such as increasing the distance over which he must travel to come or increasing the distraction with which he is faced.

After you've mastered the backyard, move to the front yard. After the front yard, move to the local park. You can train an increasingly difficult recall almost endlessly by moving to more and more distracting locations.

Tip: Avoid greedy trainer syndrome. Even professional obedience competitors work for years to get a 100 percent reliable formal recall. Go slow, build on success, and be patient.

Dog Won't Come from the Dog Park When Called

Like a six-year-old child at recess, the modern dog skips along at the dog park playing chase, roll, wrestle, and hunt with his canine buddies. You watch him bound through the tall grass, romp into the shallow water, and gleefully smile with a tongue too exhausted to stay in his mouth, and your order to "come" gets a chuckle from those around and absolutely no response from the dog.

Why

As young pups, dogs learn the value of things in their lives, and coming when called is no different than any of the other lessons they learn. Typically owners dole out praise when a dog comes, no matter what he was just summoned from or what it is he is being called to do. Other times, "Come!" is followed by "You bad dog," or nothing at all. In some cases, an owner may pony up some food, but typically the food is a dry cookie and the value is always the same.

As a dog's system of favorite and not-so-favorite things develops, he learns the value of his owner's predictable rewards or lack thereof for coming when called and fits it into his reward system. Because of this, sometimes the reward for coming trumps whatever it is he's doing and sometimes it doesn't.

Furthermore, because dogs are compulsively social by nature, the opportunity to socialize with other dogs is one of the most highly rewarding activities available.

Remedy

Before beginning this lesson refer to STARTING OUT RIGHT: THE FORMAL RECALL ON PAGE 120.

The dog park is one of the most advanced training grounds for recall. Because of this, it's best to use an informal recall or "check-in" system at first.

EASY

1. While it's imperative you supervise your dog at the park, make a subtle shift from following him around to leading him.

   Keep moving. Moving constantly through the dog park automatically requires your dog to keep his eye on you, resulting in increased attentiveness. The opposite is true when your dog has learned you will always keep your eye on him.

2. As you move through the park this way, your dog will begin to check in with you by trotting to your side and then trotting off. Depending on his personality and reinforcement/ punishment history, this may happen immediately or after a few sessions. Be patient. Use his choice to check in as a reason to verbally praise him enthusiastically. If your dog does not guard food and you are comfortable tossing him a low-value treat for a check-in, do so, but beware of potential guarding from dogs who may be nearby.

   As your dog checks in more and more, begin to take hold of his collar before you give him his praise. After praising him, let him go back to play.

3. If your dog loses sight of you, slip quickly behind a tree or other visual barrier to hide from him. A dog's eyesight is fairly poor at long distances, so a super hiding place isn't necessary. You only need hide enough to where you can still keep your eye on him and he can't see you. Watch him as he begins to eagerly search for you once he realizes you're missing. Feel free to give him some verbal prompting to keep him oriented. Once he finds you, pay off with a huge praise party.

4. As you work to increase your dog's attention to your movements through the park, consider these tips:

- Don't stay at the park longer than your dog wants to. When he begins to appear bored or he has run out of steam, leave the park.

- If the park has multiple exits, alternate the route you take.

- Try to keep your verbal cues to your dog at the park as minimal as possible until you've reached the advanced training stage. The human voice quickly becomes irrelevant at the park and saving it will help avoid this pitfall.

5. When you're finally ready to leave the park, use an informal cue such as "let's go" or "we're done" and head for the exit. Be patient as your dog may be hesitant to join you, having learned that leaving the park can be somewhat of a punishment. With patience and consistency he will learn to follow you to the edge of the park as he's learned to do by keeping his eye on you. Leash him up, and make sure you make his car ride home as enjoyable as possible with a yummy work-to-eat puzzle, long-term consumable chew item, and cozy quarters.

DIFFICULT

Training a formal recall at the dog park is considered a difficult lesson. Please refer to DOG WON'T COME FROM THE YARD OR INSIDE THE HOUSE WHEN CALLED ON PAGE 122 to train a formal recall in the dog park.

Dog Won't Come When Called in Emergency Situation

Nothing will snap an owner to attention like the sight of his dog darting into traffic or heading into an injurious dog fight. Panicking, this person says a recall cue to no avail; the dog continues his quest. Chasing him only seems to encourage him to run, and everyone involved seems at a loss for how on earth to get him back.

Why

As young pups, dogs learn the value of things in their lives, and coming when called is no different than any of the other lessons they learn. Typically owners dole out praise when a dog comes, no matter what he was just summoned from or what it is he is being called to do. Other times "Come!" is followed by "You bad dog," or nothing at all. In some cases, an owner may pony up some food, but typically the food is a dry cookie and the value is always the same.

As a dog's system of favorite and not-so-favorite things develops, he learns the value of his owner's predictable rewards or lack thereof for coming when called and fits it into his reward system. Because of this, sometimes the reward for coming trumps whatever it is he's doing and sometimes it doesn't.

If your dog has chosen to run into traffic, dart across the street, or run towards an escalating dog fight, it's highly likely he's doing so to investigate. If little or no formal recall training has taken place or if an ill-devised recall punishment history exists, the odds of him getting into trouble or being hurt are very good.

Remedy

Before beginning this lesson, please refer to STARTING OUT RIGHT: THE FORMAL RECALL ON PAGE 120.

The best way to ensure a solid recall is to train it from scratch. For instructions on doing so, please see DOG WON'T COME FROM THE YARD OR INSIDE THE HOUSE WHEN CALLED ON PAGE 122. However, if you've not yet trained a formal recall, there are two methods that can help improve the odds of a successful emergency recall. The method you prefer will depend on your dog's learning status and impulsivity, as well as your sense of self-control and reaction in an emergency situation.

OPTION 1: EMERGENCY FACE-ON RECALL

1. Unless your dog has bolted because of an acute fear of something such as lightning or a very loud sound, do not

chase him. Although it can be very tempting to do so, the chase is actually highly reinforcing and will only drive your dog away.

2. Instead, plant your feet and say his name. Be sure to say this alert in a nonthreatening way. The more threatening or upset your voice sounds, the less likely he is to come to you.

3. When your dog briefly turns his head to see what it is you're yelling to him, quickly bend at the waist while you're facing him, slap the front of your thighs enthusiastically, and whistle at him excitedly. Many dogs love to join in a good game of fanfare and will turn and rush towards the person dispensing it.

Squaring to a dog and staring him down can cause some dogs to act with aversion, and they will either lack response entirely or may actually run in the opposite direction. If your dog is one of these dogs, opt for another method.

4. When your dog arrives, bend to grab his collar, and pay off big with praise and treats if they're handy.

OPTION 2: EMERGENCY RUNAWAY RECALL

1. Unless he has bolted because of an acute fear of something such as lightning or a very loud sound, do not chase your dog. Although it can be very tempting to do so, the chase is actually highly reinforcing and will only drive your dog away.

2. Instead, plant your feet and say his name. Be sure to say this alert in a nonthreatening way. The more threatening or upset your voice sounds, the less likely he is to come to you.

3. When your dog briefly turns his head to see what it is you're yelling to him, quickly turn and run in the other direction. Most dogs cannot resist a good game of chase and the odds are good that he will run back to investigate what you're chasing.

4. When he reaches you, grab his collar and praise him like mad.

Note: Neither of these emergency recall exercises is an adequate substitution for a well-trained reliable formal recall. The purpose of these exercises is to increase the odds of saving your dog from harm in the event he should face a dangerous situation before you've fully trained a formal recall. Neither technique is 100 percent reliable as a formal recall can be.

 # Barking

ith the exception of a handful of specialized breeds from whom barking has been extinguished by breeding, every dog barks. It is a very normal, biological behavior. While all barks from an individual dog may sound very similar to the human ear, each has its own meaning and it's essential to understand the type and cause of barking in a given situation in order to effectively and kindly modify the behavior.

While canine professionals do not understand the causes driving all types of barking, we can identify a handful of common categories of barking to ensure appropriate corresponding modification techniques. These include but are not limited to alert/watchdog barking, attention/demand barking, play barking, guard barking, boredom barking, separation anxiety barking, barrier frustration barking, on-leash aggressive barking, barking while fighting, and spooky barking.

Some of these behaviors are considered *basic* or unemotional and can be modified by simple training. However, many of these behaviors are considered *advanced* because of an innate emotional component and/or the liability associated with modifying the barking. In the following sections, I will identify the behaviors as basic or advanced.

Alert/Watchdog: Barking at Visitors to the Home

This behavior is considered *basic*. More often than not, the resident dog will take a doorbell or knock as an opportunity to spout off at the mouth. Alert differs from other kinds of barking in that the dog will bark as he moves through the house either in a wide or small area, and/or he may pause between barks as he prances around. Often he will make the rounds through the house bouncing between family members and the door or through a central part of the house.

If the dog pins himself at the window or door and barks without stopping, it safe to assume he is exhibiting a more advanced behavior. See **GUARD BARKING ON PAGE 135** or **EXCITEMENT: BARKING IN THE CAR AT NOTHING IN PARTICULAR ON PAGE 138** for more information.

Why

Alert or watchdog barking has deep biological roots. It serves both to warn other residents that an intruder has arrived and to alert intruders that they have been noticed. While it's unreasonable to assume for even a second that your dog has mistaken the intruder for a dog, or that he's reverted to pack mentality, mistaking you for a dog as well, it is extremely reasonable to acknowledge the innate drive behind the behavior itself.

Remedy

If your dog is engaging in alert or watchdog barking, try the following remedies.

EASY

Teaching a dog a behavior that's incompatible with barking is an excellent way to significantly diminish alert barking. Training your dog to retrieve a toy when the doorbell rings will keep him and his mouth busy.

1. Begin by finding the toy your dog enjoys the most.
2. At home, ask your dog to sit.
3. Toss the item he loves just past him.
4. Give the command "fetch" and let him run freely after the item.

   For this lesson, it doesn't matter if your dog brings the item back to you. If he chooses to sit and settle with it, all the better.
5. Repeat this exercise a handful of times for several days. You should continue to see an increase in his apparent enjoyment in the fetch activity. If this is not the case, audition different items until you find one he really loves.
6. Next, set him up by enlisting the help of a friend.
7. From now on, keep the toy by the door or somewhere you can quickly reach it but he cannot. Have your friend knock on the door.
8. When your dog begins to bark, tell him your cue ("fetch"), pull out the special fetch toy, and toss it away from the door. When he grabs it, praise him and reward him with a few tosses if he brings the thing back to you.
9. Repeat steps 6 through 8, on scattered days and times. Use different friends to help you out, if you can.

With consistency, your dog will learn that the doorbell or knock at the door actually signals a game of fetch. Rather than you having to say the cue ("fetch"), he will simply quiet in anticipation of his reward.

DIFFICULT

Because barking is such a strong instinct, allowing your dog the opportunity to alert you to intruders is the best way to modify his behavior. However, this is not a license for him to babble on and on. Instead, he can learn to alert you with three or four barks and then settle.

Timeouts are a favorite technique to diminish alert barking.

1. Begin by deciding how many barks you'd like your dog to give. Three or more is reasonable.

2. When someone comes to the door and your dog barks, be prepared to jump up and train. You may choose to enlist the help of a friend to knock or use the doorbell rather than waiting for a visitor to come.

3. Count your dog's barks from the first one. On his third bark, or whatever number you'll allow, tell him your cue ("that's enough").

   • *If he stops barking*, praise him enthusiastically.

   • *If he doesn't stop barking*, which is likely at this stage, tell him "Too bad" and then lead him to his timeout area. The timeout area can be behind a barrier, inside, in his crate, behind a door, and the like.

4. Wait twenty seconds, then open the door to his timeout area, tell him "Okay," and allow him to come back in. Repeat from step 3 until your dog quiets the first time you say your cue ("that's enough").

With consistency, the need to say your cue ("that's enough") will diminish or go away altogether. Your dog is learning the rules to this particular situation and he will often choose to be quiet on his own rather than be punished.

Note: Long after an owner has taught and solidified this lesson, many dogs who are punished with timeouts for alert barking will occasionally belt out a huge bark after the owner says the "that's enough" cue. This is normal and should be expected. Still, follow through with the timeout for this slip. In an alarming number of cases, this dog will actually shuttle himself off to a timeout before you can get to him!

Guard Barking: Barking at Visitors to the Home

This behavior is considered *advanced*. While some dogs bark at the door to alert residents of an intruder, others take the behavior a step further by pinning themselves to the door or window while they bark. Rather than trotting around the house as the alert barker does, the guard barker plants himself at the closest point to the person on the other side of the barrier, be it solid or transparent. His posture is usually aggressive, and he exhibits any of the following: raised hackles, tense shoulders, pinned-back ears, extended and tense limbs. He hesitates in his barking only if to deliver a growl, but it generally stays loud until the person on the other side of the door goes away. The guard barker is also very hard to interrupt and he usually will not respond to his name or other orders.

Why

The aggressive display is meant to drive the intruder away rather than just to alert the residents and intruder of their mutual presence. Guard barking is a somewhat complicated behavior with multiple components and possible causes:

- **RESOURCE GUARDING:** Every dog is prone to guard his resources and the adaptive significance driving resource guarding is very normal and strong. For more information about resource guarding see **AGGRESSIVE DISPLAY DURING HANDLING ON PAGE 229.**

- **UNDERSOCIALIZATION:** As a dog matures past puppyhood he develops behaviors manifesting from discomfort and the threat of something he's undersocialized to. The behavior may be to retreat, or in the case of guard barking, to exhibit fear.

- **BARRIER FRUSTRATION:** Dogs are compulsively social animals who rely heavily on being able to investigate a stranger

very quickly or another dog up close. When he is denied
the opportunity to investigate in this way, he goes through
an anxiety response. After repeated exposure to the same
situation, he learns that a particular set of conditions equals
anxiety. In the case of guard barking, the arrival of someone
on the porch equals anxiety. It is in this dog's best interest to
drive away the thing that makes him anxious.

When visitors come and leave the house on a predictable schedule, a dog's guard behavior is reinforced greatly as he not only pre-
dicts the general time the person will arrive but also that the person
will be driven away with his display every single time. Mail carri-
ers and delivery people are perfect examples of this phenomenon.

Remedy

Because of its emotional component, it is not effective to modify
guard barking using a usual obedience command and doing so can
actually exacerbate the problem. Instead, you must instate a classical conditioning approach to tackle the problem in two parts:

1. **DESENSITIZE:** Make the threatening thing less threatening.
2. **COUNTERCONDITION:** Change the current and undesirable
   association.

EASY

If a dog has just begun to exhibit guarding behavior at the door or
window when visitors come, it may be possible to change the association the dog has with visitors to the home.

1. Begin by breaking the cycle of reinforcement. To do this,
   block visibility to the visitor if your dog can see guests
   through a window or screen door. If you execute this step
   correctly, from day one your dog should never be allowed to
   explode in a guard-barking fit again.
2. Set your dog up. Enlist the help of a friend, asking him or her
   to visit the house at predetermined times, coming to the door,

knocking or ringing the bell, waiting fifteen seconds, and then walking away.

3. When the person knocks, your dog will begin to bark and attempt to head to his usual guarding spot. The *moment* he begins, present him with some highly valuable bait such as cheese or meat, and continue to feed him as long as the person stands at the door.

4. When the visitor turns to leave, promptly stop feeding your dog.

Note: This may seem like you're rewarding your dog for barking, but this is not the case. When a dog is involved in the emotional eruption of guard barking, he is over his threshold. In other words, he's out of his mind and cannot respond reasonably to a command. This is very similar to humans who are incensed. The person cannot reasonably respond to orders to "calm down" just as a guard barking dog cannot respond to "quiet!"

This exercise changes the lesson your dog has learned from "seeing people on the porch who I cannot get to makes me uncomfortable and I want them to leave" to "when people show up on the porch great things happen and when they turn to go away the great things end."

DIFFICULT

If your dog has been guard barking for some time, if he has ever injured someone at the door, or if he will not take the food you offer him when attempting the easy technique above, consult a Certificate in Training and Counseling (CTC) professional trainer (www.sfspca.org/academy/referral.shtml) or a Certified Applied Animal Behaviorist (www.animalbehavior.org).

Important: Never let a guest into your home while your dog is exhibiting guard barking as the likelihood of him biting is great. Instead, sequester the dog in another room before ever opening the door.

Excitement: Barking in the Car at Nothing in Particular

This behavior is considered *basic*. Many dogs love to ride in the car as is obvious by how they willingly hang a head out the window, eagerly prance until the car door opens, and might let out an occasional whimper or whine while the car is in motion. However, sometimes the ride to the park is so exciting a dog cannot help but express himself with loud and persistent barking. Excitement barking is characterized by pacing, panting, and loud repetitive barking. Usually the barks are of similar loud volume with little variation in tonality or pitch.

Why

Excitatory barking is a symptom of over-the-top enthusiasm. More likely to occur in high-drive breeds and anxious individuals, it is an anxiety-relieving behavior similar to the running and screaming often exhibited by highly excited children.

Remedy

If your dog is engaging in excitement barking, try the following remedies.

MANAGEMENT

Management is the easiest method for calming an excitement barker.

- Have your dog travel in a crate in the car and cover the crate with a visual barrier such as a light sheet. Not only is this a safe way to travel but also simply limiting the visual stimulation and anticipation association with trips out can significantly diminish and even eliminate excited barking.
- Keep your dog busy in the car with something he can't resist. Fortify his travel area with a bully stick, yummy bone, or favorite toy that he doesn't have access to any other time.

EASY

Reward the behavior you want to see. Biological law says that your dog must take a breath between barks. While his barking may seem endless, it's not without occasional pause.

1. Bring a pile of dry, tossable bait in the front of the car with you.
2. Listen carefully. When your dog is quiet, even if just for a moment, praise him verbally and toss a treat. If he remains quiet continue to toss treats every few seconds.

The more often you work this lesson, the longer your dog will be quiet. Be sure to deliver bait in inconsistent intervals to prevent him from predicting your reward schedule. Before long you will be traveling great distances with a quiet dog in the car.

Tips: Relieving generalized anxiety and keeping your dog mentally and physically stimulated will help tremendously with this lesson. For ideas and instructions see **THE PRACTICAL FOUNDATION OF THE DAHL METHOD ON PAGE 65.**

Do not yell at your dog to be quiet while he is in an excited barking fit. This actually exacerbates the problem.

While car rides may be temporarily frustrating and hectic, keep at it and go often. Part of your dog's excitatory barking is due to his sensitivity to car rides. The more often a dog is exposed to something, the less novel it becomes and the more relaxed he becomes. If you see his behavior escalate, consult a private trainer.

Consider mixing up your routes to locations you know cause excitement. The anticipation of the predictable route progressively increases excitatory barking.

Barrier Frustration: Barking in the Car at Other Dogs

This behavior is considered *advanced*. A surprising number of dogs who play well with others at the park or in other situations react quite differently when they're placed in cars. Even as these dogs head to or leave the dog park, the very sight of another dog sends them into fits of very aggressive-sounding barking accompanied by erect hackles, pinned ears, noses pressed to the glass, tense shoulders, and stiff limbs. These dogs cannot be swayed by attempts to catch their attention no matter how loudly or emphatically their names or another command is yelled.

Why

Dogs are highly social and rely on their investigatory senses to quickly assess novel situations and other dogs. Their preferred method of doing so is up close as their eyesight is one of their weaker senses.

If an undersocialized* dog is repeatedly presented with the sight of another dog, but prevented from approaching it to investigate because of a physical barrier such as a fence or a window, the dog can quickly learn to associate the sight of another dog from behind a barrier with the anxiety of being unable to approach it. This feeling is so strong that it manifests itself not only mentally, but also physically. The resulting display of whirling, growling, lunging, and barking is meant to drive away the thing causing the anxiety: the other dog.

---

* The term "undersocialization" is a very individualized measure of socialization. Every dog requires a different level of exposure to novel things in order to become comfortable with them. A dog who is considered undersocialized simply hasn't had enough pleasant exposure with something (this can be anything, really) for him to be relaxed and calm in its presence.

Remedy

If your dog is engaging in barrier frustration, try the following remedies.

EASY

1. Begin by ending the cycle of reinforcement by ceasing all activities that are likely to put your dog in a situation where he may act in this way. If he must travel in the car, sequester him in a crate covered with a light sheet to create a visual barrier.

2. While working on ending the cycle of barrier frustration, continue to socialize your dog with dogs in situations where he can interact successfully with them, such as at the dog park or in small play groups with friends.

DIFFICULT

If your dog has been exhibiting barrier frustration for some time or if he has ever injured another dog as a result, consult a Certificate in Training and Counseling (CTC) professional trainer (www.sfspca.org/academy/referral.shtml) or a Certified Applied Animal Behaviorist (www.animalbehavior.org).

> *Important: Never let a dog exhibiting barrier frustration out of the car to greet an unfamiliar dog. The likelihood of the meeting escalating into a fight is very, very high.*

Prey Drive: Barking in the Car at Bikes, Motorcycles, and Joggers

This behavior is considered *advanced*. Bikes, motorcycles, scooters, skateboarders, skaters, and joggers can evoke a very aggressive-looking response from even the most docile dog. Usually the display occurs when the vehicle or person is in motion, but in some cases, the vehicle or person may be standing perfectly still.

Why

The predatory sequence seen in domesticated dogs is made up of eight primary steps: search, stalk, rush, chase, grab, kill, dissect, consume. Every dog is born with some level of predatory drive and many of the most popular breeds are even bred to exaggerate certain steps of the sequence and suppress others. The earliest Labrador Retrievers, for example, were selectively bred to accompany hunters in the field. The ideal companion exhibited strong search, stalk, chase, and grab behaviors. Those with kill (shake), dissect, and consume behaviors were undesirable and were, therefore, culled from the stock.

Today's Labrador Retriever still retains much of the predatory sequence of his ancestors. However, because of great variation in the breeding pool, the range of intensity and presence of these steps is broad and some Labrador Retrievers exhibit more or less of the sequence than the original breeding stock.

Many dogs direct their predatory urges at inanimate objects such as balls, stuffed toys, and tug tools. However, those dogs who target living things or moving vehicles can be very dangerous and you should take their predatory tendencies seriously.

Remedy

The predatory sequence in all dogs is a very strong biological drive and, as such, it cannot be eliminated without serious collateral damage. However, you can control and redirect it to avoid injury while maintaining your dog's mental and physical health. Following are two methods (Tug and Leave-it) of redirecting his drive emotions to other activities.

MANAGEMENT

Before proceeding with the easy lesson that follows, end the cycle of reinforcement by ceasing all activities that are likely to put your dog in a situation where he may display aggressively. If he must travel in the car, sequester him in a crate covered with a light sheet to create a visual barrier.

EASY (TUG)

Contrary to historical and popular belief, teaching a dog to tug does *not* teach him to be aggressive. Quite the opposite is true. If Tug is taught using a set of rules, it can achieve the following:

- **JAW PRUDENCE:** This teaches a dog be aware of where he puts his teeth.
- **DROP:** This teaches a dog how to release an item from his mouth on cue.
- **DRIVE CONTROL:** This is the most valuable of the elements of a well-designed game of Tug. Unless a dog has been taught to get into and settle out of a prey interaction, it is impossible to expect him to do so in a real-life context.

Begin by teaching your dog the correct way to play Tug. For instructions on doing so, please see **TUG ON PAGE 99.**

INTERMEDIATE/DIFFICULT (LEAVE-IT)

At the same time you teach Tug, it is also necessary to teach your dog a very strong Leave-it. The key to teaching this invaluable skill is to increase the difficulty slowly.

1. Begin by holding a yummy food treat in your hand, with your palm closed, and allow your dog to nudge it just as you say "Leave it."

   Do *not* move your hand. Your dog must learn to leave the item on his own without you pulling it away from him.

2. The *moment* he abandons his effort to pry the food out of your hand, open your hand, mark the behavior with a "yes" or "take it" and allow him to take the treat.

   "Yes" or another release cue is necessary to teach a balanced Leave-it.

   Repeat these two steps ten times.

3. Hold out your hand again as in step 1, say "Leave it," but this time open your hand when it's next to your dog's head so that he can see the food. Each time he heads for it, close your fingers over the food and only allow him to see it when he abandons it. When he actively abandons it for a second or two, say your release cue ("yes") and allow him to take the food.

4. Hold your hand cupped over yummy food on the floor, say "Leave it" just as you did in step 1. However, this time, when he abandons it you'll mark his correct behavior and treat from the *other* hand.

5. Lastly, set yummy food on the floor with your hand next to it poised and ready to cover it should your dog begin to head for it. Say "Leave it" just as you uncover it, and the moment he abandons it, mark his correct behavior and, again, treat from the *other* hand.

To increase the difficulty of Leave-it, begin at home by increasing the value of the item your dog must leave. Then move to easy items outside of your home such as sniffs on the ground. Then move onto stinky things on the ground, and so forth.

Eventually it's reasonable to begin to ask your dog to abandon his urge to chase things, but *only* train at this level when your dog is achieving 100 percent success at all other levels. Depending on your dog, this may take weeks, months, or even longer.

At this stage, you may begin to ask him to leave his urges to lunge at motorcycles, scooters, joggers, and the like. At this advanced level, aim to issue your "leave it" command *before* your dog begins his pursuit. Be prepared to reward him big time when he does. Remember, this is a *very* advanced level of training, so be patient.

OTHER GAMES

Getting control over predatory drive is all about the skill of getting into and settling out of a drive behavior. Other helpful games to strengthen this skill are:

- **FETCH:** When playing fetch, be sure to get your dog to sit still near you until you give the cue for him to fetch. When he returns with the item he's retrieved, require him to drop it in your hand or at your feet before you bend to pick it up and toss it again.

- **HIDE-AND-SEEK:** This version of hide-and-seek is one in which you hide a favorite toy or puzzle in a room without your dog seeing you hide it. Once you've hidden the toy, invite him back into the room in which it's hidden. Require him to sit before you say your cue ("find it").

  To teach this game, begin with the item in visible range. When your dog learns the cue "find it" means to seize the item, you may hide the item in more and more obscure locations.

  If at any time your dog breaks from his Sit and goes after the item before you have given him permission, retrieve him, and start over.

Boredom Barking: Barking Incessantly in Owner Absence

This behavior is considered *basic*. One of the more shocking and somewhat embarrassing quandaries is being on the receiving end of a report from neighbors that your dog barks incessantly in your absence. Many dogs who are quiet when their owners are home bark in predictable continuous patterns that are similar in volume and have little variation in tonality or pitch when they're home alone.

Why

Many of today's dogs are left with little to nothing to do for hours on end while their owners are absent. The sheer abundance of today's double-income homes means that the average dog is generally understimulated and overly anxious due to a lack of exercise, both mental and physical, and ample outlets for his biological drives. He may be toted to the dog park on weekends, or receive a token walk in the morning or evening, but even the most laid-back dog needs more activity than just that to remain happy and healthy.

Just as humans begin to manifest anxieties in unusual and often annoying ways, such as tapping pencils, rocking back and forth, or grinding their teeth, dogs do as well. When boredom and anxiety take hold, a dog will begin to develop odd and unhealthy side effect behaviors such as pacing, destructive chewing and digging, and, in many cases, boredom barking.

Remedy

The only acceptable treatment for boredom barking is beefing up your dog's mental and physical activity. There are dozens of ways to do so, a few of which include:

- Feed him only by way of work-to-eat puzzles. Instead of feeding by a bowl, trade the bowl for one of the work-to-eat puzzles featured in **PART III, RECOMMENDED TOYS AND PRODUCTS**. For double duty, leave him with one of these things when you leave to keep him busy and relaxed.

- Fortify his environment with a vast array of items such as long-term consumables, dissectibles, and puzzle toys to keep him busy.

- Consider dog daycare or a dog walker a few or all days of the week. A good caretaker during the day can do wonders for the boredom barker.

- Frequent the dog park and/or playgroups in your area or arranged by dog owners in your community.

• Consider enrolling your dog in a brain-stimulating activity such as fly ball, freestyle, or agility. Many programs of this nature are available throughout the country. Before doing so, however, make sure the facility you are considering utilizes animal learning theory and positive training methods only.

Note: Do not punish the boredom barker with positive punishment (not-so-lovely) such as yelling, or using a shaker can, throw chain, or bark collar. This will only increase his anxiety punishment threshold. It can also be extremely helpful while training is taking place to move your dog to an area of your home where your neighbors are less likely to hear him. Leaving your dog all day in a backyard is a sure recipe for boredom barking, so avoid this at all cost.

Separation Anxiety: Barking Incessantly in Owner Absence

This behavior is considered *advanced*. Fairly common is the dog who barks incessantly during owner absence as reported by neighbors or passers by. While this type of report might indicate guard barking, alert barking, or boredom barking, it might also indicate something much more serious: separation anxiety (or "sepanx"). Separation-anxiety barking is usually accompanied by other vocalizations such as extreme whining with panting, howling, and baying. Although many dogs suffer from emotional discomfort when their owners leave the house or step out of the room, actual clinical separation anxiety is indicated by at least one of the following symptoms:

• **DESTRUCTION AT EXIT POINTS:** Exit points include crate doors, door frames, and doors.

• **SELF-MUTILATION:** This includes injuries to paws, toenails, noses, and teeth, usually from attempts to break through exit points.

• **EXTREME VOCALIZATIONS:** This include howling, baying, whining, panting, and barking incessantly.

- **PANTING AND DROOLING:** Anxiety panting is characterized by small, quick breaths with the mouth slightly open, lips parted, tongue in or out.

- **ANOREXIA:** Dogs exhibiting separation anxiety will not eat food left for them in an owner's absence.

- **EXTREME GREETING RITUAL:** This differs from the usual happy-to-see-you greeting in that it is accompanied by anxiety panting, pacing, pawing, and other seemingly "desperate" behaviors.

- **BLOWING OF BLADDER AND BOWELS:** Dogs will often void their bladder and/or bowels due to extreme anxiety.

- **VOMITING:** This is a direct response to extreme anxiety.

Why

There are many causes of separation anxiety, ranging from re-homing to advancing age to injury, and so forth. But no matter the cause, sepanx results from a dog who is overly affected by the contrast between times when the owner is present and times when the owner is gone.

Contrary to popular belief, it is not the moment when the owner leaves that causes the trauma—that is simply when the symptoms show themselves most fully—but rather the build up of predeparture cues that cause a dog suffering from sepanx the most anxiety. Most owners notice their dogs getting "anxious" about five minutes before they leave, and usually they can identify an action, such as picking up keys or a purse, or even shutting the door to leave, that sets off the anxiety. We now know that a dog suffering from this condition usually shows subtle symptoms of building anxiety an average of *forty-five minutes* before the owner actually departs.

Remedy

It's important to note that dogs suffering from separation anxiety are in an emotional state—their behavior cannot be humanely modified using positive punishment. Instead, the underlying feeling associated with an owner leaving must be changed so the dog perceives it as something good instead of scary.

The great news is that you can improve or alleviate the vast majority of separation anxiety cases entirely with a well-planned and executed behavior modification plan. The goal during the training period is to keep your dog under his emotional reaction threshold at all times while extending the amount of time he can be left alone.

PREPARATION

1. Suspend all situations in which your dog may experience a separation anxiety episode without exception. To accomplish this, owner creativity and commitment is key. Consider daycare, dog walkers, bringing your dog to work, and so forth.

2. Identify a full list of predeparture rituals and systematically desensitize your dog to them.

   Begin this list of steps at the moment you get up for work in the morning: get out of bed, take a shower, make coffee, pack a lunch, and so on. At each of these steps, your dog is determining his odds of being left alone, his anticipation and anxiety mounting with each one.

   It's imperative that you complete your entire ritual with the step your dog interprets as your final departure cue. While many owners stop at locking the door, dogs actually identify walking down the steps, opening the garage, or hearing your engine drive off as the actual final cues. This is why owners almost never hear their own dog suffering from sepanx; most rely on reports from others.

3. Determine the period of time in either seconds or minutes from the moment you leave to your dog's first vocalization. Write that here: _____ minutes _____ seconds.

4. Consider medications to help boost the chances of a successful behavior modification plan. Medications such as Clomicalm can be extremely useful for keeping a dog under threshold and can greatly increase the likelihood of success. You should only use medications in conjunction with a behavior modification

plan, not as a substitute. If you need help communicating your dog's needs to your vet, enlist the help of a Certificate in Training and Counseling (CTC) professional trainer (www.sfspca.org/academy/referral.shtml) or a Certified Applied Animal Behaviorist (www.animalbehavior.org) in your area.

Before embarking on the active training plan, instate these guidelines for all absences:

• Leave your dog with very tasty and attractive treats, toys, long-term consumables, and puzzles. These should be special items that he only has access to in your absence.

• When you leave and when you return, avoid fanfare—no petting, giving out treats, and so on.

• Leave a radio or television on to blur or fill the silence of being alone.

ACTIVE TRAINING

1. Desensitize your dog to your predeparture ritual:
   • Mix up the order of your predeparture ritual.
   • Follow your current ritual to various steps and then abort before its completion.

   There is no set timeline for the success of habituation. Look for behaviors that signal your dog's anxiety is lessening, such as decreased shadowing, pacing, whining, and so forth.

2. After step 1 is complete, slowly increase the amount of time your dog can be left alone *before* he becomes upset.

   Begin with thirty seconds less than the amount of time you identified in **STEP 3 UNDER PREPARATION**. Write that number here: _____ minutes _____ seconds.

   Put your dog in his confinement area, and step out of the house for this period of time, returning after the time above has elapsed, but no longer.

Using the following worksheet, increase the amount of time your dog can be left alone every three days. Mark each day he successfully remains silent. If he vocalizes at any time during this plan, take a step back and complete the previous level.

Attention-Seeking: Barking Plus Other Behaviors

This behavior is considered *basic*. Inevitably, every dog develops some type of attention-seeking behavior, such as nudging a hand for a pet, barking to throw a ball, or even something more clever like pouting by the edge of a piece of furniture, to entice a human to retrieve some lost item for him. Equally predictable, the human target often indulges the demand just to prevent the escalation of said attention-seeking behavior or to keep peace in the house. Common attention requests and human responses are:

- Dog barks while staring at owner = owner yells at the dog to be quiet
- Dog steals something and parades it by owner = owner chases dog
- Dog whines at couch = owner bends down and retrieves lost toy
- Dog paws or nudges owner = owner pets dog
- Dog barks at the door = owner lets dog out

Why

The simple answer for why your dog behaves this way: it works. The owner responses listed previously may seem harmless, but they are actually strong reinforcements of the requests the dog is issuing. Dogs are very crafty and they learn at a young age that certain behaviors will elicit a response. They are also great sports for fun and enjoy engaging humans in play and other activities. Once something works to earn the attention from the owner, the dog will continue to issue the demand as long as it pays off.

Remedy

You can deal with attention-seeking behaviors, including barking, in two ways:

1. **EXTINGUISHING (IGNORING THE BEHAVIOR UNTIL IT GOES AWAY)**

   Simply stop giving in. In other words, no longer pay off in any way, not even with eye contact, when your dog issues any demand for attention.

   Extinguishing is very effective, but beware of common challenges:

   • Your dog will go through an *extinction burst* before the behavior goes away. This burst is defined as an increase in intensity and frequency. This is the equivalent to human behavior when a person encounters a light switch that does not turn the light on; the person will flip the switch several times in hopes of a spontaneous burst of electricity—the extinction burst. When the light doesn't come on, the person abandons the activity—the action is extinguished.

   • If you embark on an extinguishing plan, be prepared to stick to it no matter how intense the burst gets. Rewarding any time before the behavior is extinguished reinforces a higher level of attention seeking.

2. **TIMEOUTS (PUNISHING THE BEHAVIOR BY REMOVING THE OPPORTUNITY FOR REWARD)**

   Begin by identifying the behavior you are giving to reinforce your dog's attention request. When he issues his request, simply say "That's enough."

   • *If he leaves you alone*, praise him.

   • *If he continues*, tell him "Too bad" and then lead him to a timeout area such as his crate, behind a door, and so forth. Wait for ten seconds, then open the door, say "Okay," and allow him to come back in. Repeat.

You may also choose to administer a timeout without a warning. To do this, simply skip the "that's enough" step and deliver a timeout. Repeat and extend the timeout period up to no longer than thirty seconds if needed.

Tip: It can also be extremely helpful to remove *yourself* for a timeout instead of your dog. Rather than shuttling him to his timeout area, just get up and walk out when he demands attention.

Note: *As brilliant discriminators, dogs will learn who in the house will pay off for attention seeking and who will not. To eliminate attention seeking altogether, all family members must agree on the same behavior modification plan. If this does not happen, those who choose not to participate will still be regular targets for your dog!*

CHAPTER 10

Other Greeting Problems

Your home is your sanctuary, and it should be a place where people are happy to live and visit without being on the receiving end of a barrage of dog paws, noses, and licks. Even the most dog-loving guest will take offense to being lovingly mauled at the front door when simply coming by to visit. Even worse is the guest forced to endure crotch sniffing or humping while you, the embarrassed owner, yell urgent expletives at the dog to "just stop!"

Bursting through doors, jumping on visitors and family members, crotch targeting, and humping are extremely common but taboo behavior problems. By training your dog by following a few simple guidelines, you are well on your way to a happy guest, civilized dog, and relaxed home environment.

Bursting Out the Front Door upon Your Departure

Few things can be more frustrating and dangerous than a dog who dashes through the door the moment it's opened. Some dogs choose to bolt after the door is fully open while others actually take on the job themselves by forcefully pushing a snout or paw into the door jam, forcing their way past their owners, who are scrambling madly to fetch them and lock the door, while trying to avoid serious injury.

Why

Very early on, dogs learn the value of heading outside. A trip out might mean just a trot to go to the bathroom, but it also has the possibility of turning into a trip to the dog park, to visit friends, to go on a favorite walk, or any number of exceedingly wonderful things.

Being unbelievably good discriminators, dogs pick up on even the most subtle predeparture clues to your intended destination. If you're leaving in the morning and don your work pants and shoes, your dog will be less likely to want to follow you. However, reach for the leash or your dog park pants and he turns into a bouncing lunatic.

Lastly, dogs are not born bursting through doors and the behavior is not a manifestation of any deeply rooted drive. It's safe to assume that if your dog's a door dasher, he's gotten away with the behavior in the past and has learned its value.

Remedy

Ending door dashing is as easy as teaching your dog a "wait" cue. Wait is considered a less formal stay.

1. First, end the cycle of reinforcement by making sure your dog is not allowed to rush through one more doorway without first being given permission.

2. With your dog on leash, approach the door through which your dog wants to pass.

   It's absolutely imperative that you keep the leash slack here. If you hold your dog back by putting pressure on the leash, he will never learn to wait. He will learn that you will hold his body in whatever position you want it and he need not modify his behavior.

3. Say "Wait" once, and *slowly* open the door just an inch or two.

   If your dog begins to head through the door, say "Oops" and close the door quickly. Be careful not to close his snout in the door. This technique takes a bit of finesse, so go slow.

4. Do not repeat the "wait" cue, but repeat opening the door and closing it again and again until your dog visibly stays still when the door opens.

   You're retraining your dog from his old behavior (pushing at the door opens it) to a new lesson (pushing the door closes it but waiting opens it).

5. At the first door opening during which your dog hesitates, open the door fully and say "Okay" as you allow him to pass.

6. Repeat this training several days in a row. Each week, increase the distance you open the door, starting with just an inch to a few inches, then to a foot, then to a foot and a half, and then all the way, building on success each time.

Before you know it, simply arriving to the door will cause your dog to wait!

Bursting Out the Front Door as Guests Arrive

One of the most likely times a dog will escape through the front door is when guests arrive. The open door can be an irresistible beacon to the dog who is hungry to taste freedom. Few feelings are as sinking as watching a dog bolt through a guest's knees to the world outside while guest and owner are left frazzled at the door, choosing between polite greeting manners and madly chasing after the escapee to possibly save his life.

Why

Very early on, dogs learn the value of heading outside. A trip out might mean just a trot to go to the bathroom, but it also has the possibility of turning into a trip to the dog park, to visit friends, to go on a favorite walk, or any number of exceedingly wonderful things.

Being unbelievably good discriminators, dogs pick upon even the most subtle predeparture clues to your intended destination. If you're leaving in the morning and don your work pants and shoes, your dog will be less likely to want to follow you. However, reach for the leash or your dog park pants and he turns into a bouncing lunatic.

Lastly, dogs are not born bursting through doors and the behavior is not a manifestation of any deeply rooted drive. It's safe to assume that if your dog's a door dasher, he's gotten away with the behavior in the past and has learned its value.

Incidentally, repeated running away is credited as one of the top three reasons given by owners when relinquishing their dog to a shelter. Owners often incorrectly interpret the behavior as the dog's dislike for his home and family. To the contrary, most dogs like their families very much but they will always seize the chance to experience something new and fun, not unlike a child who wants to visit Disneyland.

Remedy

If your dog bursts through the door when guests arrive, try the following remedies.

MANAGEMENT

Managing your dog's access to the front door is the easiest way to avoid escape. When the doorbell rings, you may decide to put him in another room, into his crate, or behind an expen until the guest enters. Just temporarily holding him by the collar or leash before opening the door can help save your dog's life.

EASY

Teaching your dog to wait at the door rather than rush it when it opens can do wonders for preventing escape.

1. Begin by setting your dog up. Enlist the help of some friends to come by at prearranged times.

2. When the doorbell rings or your guest knocks, walk your dog to the door on leash.

   It's absolutely imperative that you keep the leash slack here. If you hold your dog back by putting pressure on the leash, he will never learn to wait. He will learn that you will hold his body in whatever position you want it and he need not modify his behavior.

3. Say "Wait" once, and *slowly* open the door just an inch or two.

   If your dog begins to head through the door, say "Oops" and close the door quickly. Be careful not to close his snout in the door. This technique takes a bit of finesse, so go slow.

4. Do not repeat the "wait" cue, but repeat opening the door and closing it again and again until your dog visibly stays still when the door opens.

   After a few repeats, you will open the door and your dog will hesitate or even step away from it. At this point, say "Okay" and fully open the door to your guest so he or she may enter. Praise your dog like crazy.

5. Repeat this training several days in a row. Each week, increase the distance you open the door, starting with just an inch to a few inches, then to a foot, then to a foot and a half, and then all the way, building on success each time.

Because the potential for injury if this cue fails is so great, keep the dog on leash and practice this lesson until you are certain you can open the door without having your dog bolt.

DIFFICULT

A very useful and safe technique in avoiding door dashing is teaching the dog to go to his mat away from the door and settle while guests arrive. For instructions on doing so, please see **GO TO MAT ON PAGE 96.**

Jumping Up upon Your Arrival Home

Every owner knows the experience of returning home to his loyal canine only to be greeted by flailing paws, sloppy kisses, and relentless jumping. With not even a foot across the threshold, the owner's gregarious companion throws himself against the door, knocks packages and keys from his owner's arms, and makes entering the house equivalent to crossing a battlefield under fire.

Why

Jumping on people is a highly rewarding behavior for your dog. When he jumps, he is seeking attention. Predictably, when he jumps you respond, albeit with a glare, a "No," a yell, a knee to the chest, or some other deflective attempt. Although all of these responses seem to us like punishments, your dog only sees this as the coveted "attention" he is seeking.

Think about what is reinforcing your dog at the moment he's jumping. Assuming he doesn't spend eight hours a day in your absence bouncing from wall to wall in an apparent sugar-induced craze, it's clear that your arrival is the greatest thing to happen to him all day.

Remedy

As his punishment, remove your dog's topmost reward. In other words, remove from him the most rewarding thing possible at that moment: your attention.

1. Upon your arrival home from work, key the front door as you usually would, open the screen just a few inches, and attempt to enter.

2. The *moment* your dog takes his front feet off the ground, quickly back out of the door. Wait.

3. The *moment* all four feet hit the ground, attempt your entry again. If his feet come off the floor, back out and shut the door. Only when he behaves like a gentleman, with all four feet on the floor, will you enter fully.

This may take four or five tries on your first attempt to enter, but be patient. Your dog will quickly learn that his less-than-civilized behavior actually drives you away. At the same time, he's learning that good behavior is rewarded with the greatest thing ever: you!

Jumping Up on Visitors to Your Home

A dog cannot resist the opportunity to put his paws up on visitors to his home. Often, his enthusiastic greeting is paired with face licks, a ferociously beating tail, and a shameless display of delight and worship.

Why

Jumping on people is a highly rewarding behavior for your dog. When he jumps, he is seeking attention. Predictably, when he jumps, the person on whom he is jumping responds, albeit with a glare, a "No," a yell, a knee to the chest, or some other deflective attempt. Although all of these responses seem to us like punishments, your dog only sees the coveted "attention" he is seeking.

Remedy

If your dog jumps up on visitors to your home, try the following remedies.

EASY

1. If you're expecting a number of casual guests who are likely to help in your training, start by tacking a note to the outside of your front door that reads:

Help me train my dog!

- Ring doorbell.
- After door opens, if dog jumps, ignore him. If he sits, pet him.

This may seem odd, but it is amazing how many of your friends will be delighted with their new and helpful task.

2. Sit back and watch the learning happen. Your guests will take an erect posture and with flawless timing will ignore your dog when he jumps. Eager to help, they bend with equally great timing to reward your dog with pets for polite manners. A number of my students have reported to me that often a friendly competition will break out among guests to call each other out for poor training techniques!

INTERMEDIATE

1. If you are expecting visitors who are not likely to participate in the previous activity, begin by teaching and perfecting a solid Sit. For instructions, see **SIT ON PAGE 87.**

2. When the doorbell rings, ask your dog to sit. Reward him with a cookie.

3. While he is sitting, open the door just a few inches:

- *If he stays in the sit position*, open the door fully and allow your guest in. As long as your dog sits, reward him with periodic cookies and praise.
- *If he gets up* from the Sit before your visitor enters, gently close the door for another moment.

Guests are often grateful to meet an owner who is actively training his dog not to jump on visitors and they don't seem to mind waiting the few extra seconds it takes to do so.

4. Ask your dog to sit again and repeat step 2 until your guest is inside.

5. If at any time during your guest's visit your dog jumps on him, issue your dog a firm but calm and unemotional "Too bad" the very *moment* his paws touch the visitor. Walk calmly and quietly to him, gently grab hold of his collar and lead him from the room into an area in which he does not have access to the guest.

6. After thirty seconds the dog may return or he may be left in the confinement area for the duration of the guest's visit.

With practice and consistency, the doorbell itself will become a signal to your dog to keep all four feet on the ground or sit.

Jumping Up on Adult Family Members

It doesn't take much encouragement for a dog to rear up and place a couple of happy paws on a family member. Just pulling the leash from its hook or tucking the Chuckit! under an arm will send even the best-behaved canine into fits of jumping joy. Even a key piece of clothing indicating a special trip out may trigger a bouncing attack.

Why

In these situations, jumping up is a symptom of excitement. Two things reinforce this behavior: the continuation of the exciting activity and your attention.

When your dog jumps on an adult family member in the home, the family member responds, albeit with a glare, a "No," a yell, a knee to the chest, or some other deflective attempt. Although all of these responses seem to us like punishments, your dog only sees the coveted "attention" he is seeking.

Often making this type of jumping even more reinforcing is the item just brandished such as a leash or Chuckit!, or the cues to an intended dog-friendly activity such as heading for a walk or to the dog park.

Remedy

As his punishment, remove your dog's topmost reward. In other words, remove from him the most rewarding thing possible at that moment: you. This technique is effective for in-home jumping regardless of the activity that has sparked the jumping.

EASY

1. The *moment* your dog places his paws on your body, quickly turn your back and be still and quiet. Wait.

2. The *moment* all four feet hit the ground, turn around and continue your activity. If his feet come off the floor, repeat step 1. Only when he behaves like a gentleman, with all four feet on the floor, will you continue your exciting activity.

INTERMEDIATE

1. If your dog doesn't respond when you turn your back twice, then decide what specifically is reinforcing his behavior: the leash, putting on your boots, grabbing your coat or keys, and so on.

2. Instead of turning your back in step 1 under the EASY steps, when his toes come off the ground to jump on you, reverse the dog-friendly activity:

   Examples:

   - If you are putting on his leash, stop and put it back on the hook.
   - If you are putting on your dog park pants, take them off and put them away.
   - If you are playing with his favorite toy, place it back in its bin.

Always give your dog a few chances to get this right while he's still learning. When you reverse the activity, restart the activity two or three more times in a row. With repetition, he will learn that putting his paws on you makes good things go away. Likewise, keeping his paws on the ground keeps the great activities going!

Jumping Up on Children in the Family

There is something about a child that a playful dog cannot resist. Children are endless partners in chase-and-be-chased games, Tug, fetch, and all other types of fun activities. However, unlike your dog's canine play partners, human play pals of the child variety are more fragile and need extra care to avoid being flattened during chase, thrown during Tug, or toppled for no apparent reason.

Why

Children really do make more natural play partners for dogs than adults. Surprisingly this has little to do with their size. Instead, dogs are highly rewarded by kids' energetic movements, flapping arms, squealing, screaming, quick movements, bouncy agility, and merriment. Even more rewarding is their endless willingness to play any game for hours on end.

Remedy

If your dog jumps up on children, try the following remedies.

Important: Only proceed with this lesson after consulting SPE-CIAL INSTRUCTIONS FOR KIDS ON PAGE 100 *for details about teaching kids and dogs to play and train together. It is unsafe to proceed without doing so.*

EASY

1. The *moment* your dog jumps on your child, the child is to stop whatever activity he was just doing and stand still and quiet. If he was holding a toy that enticed the dog, he is to drop the toy, and stand still and quiet. It does not matter if

the dog accidentally gets the toy. This is less rewarding than having the child engage in play.

Teaching the child to "be a tree" is a helpful way for him to learn his part in the dog's training. To "be a tree," the child must stand still with his feet planted firmly on the ground, his arms (the branches) crossed in front, and remain silent.

2. While the child is still and quiet, he must count to ten. Play may then resume.

It is reasonable to repeat these steps two or three times before proceeding to the intermediate method.

INTERMEDIATE

1. If your dog's behavior does not improve as a result of your child's staying still, say a firm but calm and unemotional "Too bad" the very *moment* your dog's paws touch the child.

2. Walk calmly and quietly to your dog, gently grab hold of his collar and lead him from play into an area in which he does not have access to the child. This area may be just inside, in a gated room, or behind a door. It is not necessary to put the dog in his crate or in another official timeout area.

3. Play may end for the day, or may resume in five to ten minutes.

Always give your dog a few chances to get this right while he's still learning. Be patient and consistent. With a little practice your dog will learn the intended lesson: "I lose my favorite play partner when I jump on him. When I have all four feet on the ground, I get to play with my best buddy!"

Jumping Up on Strangers in Public

Despite earnest efforts to encourage only the best behavior, walking the family dog through the neighborhood can be a frustrating, embarrassing, and seemingly uncontrollable situation. Your friendly companion seizes every opportunity during his walk to jump up on passersby or neighbors who pause to chat.

Why

Jumping on people is a highly rewarding behavior for your dog. When he jumps, he is seeking attention. Predictably, when he jumps, the person on whom he is jumping responds, albeit with a glare, a "No," a yell, a knee to the chest, or some other deflective attempt. Although all of these responses seem to us like punishments, your dog only sees the coveted "attention" he is seeking. With continued reinforcement such as this, he is actually learning to jump on strangers in public.

Remedy

1. When a stranger begins to approach for a chat or to pet your dog, politely and enthusiastically ask that he or she help you with your training. A quick, "Hello, do you want to help my dog with his training?" is usually all you'll have time for. (Strangers approaching to pet your dog almost always enjoy the opportunity to engage with a dog rather than just pat him and move on.)

2. Invite the stranger to pet your dog but only if he's not jumping.

3. Your job is to hold the leash tight at your center of gravity. For instructions, see **PULLING ON LEASH ON PAGE 213**. The leash should be just short enough that when fully extended your dog's feet cannot reach the stranger. Expect him to strain at the end of the leash at first.

4. Plant yourself and watch the learning happen. The stranger will most often take on an erect posture just out of your dog's reach, eagerly waiting for his or her chance to pet a well-behaved non-jumping dog. The timing is perfect as the stranger is poised and ready to quickly bend and deliver

the attention your dog seeks when all four paws are on the ground.

With practice and consistency, the sight of strangers will automatically elicit good manners and, with time, your dog is even likely to develop a Sit when he sees strangers who might dish out pats and other forms of attention.

Crotch Targeting You and Family Members

Both embarrassing and humanly inappropriate, many dogs have masterful precision when it comes to jamming their snouts forcefully into the privy parts. While a dog may choose to deliver this punch anytime during the day, his favorite time to do so is upon his owner's arrival home or during play. This behavior is not left solely to those breeds capable of reaching their target without jumping, but is an equal opportunity offense that adds the bonus of a hurling jump for those dogs too short to reach without a boost.

Why

Dogs are equipped with noses designed to pick up the most imperceptible of smells. The very structure of the nose allows a dog to take fresh air into his nostrils from the front of his face, drawing odor molecules into a specialized shelflike structure inside his nasal cavity where the molecules pause to be analyzed. The dog exhales contaminated air through the curved side structure of the nose, avoiding the front of his face; this ensures the air being drawn into the front of the nostrils remains contaminant-free.

Dogs are masters at reading body language through both visual and scent signals. Dog nature requires him to find out as much about his environment through these means as quickly as possible to assess possible threats and benefits.

A dog can get a tremendous amount of information about an individual from sniffing him, especially in his most intimate areas. The smells a person gives off are as individual as a fingerprint, and when a dog takes a header for the crotch, he's getting a very

concentrated sense of the person's identity in a very quick investigation. Because of this, the behavior is highly self-reinforcing.

Remedy

Although this behavior is extremely normal, it can be very uncomfortable both physically and emotionally for humans.

EASY

Giving a dog something to do that's incompatible with the behavior you'd like to see end is often the easiest way to fix a problem
behavior. Teaching your dog to target a person's hand instead of
his crotch can be just the remedy needed.

1. Sit *silently* with your dog in your home with a clicker, or use
   a marker word, and some bait. Flatten the hand your dog
   will be bumping as if you're raising your hand to be sworn in,
   with all of your fingers straight and together.

2. Present your hand to your dog to the side of his face, about
   three inches from his nose, at a slight angle (not flat as if
   offering him a treat and not vertical).

3. He's curious, so wait until he sniffs your hand. The *moment*
   his nose bumps your hand to investigate, mark the behavior
   with a click or marker word and treat.

4. Repeat these steps several days in a row, moving your hand
   around in front of him until he quickly rushes to bump it the
   moment you present it.

5. Only after you can be 90 percent certain he'll bump your
   hand when you present it, say your cue ("say hi") and present
   your hand. You should be following this training string: *say
   verbal cue ("say hi"), present your hand, dog bumps hand
   with his nose, you treat.*

6. After several repetitions, you're ready to generalize the
   behavior. To do so, simply begin asking for him to "say hi" at
   various times throughout the house.

7. Now you'll put the verbal cue in context. When you arrive home, come in calmly, say his name to get his attention, say your cue ("say hi"), and present your hand. It is very helpful at this stage to keep some cookies in your pocket to reinforce this difficult switch.

With consistency he will learn to target your palm instead of your crotch.

DIFFICULT

While teaching a dog to target your hand instead of your crotch can be very effective for most dogs, some dogs are more persistent and may need a little more help learning. A timeout without a warning can be exceptionally useful.

1. The *moment* your dog bumps your crotch with his nose, say "Too bad" and lead him gently to a timeout area such as his crate or behind a door. Having the opportunity to investigate you at all is what's reinforcing him, so removing that opportunity is a punishment.

   Good timing is absolutely crucial, so be sure to say "Too bad" at the very *moment* your dog's nose touches your crotch.

2. Wait for twenty to thirty seconds, then open the door to his timeout area, say "Okay," and allow him to come back in. Repeat.

If he comes back in and doesn't target your crotch right away, praise, praise, praise.

Many dogs will cease crotch targeting in just a few days, though some may take longer. Be patient and consistent and you will succeed!

Crotch Targeting Visitors to the Home

More embarrassing than being personally on the end of a well-aimed crotch investigation is witnessing guests undergo the most intimate of handshakes: a snoot to the groin by the beloved resident dog. This dog may decide to deliver this welcome at the moment the guest enters, or he may delivery sporadic investigative attempts during the visitor's stay.

Why

Dogs are equipped with noses designed to pick up the most imperceptible of smells. The very structure of the nose allows a dog to take fresh air into his nostrils from the front of his face, drawing odor molecules into a specialized shelflike structure inside his nasal cavity where the molecules pause to be analyzed. The dog exhales contaminated air through the curved side structure of the nose, avoiding the front of his face; this ensures the air being drawn into the front of the nostrils remains contaminant-free.

Dogs are masters at reading body language through both visual and scent signals. Dog nature requires him to find out as much about his environment through these means as quickly as possible to assess possible threats and benefits.

A dog can get a tremendous amount of information about an individual from sniffing him, especially in his most intimate areas. The smells a person gives off are as individual as a fingerprint, and when a dog takes a header for the crotch, he's getting a very concentrated sense of the person's identity in a very quick investigation. Because of this, the behavior is highly self-reinforcing.

Remedy

Although this behavior is extremely normal, it can be very uncomfortable both physically and emotionally for humans.

MANAGEMENT

One of the best approaches to any display of poor manners while entertaining is to give your dog a long-term project while guests are around. This may be teaching him to settle in his bed while chewing on a favorite bone or giving him a work-to-eat puzzle to keep him occupied. Popular management strategies include:

- Sequester your dog behind a barrier such as a baby gate or in his crate with a bone or bully stick.

- Teach your dog to go to his mat and settle while guests are around. For instructions on doing so, please see GO TO MAT ON PAGE 96.

EASY

Second to management, giving a dog something to do that's incompatible with the behavior you'd like to see end is an excellent way to fix a problem behavior. Teaching your dog to target a person's hand instead of his crotch can be just the remedy needed.

1. Sit *silently* with your dog in your home with your clicker, or use a marker word, and some bait. Flatten the hand your dog will be bumping as if you're raising your hand to be sworn in, with all of your fingers straight and together.

2. Present your hand to your dog to the side of his face, about three inches from his nose, at a slight angle (not flat as if offering him a treat and not vertical).

3. He's curious, so wait until he sniffs your hand. The *moment* his nose bumps your hand to investigate, mark the behavior with a click or marker word and treat.

4. Repeat these steps several days in a row, moving your hand around in front of him until he quickly rushes to bump it the moment you present it.

5. Only after you can be 90 percent certain he'll bump your hand when you present it, say your cue ("say hi") and present your hand. You should be following this training string: *say verbal cue ("say hi"), present your hand, dog bumps hand with his nose, you treat.*

6. After several repetitions, you're ready to generalize the behavior. To do so, simply begin asking for him to "say hi" at various times throughout the house.

7. Now you'll put the cue in context. Set your dog up by having visitors participate in your training goal. Have each guest

enter and exit a few times in a row until your dog learns to bump the guest's hand instead of his groin.

With consistency he will learn to target guest's palms instead of crotches.

DIFFICULT

While teaching a dog to target a hand instead of a crotch can be very effective for most dogs, some dogs are more persistent and may need a little more help learning. A timeout without a warning can be exceptionally useful.

1. Be ready at the door with your dog when a guest arrives. The *moment* your dog bumps the visitor's crotch with his nose, say "Too bad" and lead him gently to a timeout area such as his crate or behind a door. Having the opportunity to investigate your visitor at all is what's reinforcing him, so removing that opportunity is a punishment.

   Good timing is absolutely crucial, so be sure to say "Too bad" at the very *moment* your dog's nose touches your guest.

2. Wait for twenty to thirty seconds, then open the door to his timeout area, say "Okay" and allow him to come back in. Repeat.

If he comes back in and doesn't target your guest right away, praise, praise, praise.

Many dogs will cease crotch targeting in just a few days, though some may take longer. Be patient and consistent and you will succeed!

Crotch Targeting Strangers in Public

Because of their innate appeal, most dogs attract requests for pets during walks through the neighborhood or when meeting with acquaintances while out in public. While a number of behaviors exhibited by a dog can make greeting someone uncomfortable, crotch targeting takes the cake.

Why

Dogs are equipped with noses designed to pick up the most imperceptible of smells. The very structure of the nose allows a dog to take fresh air into his nostrils from the front of his face, drawing odor molecules into a specialized shelflike structure inside his nasal cavity where the molecules pause to be analyzed. The dog exhales contaminated air through the curved side structure of the nose, avoiding the front of his face; this ensures the air being drawn into the front of the nostrils remains contaminant-free.

Dogs are masters at reading body language through both visual and scent signals. Dog nature requires him to find out as much about his environment through these means as quickly as possible to assess possible threats and benefits.

A dog can get a tremendous amount of information about an individual from sniffing him, especially in his most intimate areas. The smells a person gives off are as individual as a fingerprint, and when a dog takes a header for the crotch, he's getting a very concentrated sense of the person's identity in a very quick investigation. Because of this, the behavior is highly self-reinforcing.

Remedy

Although this behavior is extremely normal, it can be very uncomfortable both physically and emotionally for humans.

MANAGEMENT

If you know your dog is a crotch-targeter, start out by limiting his reach to people he meets. Simply shortening the leash or requiring him to sit when you stop can head off the undesirable behavior altogether. For instructions on teaching Sit, SEE SIT ON PAGE 87, and for leash guidance, SEE PULLING ON LEASH ON PAGE 213.

EASY

Second to management, giving a dog something to do that's incompatible with the behavior you'd like to see end is an excellent way to fix a problem behavior. Teaching your dog to target a person's hand instead of his crotch can be just the remedy needed.

1. To begin, sit *silently* with your dog in your home with your clicker, or use a marker word, and some bait. Flatten the hand your dog will be bumping as if you're raising your hand to be sworn in, with all of your fingers straight and together.

2. Present your hand to your dog to the side of his face, about three inches from his nose, at a slight angle (not flat as if offering him a treat and not vertical).

3. He's curious, so wait until he sniffs your hand. The *moment* his nose bumps your hand to investigate, mark the behavior with a click or marker word and treat.

4. Repeat these steps several days in a row, moving your hand around in front of him until he quickly rushes to bump it the moment it's presented.

5. Only after you can be 90 percent certain he'll bump your hand when you present it, say your cue ("say hi") and present your hand. You should be following this training string: *say verbal cue ("say hi"), present your hand, dog bumps hand with his nose, you treat.*

6. After several repetitions, you're ready to generalize the behavior. To do so, simply begin asking for him to "say hi" at various times throughout the house.

7. Now you'll put the cue in context. While in public, when you see a person approaching to say hello to your dog, say your cue ("say hi") directly to your dog but do not present your hand. Instead, watch your dog head for the other person's hand as he reaches to pet your dog.

With consistency he will learn to target palms instead of crotches.

Humping Family Members and Guests

Humiliating and shocking, it only takes being humped once by the family dog to force an owner to search for a solution to make sure it never happens again. A humper may have a preferred family member whom he always targets, or he may be an equal opportunity offender, targeting all members without prejudice. The humper may be male, female, young, old, intact or altered, and of any breed and temperament. Adding insult to being humped, attempts to push the dog off or holler at him usually only incite a more enthusiastic humping episode.

Why

Humping is a very normal dog behavior. Normal, normal, normal, yet one that seems to send owners into a freaked out frenzy more than any other. Speculation about American views of sex, outdated but persisting beliefs of potential aggression resulting from humping, and other suggested but anecdotal theories of world domination by the humper are common explanations for this hysteria.

As puppies, dogs begin humping one another as part of normal play and socialization. Mounting another dog is part of ritualized play and practice just as roughhousing is ritualized aggression in human children. Unless a dog is sexually mature and he is humping another dog of the opposite sex who is in season, he is not doing so to mate. Unless we develop mind-reading skills, we will never know the exact reasons for humping in a nonsexual situation, but we do know that something about the behavior is rewarding. It may be fun, it may feel good, or it may improve bonding or communication. Regardless, it's unnecessary to know the very cause of humping in order to modify it.

Remedy

While acknowledging humping is normal, we also must acknowledge that it's almost always socially uncomfortable.

EASY

Interruption and redirection is a very effective, labor-light method for modifying humping.

1. When your dog mounts his target, say a firm but controlled "Ah-ah."

2. Direct him to another activity such as Tug, fetch, or a long-term chew item.

   When he settles into his new activity, praise him.

3. Repeat. As you continue to repeat this exercise, your dog will learn to direct his own urge to a behavior other than humping as being interrupted while humping is a punishment.

INTERMEDIATE

Timeouts are also very effective but are slightly more labor-intensive.

1. When your dog mounts his target, say "That's enough."

   • *If he leaves you alone*, praise him.

   • *If he continues*, tell him "Too bad" and then lead him to a timeout area such as his crate, behind a door, and so on. Wait for ten seconds, then open the door, say "Okay" and allow him to come back in. Repeat.

2. You may also choose to administer a timeout without a warning. This technique is particularly helpful with guests.

   To do this, simply skip the "that's enough" step and deliver a timeout as stated previously. Repeat and extend the timeout period up to but no longer than thirty seconds if needed.

Humping Other Dogs

Few things cause more caustic stares, unsolicited advice, or even outright aggression in humans than the sight of a humping dog at the dog park or other public setting. It can be shocking and embarrassing for the owner of the dog on the receiving end of the humping, but it can be downright humiliating and confusing for the owner of the humper himself.

Why

Humping is a very normal dog behavior. Normal, normal, normal, yet one that seems to send owners into a freaked out frenzy more than any other. Speculation about American views of sex, outdated but persisting beliefs of potential aggression resulting from humping, and other suggested but anecdotal theories of world domination by the humper are common explanations for this hysteria.

As puppies, dogs begin humping one another as part of normal play and socialization. Mounting another dog is part of ritualized play and practice just as roughhousing is ritualized aggression in human children. Unless a dog is sexually mature, he is not humping to mate. Unless we develop mind-reading skills, we will never know the exact reasons for humping in a nonsexual situation but we do know that something about the behavior is rewarding. It may be fun, it may feel good, or it may improve bonding or communication. Regardless, it's unnecessary to know the very cause of humping in order to modify it.

Remedy

The best rule of thumb for the occasional humper is to allow the dog he his humping to tell him to stop. Usually this is enough of a punishment and the humper will dismount and avoid the behavior again.

If you know your dog is a humper, a more hands-on modification plan of a timeout without warning is the best approach in these situations:

- If the owner of the dog being humped is uncomfortable
- If the dog on the receiving end is not telling your dog to stop
- If the dog on the receiving end is telling your dog to stop but your dog isn't listening

When issuing a timeout, follow these steps:

1. The *moment* your dog mounts another dog, say "Too bad."

2. Quickly walk to your dog calmly and quietly, grab his collar, and pull him from play away from other dogs.

   Require him to sit in this spot for twenty seconds or until he is visibly relaxed.

3. Release him to play again.

It's very likely at first he will re-offend. This is normal and expected and is key to teaching and learning. Simply repeat this exercise from step 1 until his humping behavior diminishes.

Tips: Don't forget to verbally praise your dog for non-humping social interaction.

If after several days practicing timeouts your dog continues to hump, consider leaving play altogether at the first offense. This is labor-intensive and tedious for owners, but it is tremendously effective.

Humping Furniture and Other Home Accessories

Many dogs will take the opportunity to express their urge to hump inanimate objects such as pillows, stuffed animals, armchairs, or even thoughtfully arranged blankets. While the activity seems random, it's clearly purposeful and most dogs take on a posture and set of facial expressions often interpreted as enjoyment.

Why

Humping is a very normal dog behavior. Normal, normal, normal, yet one that seems to send owners into a freaked out frenzy more than any other. Speculation about American views of sex, outdated but persisting beliefs of potential aggression resulting from humping, and other suggested but anecdotal theories of world domination by the humper are common explanations for this hysteria.

As puppies, dogs begin humping one another as part of normal play and socialization. Mounting another dog is part of ritualized play and practice just as roughhousing is ritualized aggression in human children. Sometimes the humper will target people and even furniture or other soft items resembling a dog torso. Unless a dog is sexually mature and he is humping another dog of the opposite sex who is in season, he is not doing so to mate. Unless we develop mind-reading skills, we will never know the exact reasons for humping in a nonsexual situation but we do know that something about the behavior is rewarding. It may be fun, it may feel good, or it may improve bonding or communication. Regardless, it's unnecessary to know the very cause of humping in order to modify it.

Remedy

While seemingly irresponsible, it's actually perfectly acceptable and healthy for your dog if you allow him to hump a soft inanimate object if he has chosen to do so—as long as the humping is not excessive and accompanied by anxiety or followed by aggression. However, if you choose not to allow it, a simple interruption and redirection will do the trick.

EASY

Interruption and redirection is a very effective, labor-light method for modifying humping.

1. When your dog mounts his target, say a firm but controlled "Ah-ah."

2. Direct him to another activity such as Tug, fetch, or a long-term chew item.

   When he settles into his new activity, praise him.

3. Repeat. As you continue to repeat this exercise, your dog will learn to direct his own urge to a behavior other than humping as being interrupted while humping is a punishment.

INTERMEDIATE

Timeouts are also very effective but are slightly more labor-intensive.

1. When your dog mounts his target, say "That's enough."
   - *If he leaves your furniture alone*, praise him.
   - *If he continues*, tell him "Too bad" and then lead him to a timeout area such as his crate, behind a door, and so on. Wait for ten seconds, then open the door, say "Okay" and allow him to come back in. Repeat.

2. You may also choose to administer a timeout without a warning. This technique is particularly helpful with guests.

   To do this, simply skip the "that's enough" step and deliver a timeout as stated previously. Repeat and extend the timeout period up to but no longer than thirty seconds if needed.

 **Chewing**

Few behavior problems ignite an owner's anger more than an indiscriminate chewer. It only takes the mutilation of one kitchen cabinet, one antique table leg, or one shoe to send an owner into a whirling mess of hollering and gasping as his dog bolts from the room to take cover from whatever punishment is bound to descend upon him.

While most types of chewing are perfectly normal, it can seem that your dog, especially if he is young, has a seemingly insatiable urge to chew anything and everything. Luckily, helping direct your dog to appropriate outlets for his urges is relatively straightforward. A good plan and consistency are all that are needed to keep your home intact and your canine/human family happy.

Chewing on Shoes

Almost every canine has an almost unexplainable appetite for shoes. Whether the shoes are tossed carelessly on the living room floor, aligned neatly by the front door, or tucked safely in the closet, your dog will pass up all approved chew items to settle into a gleeful chewing episode with footwear.

Why

Chewing is a strong drive behavior very similar to one of your favorite rituals: perhaps it's having your morning cup of coffee, doing yoga, or relaxing in the evening with a glass of wine and a good book. Just as you are rewarded by these calming and repetitive activities, your dog is rewarded by the soothing nature of chewing. Shoes are attractive because they contain smells from your whereabouts, provide fabulous chewing surfaces, and are portable.

Because chewing is a drive behavior born into every dog, you cannot stop it without undesirable side effects. But, you can modify it so that you and your pup remain the best of friends and your adorable satin slippers or running shoes remain intact.

Remedy

1. You must first manage his environment to prevent him from exercising his urges on your favorite footwear. To do this, simply be sure to put your shoes where he cannot get them.

2. During this management period, inundate him with items that are even more interesting than your shoes. Populate his environment with an array of legal (acceptable) chew items to satiate every chewing urge: tasty items, chewy items, hard items, squishy items, squeaky items, furry items, and the like. Don't forget to praise him with jolly talk when he settles in with one of these things.

3. If at any time he heads for a shoe that has found its way out of its hiding place, simply interrupt him with an "Ah-ah" and quickly present him with one of his approved chewing items.

Because it is unpleasant for your dog to be interrupted by you in the middle of a chewing episode, with guidance and consistency he will quickly learn to direct himself to his chew items instead of your shoes.

Chewing on Soft Furniture

It is not unusual to find your dog, especially when he's young, chewing on the edge of a couch, stuffed chair, or pillow. He may even find the mattress particularly appealing or choose to sink his teeth into an ottoman. He may prefer fabric over leather, or he may be an equal opportunist choosing anything soft despite its material.

Why

Chewing is a strong drive behavior very similar to one of your favorite rituals: perhaps it's having your morning cup of coffee, doing yoga, or relaxing in the evening with a glass of wine and a good book. Just as you are rewarded by these calming and repetitive activities, your dog is rewarded by the soothing nature of chewing.

Your dog has preferences for what he chews just as you have favorite foods and pastimes. He has chosen to chew on something soft because it's to his liking.

Because chewing is a drive behavior born into every dog, you cannot stop it without causing undesirable side effects. But you can modify it so that you and your pup remain the best of friends and your perfect living room remains intact.

Remedy

1. First, manage his environment to prevent him from exercising his urges on your furniture. To do this, either

temporarily remove the piece of furniture he's chosen to chew, erect a barrier around the particular piece, or limit his exposure to the room in which the furniture is placed.

2. During this management period, inundate him with items that are even more interesting than the furniture. Populate his environment with an array of legal (acceptable) chew items to satiate every chewing urge: tasty items, chewy items, hard items, squishy items, squeaky items, furry items, and the like. Don't forget to praise him with jolly talk when he settles in with one of these things.

Tip: Taking cues from his apparent taste for soft furniture, find chew items similar to the furniture he's previously chewed on such as hard stuffed canvas toys, leather tosses, and stuffed plush toys. Contrary to the belief that this will encourage your dog to head back to the furniture, the truth is that it will instead satiate his need for this particular chewing material and it will actually preserve your things.

3. After a week or two of keeping him away from the furniture and allowing him to chew on his approved items, slowly allow him supervised access to the furniture again. This is your opportunity to give him that essential feedback he needs to learn. If he heads for the furniture again, quickly and calmly interrupt him with an "Ah-ah" and present him with one of his approved chewing items.

Because it is unpleasant for your dog to be interrupted by you in the middle of a chewing episode, with guidance and consistency he will quickly learn to direct himself to his chew items instead of your furniture.

Chewing on Hard Furniture and Fixtures

Despite dollars and effort invested in making available every wonderful chew item known to man, it is not uncommon to find the family dog gnawing on the kitchen molding, counter cabinets, edge of the futon, or dining room table leg.

Why

Chewing is a strong drive behavior very similar to one of your favorite rituals: perhaps it's having your morning cup of coffee, doing yoga, or relaxing in the evening with a glass of wine and a good book. Just as you are rewarded by these calming and repetitive activities, your dog is rewarded by the soothing nature of chewing.

Your dog has preferences for what he chews just as you have favorite foods and pastimes. He has chosen to chew on something hard, such as wood or plastic, because it's to his liking.

Because chewing is a drive behavior born into every dog, you cannot stop it without causing undesirable side effects. But you can modify it so that you and your pup remain the best of friends and your home remains intact.

Remedy

1. First, manage his environment to prevent him from exercising his urges on your hard furniture and fixtures. To do this, either temporarily remove the thing he's chosen to chew, erect a barrier around it, or limit his exposure to the room in which it is placed.

2. During this management period, inundate him with items that are even more interesting than the furniture or fixture. Populate his environment with an array of legal chew items to satiate every chewing urge: tasty items, chewy items, hard items, squishy items, squeaky items, furry items, and the like. Don't forget to praise him with jolly talk when he settles in with one of these things.

Tip: Taking cues from his apparent taste for hard furniture and fixtures, find chew items similar to the items he's previously chewed on such as beef bones, hard Nylabones, and bully sticks. Contrary to the belief that this will only spark your dog's interest in nonapproved hard chew items, it will instead satiate his need for this particular chewing material and actually preserve your things.

3. After a week or two of keeping him away from the hard furniture and fixtures and encouraging him to chew on his approved items, slowly allow him supervised access to the previously chewed items again. This is your opportunity to give him that essential feedback he needs to learn. If he heads for the furniture again, quickly and calmly interrupt him with an "Ah-ah" and present him with one of his approved chewing items.

Because it is unpleasant for your dog to be interrupted by you in the middle of a chewing episode, with guidance and consistency he will quickly learn to direct himself to his chew items instead of your things.

Chewing on Clothes, Blankets, Towels, and Rugs

Although it's not as common as chewing on furniture, fixtures, or shoes, many dogs develop a taste for clothes, blankets, towels, and rugs, especially those with tassels. They may have a favorite thing they like to drag around and chew regularly, or they may be equally impressed by anything that falls into this category.

Why

Chewing is a strong drive behavior very similar to one of your favorite rituals: perhaps it's having your morning cup of coffee, doing yoga, or relaxing in the evening with a glass of wine and a good book. Just as you are rewarded by these calming and repetitive activities, your dog is rewarded by the soothing nature of chewing.

Your dog has preferences for what he chews just as you have favorite foods and pastimes. He has chosen to chew on clothes (socks are very popular), blankets, towels, and rugs because these items are to his liking.

Because chewing is a drive behavior born into every dog, you cannot stop it without undesirable side effects. But, you can modify it so that you and your pup remain the best of friends and your things remain intact.

Remedy

1. First, manage his environment to prevent him from exercising his urges on these unapproved items. To do this, simply be sure to put clothes away or in closed hampers, place blankets up above his reach, and temporarily roll up any rugs he's chosen to chew.

2. During this management period, inundate him with items that are even more interesting than these things. Populate his environment with an array of legal (acceptable) chew items to satiate every chewing urge: tasty items, chewy items, hard items, squishy items, squeaky items, furry items, and the like. Don't forget to praise him with jolly talk when he settles in with one of these things.

Tip: Taking cues from his apparent taste for these fabric items, find chew items similar to the things he's previously chewed on such as a tennis ball tied in an old sock, a plush toy equipped with floppy legs or other cloth appendages, or a second-hand potholder. Contrary to the belief that this will encourage your dog to head back to chewing on your fabric items, the truth is that it will instead satiate his need for this particular chewing material and will actually preserve your things.

3. After a week or two of keeping him away from illegal (unacceptable) chew things while encouraging him to chew on approved items, slowly allow him supervised access to the items he previously chewed again. This is your opportunity to give him that essential feedback he needs to learn. If he heads for your clothing or linens again, quickly and calmly interrupt him with an "Ah-ah" and present him with one of his approved chewing items.

Because it is unpleasant for your dog to be interrupted by you in the middle of a chewing episode, with your guidance and consistency he will quickly learn to direct himself to his chew items instead of your things.

Note: If your dog sucks on blankets and towels and this behavior is accompanied by self-mutilation or destruction, consult a Certificate in Training and Counseling (CTC) professional trainer (www.sfspca.org/academy/referral.shtml) or a Certified Applied Animal Behaviorist (www.animalbehavior.org).

CHAPTER 12

 **Stealing**

specially as puppies and young adults, most every dog will steal something with regularity; laundry, trash, facial tissue, dryer sheets, or any other prohibited item seems fair game.

In many cases, the dog will not only steal the item and abscond with it, but he will actually parade the item past his owner and a game of chase will ensue. While this behavior may be interpreted as devious and naughty, it's actually quite normal and has significant and deep biological roots.

To curb the behavior, it is only necessary to understand the root of the behavior and instate a few simple training techniques. With consistency and a great modification plan, stealing will be a rare occurrence.

Stealing Laundry

Laundry, clean or otherwise, is an irresistible beacon to most dogs. Nothing is more desirable than a sock left on the floor or a pair of skivvies dangling enticingly from the edge of the hamper. Once a dog has discovered the joy of the clothes basket, he can be seen regularly streaking past, stimulating a hot game of chase and keep-away. The stealing dog likes to stockpile his treasures and even just cleaning the thief's bed will uncover a small fortune of lost items.

Why

Scavenging is one of the strongest biological drives born into the domesticated dog. It has tremendous adaptive significance as the better scavengers in the canine ancestral line are the ones who've successfully reproduced to create the domesticated dog. It is a hardwired drive and cannot be turned off without affecting behavioral health or damaging the human/canine relationship.

Laundry, even after it has been laundered, still retains some of its very interesting smell. Your dog can detect smells up to 100,000 times better than the average human.[1] So if clean laundry is enticing, dirty laundry is heaven!

Remedy

If your dog steals laundry, try the following remedies.

EASY

1. You must set him up for success by keeping laundry and other clothing out of his reach. This is considered management, not training.

2. Give him legal outlets for his scavenging drive. Replace his food bowl with work-to-eat tools such as the Tricky Treat Ball, Buster Cube, or Waggle. Instead of filling his bowl and laying it down each meal, fill one of these dispensers and lay it down.

Tip: Your dog can smell the food inside his work-to-eat puzzle. If he's not used to the concept of eating out of anything other than a bowl, be patient. Make the tool especially interesting by smearing a bit of peanut butter or squeeze cheese in the opening to encourage him to move it. Usually after he's moved it enough to spit out a kibble or two, he's hooked.

3. If there is a breakdown in the management system and laundry finds its way into circulation, do not chase him for it. Chase is highly rewarding as his scavenging feat has now turned into a fabulous game. Calmly get up and find favorite items he finds more wonderful than laundry, such as a tennis ball or favorite toy. Quietly walk over to him, interest him in the favorite thing, and toss it a few feet from him. He will drop the item and run over to it. When he does, pick up the laundry and put it away.

DIFFICULT

You may also decide to teach your dog a rock-solid Drop. To do so, please see **DROP ON PAGE 95.**

Note: If your dog has guarded his toys, laundry, bed, or other resources in the past with signs such as a growl, snarl, snap, or bite, do not attempt this lesson. Consult a Certificate in Training and Counseling (CTC) professional trainer (www.sfspca. org/academy/referral.shtml) or a Certified Applied Animal Behaviorist (www.animalbehavior.org).

Stealing and Scavenging Through Garbage

Few things outrank garbage in the eyes of a dog. The nastier or more stinky and rotten it is, the better. The average dog becomes Super Sleuth at the sight of a garbage can left unattended and will turn into a raging, uncivilized ravenous beast if allowed just a few minutes alone with the trash.

Why

Scavenging is one of the strongest biological drives born into the domesticated dog. It has tremendous adaptive significance as the better scavengers in the canine ancestral line are the ones who've successfully reproduced to create the domesticated dog. It is a hardwired drive and cannot be turned off without affecting behavioral health or damaging the human/canine relationship.

Not only is scavenging itself highly rewarding, but also consider the sheer greatness of garbage: all those smells and surprises, food, and neat things a dog would never usually have access to. It's really just irresistible! Because of this, stealing garbage is one of the harder behaviors to curb, so be patient.

Remedy

If your dog steals garbage, try the following remedies.

EASY

1. First set him up for success by keeping garbage out of his reach. This is known as management. Consider keeping wastebaskets up high, using a latching garbage can with a metal lid, or keeping trash behind a childproof kitchen cabinet door.

2. Give him legal outlets for his scavenging drive. Replace his food bowl with work-to-eat tools such as the Tricky Treat Ball, Buster Cube, or Waggle. Instead of filling his bowl and laying it down each meal, you'll fill one of these dispensers and lay it down.

Tip: Your dog can smell the food inside his work-to-eat puzzle. If he's not used to the concept of eating out of anything other than a bowl, be patient. Make the tool especially interesting by smearing a bit of peanut butter or squeeze cheese in the opening to encourage him to move it. Usually after he's moved it enough to spit out a kibble or two, he's hooked.

3. If there is a breakdown in the management system and somehow your dog comes into contact with the garbage, do not chase him unless he has stolen an item that can hurt him. Instead, calmly walk to him and say "Ah-ah," and be ready to hand him a tasty bone or other high-value item as a trade. Contrary to popular belief, this act is not actually rewarding to him, as it is difficult to trump trash rooting and any exchange he makes will be less rewarding than digging in the trash itself.

DIFFICULT

You may also decide to teach your dog a rock-solid Drop. To do so, please see **DROP ON PAGE 95.**

> *Note: If your dog has guarded his toys, laundry, bed, or other resources in the past with signs such as a growl, snarl, snap, or a bite, do not attempt this lesson. Consult a Certificate in Training and Counseling (CTC) professional trainer (www .sfspca.org/academy/referral.shtml) or a Certified Applied Animal Behaviorist (www.animalbehavior.org).*

Stealing Food from Plates and Counters

No matter how many times a dog has been scolded for surfing the counters or swatted for grabbing a tasty morsel off your plate, he cannot seem to resist the call of treasures to be found by sniffing and stealing. Even more shocking is his disregard of the value of the item he is stealing; bread, veggies, meat, and even dishrags seem equally fabulous when he steals them off the counter.

Why

Scavenging is one of the strongest biological drives born into the domesticated dog. It has tremendous adaptive significance as the better scavengers in the canine ancestral line are the ones who've successfully reproduced to create the domesticated dog. It is a hardwired drive and cannot be turned off without affecting behavioral health or damaging the human/canine relationship.

Not only is scavenging itself highly rewarding, but also consider the sheer greatness of things to be found on plates and counters: all those smells and surprises, food, and neat things your dog would never usually have access too. It's really just irresistible! Because of this, stealing from the counter or off plates is one of the harder behaviors to curb, so be patient.

Remedy

If your dog steals food, try the following remedies.

EASY

1. Before you do anything else, set up his environment to succeed: push tempting items to the back of the counter and put food items back in the fridge or cupboard when they're not in use. If you decide to get up from the table while in the middle of a meal, take your plate with you or keep the dog in another area so he's not tempted by the steaming plate in your absence. You may also choose to keep your dog out of the kitchen entirely. The easiest way to accomplish this is to erect a baby gate at the opening of the kitchen.

2. Give your dog legal outlets for his scavenging drive. Replace his food bowl with work-to-eat tools such as the Tricky Treat Ball, Buster Cube, or Waggle. Instead of filling his bowl and laying it down each meal, fill one of these dispensers and lay it down.

Tip: Your dog can smell the food inside his work-to-eat puzzle. If he's not used to the concept of eating out of anything other than a bowl, be patient. Make the tool especially interesting by smearing a bit of peanut butter or squeeze cheese in the opening to encourage him to move it. Usually after he's moved it enough to spit out a kibble or two, he's hooked.

3. If there is a breakdown in the management system and somehow your dog comes into contact with an item from the counter, do not chase your dog unless he has stolen something that can hurt him. Chalk this up as a learning experience and be prepared next time.

DIFFICULT

You may also teach your pup that putting his toes into the kitchen is forbidden unless he is invited:

1. Begin by deciding what is legal and what is illegal. For example, if you have carpet leading up to the kitchen and tile in the kitchen itself, it's legal for toes to stay on the carpet but illegal for them to touch the tile.

2. When your dog approaches the kitchen, say "Too bad" the *moment* his toes touch the tile. Then calmly lead him to a timeout area such as a bathroom or bedroom for no more than ten seconds.

   Repeat this several times until he learns the intended lesson: he can enjoy your company as long as he doesn't cross the threshold to the kitchen. When he crosses the threshold, he earns himself a timeout.

If after working the lesson consistently for several days, your dog seems to disregard the threshold rule, simply increase the timeout period by five-second increments. Timeouts should never be longer than thirty seconds.

Tip: More important than teaching your dog what *not* to do is teaching him *what to do instead*. It's imperative that you periodically reward him for good behavior. When he's sitting calmly at the edge of the kitchen, praise him. If you have a particularly tasty meal on the table and he decides to turn away and snooze elsewhere, give him your praise.

Stealing Paper Products

Paper has an almost unexplainable appeal to most dogs. Whether the payoff promises facial tissues, cotton swabs, or dryer sheets, dogs will gleefully paw through a trash basket for a scrap of tissue, hunt with unmeasured intensity through the laundry for a hidden fabric softener, and proudly drag the end of the toilet paper roll out of the bathroom and down the hall.

Why

Scavenging is one of the strongest biological drives born into the domesticated dog. It has tremendous adaptive significance as the better scavengers in the canine ancestral line are the ones who've successfully reproduced to create the domesticated dog. It is a hardwired drive and cannot be turned off without affecting behavioral health or damaging the human/canine relationship.

Scavenging is highly rewarding in part because of its very strong roots, but also because of the value of the stolen item. Because of this, stealing paper is one of the harder behaviors to curb, so be patient.

Remedy

If your dog steals paper products, try the following remedies.

EASY

1. First you must set him up for success by keeping trash and other paper products out of his reach. Consider keeping wastebaskets up high, putting toilet paper above his stretch, and tidying up other paper refuse as soon as possible.

2. Give him legal outlets for his scavenging drive. Replace his food bowl with a work-to-eat tool such as the Tricky Treat Ball, Buster Cube, or Waggle. Instead of filling his bowl and laying it down each meal, you'll fill one of these dispensers and lay it down for him.

Tip: Your dog can smell the food inside his work-to-eat puzzle. If he's not used to the concept of eating out of anything other than a bowl, be patient. Make the tool especially interesting by smearing a bit of peanut butter or squeeze cheese in the opening to encourage him to move it. Usually after he's moved it enough to spit out a kibble or two, he's hooked.

3. If there is a breakdown in the management system and somehow your dog comes into contact with a paper product, do not chase him unless he has stolen something that can harm him. Instead, calmly walk to him, say "Ah-ah," and be ready to hand him a tasty bone or other high-value item as a trade. Contrary to popular belief, this act is not actually rewarding to him, as it is difficult to trump anything stolen and any exchange he makes will be less rewarding than scavenging for the item in the first place.

DIFFICULT

You may also decide to teach your dog a rock-solid Drop. To do so, please see DROP ON PAGE 95.

Note: *If your dog has guarded his toys, laundry, bed, or other resources in the past with signs such as a growl, snarl, snap, or a bite, do not attempt this lesson. Consult a Certificate in Training and Counseling (CTC) professional trainer (www .sfspca.org/academy/referral.shtml) or a Certified Applied Animal Behaviorist (www.animalbehavior.org).*

1. The Associated Press, "Study Shows Dogs Able to Smell Cancer," (September 24, 2004), http://www.usatoday.com/news/health/2004-09-24-cancer-sniffing_x.htm.

CHAPTER 13

Digging and Burying

While not every dog exhibits digging and burying behaviors, if you have a digger or burrier, they can seem two of the most difficult behaviors to curb.

The opportunistic dog prone to digging and burying will destroy not only the backyard, but also furniture, carpets, pillows, linens, and other soft, dirtlike materials. Many owners deem the digger/burrier defiant, devious, or downright naughty, but the truth is, he is simply exercising two very deeply rooted biological behaviors. By teaching him the appropriate way to exercise his urges, it is possible to achieve a hole-free home while keeping your family and your dog happy and healthy.

Digging in the Garden

There is nothing more aggravating than watching a dog blissfully digging in a freshly planted garden. Even more upsetting is his need

201

to dig multiple holes throughout the yard, leaving it more closely resembling a missile testing site than a well-landscaped oasis.

Why

Digging is a hardwired biological drive and is strong in some dogs and practically nonexistent in others. Early in dog history, those who could dig to hide or find food survived better than those who lacked digging skills. Digging is also a very enjoyable activity. You have only to observe a digging dog once to appreciate his delight and merriment in the act alone.

Remedy

1. If your living situation will allow it, designate a legal digging pit. This should be an area about three feet by three feet by three feet, set apart from the rest of the yard with bricks, stones, or logs. The pit can be filled with loose dirt and/or sand. It should be fortified with something novel and exciting such as toys, kibble, or other treats for your pooch to discover.

2. Until he has leaned to direct himself to the digging pit to release his digging energy, only allow him access to the backyard if he is supervised. If he cannot be supervised, limit his backyard access to areas in which he cannot dig.

3. When he begins to dig in any area other than the digging pit, interrupt him with an "Ah-ah" and lead him to his pit. Encourage him to dig at the pit by digging a bit with your hand and using jolly talk. Don't forget to praise him when he begins to dig.

4. As being interrupted when digging is unpleasant to a dog, with consistency he will begin to direct himself to the pit and avoid other parts of the yard entirely.

If your living situation is not conducive to a legal digging pit, management is essential. If a dog is allowed to dig even once, he will learn the joy of doing so and he will take any opportunity to dig no matter its legality.

- In this case, put all potted plants up where he cannot reach them, and erect barriers, such as chicken wire or fencing, around other plantings to which he has access.

- Because this dog is not allowed to exercise one of his biological drives, he may, as a result, be more susceptible to generalized anxiety and behavioral problems. You can minimize the impact of his pent-up energy by offering him more legal drive outlets in his other drive behaviors, such as scavenging and chewing, or by allowing him more mental and physical exercise.

Digging in Grass

For some dogs, digging in the grass seems more sport than hobby. Rather than opt for a soft dirt bed or gravel drain way, this dog tears grass from its roots and snorts around in the freshly uncovered substrate for smells only he can detect.

Why

Digging is a hardwired biological drive, strong in some dogs and practically nonexistent in others. Early in dog history those who could dig to hide or find food survived better than those who lacked digging skills. Digging is also a very enjoyable activity. You have only to observe a digging dog once to appreciate his delight and merriment in the act alone.

Remedy

1. If your living situation will allow it, designate a legal digging pit. This should be an area about three feet by three feet by three feet, set apart from the rest of the yard with bricks, stones, or logs. The pit can be filled with loose dirt and/or sand. It should be fortified with something novel and exciting

such as toys, kibble, or other treats for your pooch to discover. For the dog who digs in grass, take your cue from him and fortify this pit with a square of sod or patches of grass trimmings from the yard.

2. Until he has learned to direct himself to the digging pit to release his digging energy, only allow him access to the backyard if he is supervised. If he cannot be supervised, limit his backyard access to areas in which he cannot dig.

3. When he begins to dig in any area other than the digging pit, interrupt him with an "Ah-ah" and lead him to his pit. Encourage him to dig at the pit by digging a bit with your hand and using jolly talk. Don't forget to praise him when he begins to dig in the pit.

4. As being interrupted when digging is unpleasant to a dog, with consistency he will begin to direct himself to the pit and avoid other parts of the yard entirely. When this begins to happen, you may slowly and methodically reopen the rest of the yard to him, building on success.

If your living situation is not conducive to a legal digging pit, management is essential. If a dog is allowed to dig even once, he will learn the joy of doing so and will take any opportunity to dig no matter its legality.

- In this case, put all potted plants up where he cannot reach them, and erect barriers, such as chicken wire or fencing, around other plantings to which your dog has access.

- Because this dog is not allowed to exercise one of his biological drives, he may, as a result, be more susceptible to generalized anxiety and behavioral problems. You can minimize the impact of his pent-up energy by offering him more legal drive outlets in his other drive behaviors or by allowing him more mental and physical exercise.

Digging in Furniture

Many dogs choose to dig in couch cushions, beds, and carpets, and on pillows. The furniture-digger usually has his favorites, often directing his efforts to a couch made of soft material or corduroy, or to a set of pillows made of cotton or felt. No matter his preference, one thing's for sure: he digs, and hard, into home furnishings and the furniture shows marks of his destructive talents.

Why

Digging is a hardwired biological drive that is strong in some dogs and practically nonexistent in others. Early in dog history those who could dig to hide or find food survived better than those who lacked digging skills. Digging is also a very enjoyable activity. You have only to observe a digging dog once to appreciate his delight and merriment in the act alone.

Remedy

Begin by setting your dog up to succeed: limit his access to his favorite digging substrates either by erecting barriers around the pieces or by removing the pieces until he has learned the correct way to dig.

1. If your living situation will allow it, designate a legal digging pit outside. This should be an area about three feet by three feet by three feet, set apart from the rest of the yard with bricks, stones, or logs. The pit can be filled with loose dirt and/or sand. It should be fortified with something novel and exciting such as toys, kibble, or other treats for your pooch to discover. For the dog who digs in furniture, take your cue from him and fortify this pit with soft loose dirt.

   If your dog doesn't do much damage when he digs, you may wish to provide him with a digging pillow of his own in place of or in addition to the outdoor digging pit. Place the pillow somewhere indoors, where it can stay, to allow him to exercise his drive when he feels the urge to do so.

   Note: Contrary to popular belief, giving your dog a pillow for a legal outlet does not teach him to dig in other pillows around your home. The opposite is actually true. This lesson will help him satiate a very strong drive while he learns to discriminate legal from illegal items throughout your house.

2. When he begins to dig in your furniture, interrupt him with an "Ah-ah" and lead him to his pit or indoor pillow. Encourage him to dig at the pit or pillow by digging a bit with your hand and using jolly talk. Don't forget to praise him when he begins to dig in the pit.

3. As being interrupted when digging is unpleasant to a dog, with consistency he will begin to direct himself to the pit or legal pillow and avoid other digging substrates entirely. When this begins to happen, you may slowly and systematically reopen the house to him, building on success.

If your living situation is not conducive to a legal digging pit or pillow, management is essential. If a dog is allowed to dig even once, he will learn the joy of doing so and will take any opportunity to dig no matter its legality.

Don't forget that because this dog is not allowed to exercise one of his biological drives, he may, as a result, be more susceptible to generalized anxiety and behavioral problems. You can minimize the impact of his pent-up energy by offering him more legal drive outlets in his other drive behaviors or by allowing him more mental and physical exercise.

Burying in the Yard

Shortly after a dog passes through puppyhood, he may begin to abscond with treasured items from the house, legal or illegal, only to dig a hole in the backyard, place the items in it, and bury them never to be found again. At least, that is, the items are not to be found in the same condition in which they were buried.

Why

Burying has deeply rooted adaptive significance. As with digging, those dogs who can effectively bury and store food and other resources for later consumption have a better chance of survival. Burying is considered a Fixed Action Pattern (FAP), also known as a Modal Pattern. These patterns are defined as those that are so engrained in a dog's brain, they are not taught; instead, it only takes a physical stimulus to trigger a predictable sequence of events. The trigger in the act of burying in the yard is the possession of a high-value item and the presence of a substrate resembling dirt (dirt, gravel, sand, and so on).

The burying sequence in the domesticated dog is something like this:

1. Dog acquires high-value treasure such as a treat, bone, shoe, sock, or other special item. The item may be handed to him or he may have stolen it for extra value.

2. He carries the item around the yard in a seemingly random parade.

3. Once he's found the desired location where he'll bury this item, he will set at digging into the chosen substrate.

4. He will place the item into the hole and will then use his nose as a shovel to shovel dirt into the hole to cover the item.

Remedy

If your dog buries items in the yard, try the following remedies.

EASY (REDIRECTION)

1. Begin by eliminating his access to the area in which he currently buries. You may need to erect a barrier around a flowerbed, gate off an area of the yard, or only allow him access to the yard on leash.

2. Establish a legal substrate in which your dog may bury his things. You may also choose to build a digging pit in the yard. This should be an area about three feet by three feet by three feet identified from the rest of the yard with bricks, stones, or logs. The pit can be filled with loose dirt and/or sand.

3. Set him up. Give him a legal item you know he is likely to bury. Then follow him as he walks around to find a place to put it.

4. Without touching him, urge him to the approved burying area/pit and dig a bit with your hands. This will pique his interest. Then leave him alone to explore the act of burying in your suggested substrate.

5. After several weeks of burying in this new area and several setups, reintroduce his old burying site. Supervise him 100 percent during this reintroduction.

6. Set him up again after the old area is reintroduced. When he heads for it, interrupt him with an "Ah-ah" and redirect him to the approved pit. Being interrupted in the middle of an FAP is a punishment, and with consistency he will learn to direct himself to his approved area to avoid being bothered.

DIFFICULT (CESSATION)

Because burying is a biological drive, terminating the behavior is considered the most difficult and least-desirable remedy.

1. Begin by eliminating his access to the area in which he currently buries. You may need to erect a barrier around a flowerbed, gate off an area of the yard, or only allow him access to the yard on leash.

2. Anxiety and built-up energy are unavoidable results of putting an end to a biological drive. Because of this, you will need to beef up your dog's other drive outlets by making sure he has plenty of novel and interesting items to chew, scavenge, exercise, with, and so on. Refer to **PART III, RECOMMENDED TOYS AND PRODUCTS**, for examples and ideas.

3. When he heads for his favorite burying spot, interrupt him with an "Ah-ah" and redirect him to another drive outlet activity such as chewing or scavenging with a work-to-eat puzzle. Being interrupted in the middle of an FAP is a punishment and with consistency he will learn to avoid the behavior altogether.

Please note that some dogs who bury items will voraciously guard their pile of treasures from both people and other dogs. It is not recommended that these dogs be allowed to bury because of the potential collateral damage when their stash is inadvertently discovered or encroached upon. Cessation is the reasonable remedy. Consult a Certificate in Training and Counseling (CTC) professional trainer (www.sfspca.org/academy/referral.shtml) or a Certified Applied Animal Behaviorist (www.animalbehavior.org) if you wish to modify this behavior.

Burying in Furniture and Linens

Shortly after a dog passes through puppyhood, he may begin to use piled linens, hampers of laundry, and furniture cushions as storage spots for some of his favorite things. The entire burying sequence is very well defined and honed in some dogs while others seem to lack finesse or entire steps of the process altogether.

Why

Burying has deeply rooted adaptive significance. As with digging, those dogs who can effectively bury and store food and other resources for later consumption have a better chance of survival. Burying is considered a Fixed Action Pattern (FAP), also known as a Modal Pattern. These patterns are defined as those that are so engrained in a dog's brain, they are not taught; instead, it only takes a physical stimulus to trigger a predictable sequence of events. The trigger in the act of burying in the home is the possession of a high-value item and the presence of a substrate resembling dirt (cushion, laundry, and so on).

The burying sequence in the domesticated dog is something like this:

1. Dog acquires high-value treasure such as a treat, bone, shoe, sock, or other special item. The item may be handed to him or he may have stolen it for extra value.

2. He carries the item around the house in a seemingly random parade.

3. Once he's found the desired location where he'll bury this item, he will set at digging into the chosen substrate.

4. Several times he will place the item "into the hole," although no hole exists, and will then use his nose as a shovel to shovel invisible "dirt" into the hole to cover the item. Because laundry, linens, and cushions more closely resemble dirt than other household items, they are favorite burying locales.

Remedy

It is perfectly reasonable to allow your dog to bury if he is not doing any harm to your home and you find it intriguing. Because burying is a biological drive, this is the best approach. However, if you prefer to modify the behavior, there are two excellent options for doing so:

EASY (REDIRECTION)

1. Begin by eliminating his access to the area in which he currently buries. You may need to tip a cushion up on end, keep linens in the closet, or remove a piece of furniture altogether.

2. Establish a legal substrate in which your dog may bury his things. This may be a remote furniture cushion indoors, a blanket folded in a discreet area, or anything resembling the area in which he prefers to bury. You may also choose to build a digging pit in the yard. This should be an area about three feet by three feet by three feet identified from the rest of the

yard with bricks, stones, or logs. The pit can be filled with loose dirt and/or sand.

3. Set him up. Give him a legal item you know he is likely to bury. Then follow him as he walks around to find a place to put it.

4. Without touching him, urge him to the approved burying area/pit and dig a bit with your hands. This will pique his interest. Then leave him alone to explore the act of burying in your suggested substrate.

5. After several days of burying in this new area, and several setups, reintroduce his old burying site. Supervise him 100 percent during this reintroduction.

6. Set him up again after the old area is reintroduced. When he heads for it, interrupt him with an "Ah-ah" and redirect him to the approved pit. Being interrupted in the middle of an FAP is a punishment and with consistency he will learn to direct himself to his approved area to avoid being bothered.

DIFFICULT (CESSATION)

Because burying is a biological drive, terminating the behavior is considered the most difficult and least-desirable remedy.

1. Begin by eliminating access to the area in which he currently buries. You may need to tip a cushion up on end, keep linens in the closet, or remove a piece of furniture altogether.

2. Anxiety and built-up energy are unavoidable results of putting an end to a biological drive. Because of this, you will need to beef up your dog's other drive outlets by making sure he has plenty of novel and interesting items to chew, scavenge, exercise with, and so on. Refer to **PART III, RECOMMENDED TOYS AND PRODUCTS**, for examples and ideas.

3. When he heads for his favorite burying spot, interrupt him with an "Ah-ah" and redirect him to another drive outlet activity such as chewing or digging. Being interrupted in the middle of an FAP is a punishment and with consistency he will learn to avoid the behavior altogether.

Please note that some dogs who bury items will voraciously guard their pile of treasures from both people and other dogs. It is not recommended that these dogs be allowed to bury because of the potential collateral damage when their stash is inadvertently discovered. Consult a Certificate in Training and Counseling (CTC) professional trainer (http://www.sfspca.org/academy/referral.shtml) or a Certified Applied Animal Behaviorist (http://www.animalbehavior.org).

 # Leash Problems

eash problems are seen as some of the most urgent behavior problems faced by owners today. Owning a dog with less-than-wonderful leash manners can be frustrating, embarrassing, and absolutely unpleasant. The dog who has been deemed a poor leash walker is sentenced to a lifetime of being yanked around—as is his owner—or worse yet, relegated to his home for eternity.

Luckily, there are some wonderful techniques to tackle the most common on-leash problems. By identifying the particular problem you are facing and then implementing the recommended training plan, walks with your dog can be enjoyable and soothing.

Pulling on Leash

Knowing that perusing the neighborhood is one of a dog's favorite activities, owners readily head out the door to indulge their beloved companion's love of the outdoors. But for some reason, the fresh air turns this animal into a pulling, drooling, heaving beast. All too often, the intended leisurely walk turns into a tug match while the dog drags his chaperone around the neighborhood.

Why

Your dog pulls on his leash for a simple reason: dogs do it because it works. When a dog pulls, he gets to move forward, investigate whatever it is he's interested in, and, as an added bonus, the human on the other end of the leash follows wherever he goes.

Remedy

Begin by becoming a tree. Hold your leash tight against your diaphragm. This is your center of gravity and will make managing your dog's pulling easier. It will also give him clear feedback about what it is you're teaching him.

EASY

From now on, when the leash is tight, plant yourself firmly to the ground. Watch the leash, not your dog. When you see even the slightest bit of slack, move forward. This step teaches him that pulling no longer gets him where he wants to go, and, in fact, it stops him altogether.

All of this starting and stopping can be time-consuming. Give yourself ample time for your walks when training this skill.

For relief between loose-leash walking training sessions, manage your dog's behavior with either a Gentle Leader or Sensation Harness. You may also use these tools during training. Each of these devices will prevent pulling when you don't have time to actively train. When fitted correctly, they work immediately and are an alternative to the usual anti-pull devices.

DIFFICULT

You may also choose to combat your dog's pulling on leash by teaching a casual heel. A casual heel is less formal than an obedience heel as your dog is only required to settle comfortably at one side of your body, not cross in front of you, and walk without pulling. By contrast, an obedience heel is more structured and requires a dog to remain very close to his handler's knee.

1. To begin, ask your dog to sit.

2. While he's in the sitting position, *you* move your body to *his* side. If, at first, he pops out of the Sit, simply get him back into the sitting position, and try again.

3. With the leash in your right hand, dog on your left side, and a tasty treat in your left hand, place the treat directly in front of and touching his nostrils, and say "Let's go."

4. Keep the treat touching his nose and walk five steps, stop, and then move your hand up and back to get him back into his sit position.

Tip: At this point, it's important to move your hand in an upward, backward-arching direction, much like shifting a car into reverse. Keep your hand low to avoid tempting a jump. Remain silent during this move so that your dog learns to sit when you stop without having to be asked.

5. When he sits, praise him and give him the treat.

6. Repeat.

To continue to make casual heel more and more challenging, increase the number of steps you take, and work to get your hand with the treat further and further from his nose. In no time, you'll say "Let's go" and your fuzzy canine will walk politely, automatically sitting at your side each time you stop.

Playful Lunging on Leash at Other Dogs

Very common among young dogs, and somewhat common among older dogs, is the dog who cannot seem to contain his on-leash excitement when faced with the opportunity to meet other dogs. Usually he displays this behavior at the entrance to a dog park, at the house of a dog buddy, when first arriving at daycare, and so on. He will often lunge playfully at the end of the leash while dancing on his toes, barking and vocalizing, and will even throw in normal play behaviors such as play bows, hip checks, bouncy movements, and elbow bends. For more information on puppy play behaviors, SEE PLAY ON PAGE 257.

This dog's behavior is very different than the dog lunging because of on-leash aggression (SEE EXTREME LUNGING ON LEASH AT OTHER DOGS ON PAGE 218). This is usually because he bounces around on leash rather than pinning himself at the end of it, and the sheer presence of play behaviors indicates an intention other than aggression.

Why

Because dogs are so compulsively social, the opportunity to interact with other dogs is a top reward for many, many dogs, especially younger and more energetic pups. The behavior that the on-leash lunger shows in this situation is purely a manifestation of over-the-top excitement, a lack of impulse control, and rude manners. Complicating the behavior is the fact that it's very common for there to be a reinforcement history for this behavior. When a dog behaves like this, he is often let off the leash to play in an effort to end the behavior.

Remedy

If your dog lunges playfully on his leash at other dogs, try the following remedies.

EASY

1. Begin by teaching your dog a strong Sit and/or Lie Down. For instructions on doing so, please see SIT ON PAGE 87 and LIE DOWN ON PAGE 92.

2. Before letting your dog into play, require a Sit. Be persistent and patient at first, making sure that you only issue your verbal cue once, waiting up to ten seconds if your dog doesn't respond at first. Please note that it can be difficult socially for some dogs to lie down around other dogs. If your dog is particularly resistant to this, use a Sit instead.

   The *moment* he sits, even if just for a second, praise him and immediately let him off leash.

   If he doesn't sit, consider moving him further away from the excitement and asking him again. Decreasing proximity to a stimulus can improve the success of this exercise tremendously.

3. After a few practice trials, your dog should sit almost immediately when you issue your "sit" or "down" cue. When this begins, begin building duration one second at a time until he's sitting a pleasant ten to fifteen seconds before being released.

INTERMEDIATE

After your dog is sitting in these situations, begin to ask for other behaviors in addition to Sit, either on their own or as a string, before he's rewarded by being let off leash. Try basic obedience such as sit, stand, lie down as well as fun behaviors such as high-five, kiss, or roll over.

> *Note: Allowing your dog to engage in an activity he loves is considered an "environmental" or "life" reward. While food can be very effective for training many cues, especially in the beginning, these life rewards can also be very effective if they are rewarding enough and consistent.*

Extreme Lunging on Leash at Other Dogs

Many dogs who play very well with dogs off leash turn into a completely different animals when faced with another dog while on leash. The alarmingly common problem of on-leash aggression is characterized by a very strong lunge, persistent loud barking, growling, raised hackles, a stiff tail (wagging or otherwise), and tense posture.

Why

Dogs are highly social and rely on their investigatory senses to quickly assess novel situations and other dogs. Their preferred method of doing so is up close as their eyesight is one of their weaker senses.

If an undersocialized* dog is repeatedly presented with the sight of another dog, but is prevented from approaching him to investigate because of the leash, the dog can quickly learn to associate the sight of another dog while he's on the leash with the anxiety associated with being unable to approach it. This feeling is so strong that it manifests itself not only mentally but also physically. The resulting display of whirling, growling, lunging, and barking is meant to drive away the thing causing the anxiety: the other dog.

The leash complicates this association even further by limiting a dog's usual fight or flight options to just fight. Even if this dog wanted to flee, the leash does not allow it. The leash is literally a catalyst for the undersocialized dog in an on-leash dog-dog sighting.

---

* The term "undersocialization" is a very individualized measure of socialization. Every dog requires a different level of exposure to novel things in order to become comfortable with them. A dog who is considered undersocialized simply hasn't had enough pleasant exposure with something (this can be anything, really) for him to be relaxed and calm in its presence.

Remedy

The most appropriate remedy for treating on-leash aggression involves a comprehensive behavior modification plan comprised of both desensitization and counterconditioning components. The fix for on-leash aggression is very achievable, but because of its emotional nature and the liability and complexity of the remedy, I recommend that you get in touch with a Certificate in Training and Counseling (CTC) professional trainer (www.sfspca.org/academy/referral.shtml) or a Certified Applied Animal Behaviorist (www.animalbehavior.org) rather than attempt modification on your own.

Note: Beware of a behavior modification plan that uses positive punishment methods to fix on-leash aggression. These methods include scare, dominance, or startle techniques such as yelling, scruff grabs, holding a dog in place, snout swats, chain throws, choke/pinch/prong collars, shaker cans, ear pinches, and electric collars. These tools will only make this serious behavior worse, and in many cases, they are considered inhumane.

Lunging on Leash After Squirrels and Other Non-Dogs

While he is out for a leisurely walk, even the best behaved dog will lose his mind if he is presented with a cat, bird, squirrel, or other small animal. Even better than reaching for this little animal while it's standing still, is the chase if it should flee, quickly, in the opposite direction. Many an owner has been left with a bruised wrist or broken finger from desperately holding onto the leash in just such a situation. Scolding, shouting, and even reeling in the leash does little to calm the dog in hot pursuit and forget the chance of getting his attention until the thing is long gone.

Why

The predatory sequence seen in domesticated dogs is made up of eight primary steps: search, stalk, rush, chase, grab, kill, dissect, consume. Every dog is born with some level of predatory drive and many of the most popular breeds are even bred to exaggerate certain steps of the sequence and suppress others. The earliest Labrador Retrievers, for example, were selectively bred to accompany hunters in the field. The ideal companion exhibited strong search, stalk, chase, and grab behaviors. Those with kill (shake), dissect, and consume behaviors were undesirable and were, therefore, culled from the stock.

Today's Labrador Retriever still retains much of the predatory sequence of his ancestors. However, because of great variation in the breeding pool, the range of intensity and presence of these steps is great, and some exhibit more or less of the sequence than the original breeding stock.

Remedy

The predatory sequence in all dogs is a very strong biological drive and, as such, it cannot be eliminated without serious collateral damage. However, it can be controlled and redirected to avoid injury while maintaining your dog's mental and physical health. Following are methods to manage his behavior and to curb his predatory drive to the games of Tug and Leave-it.

MANAGEMENT

Before proceeding with the easy lesson here, try very hard to end the cycle of reinforcement by ceasing all activities that are likely to put your dog in a situation where he may display in this way. While it's impossible to control the wanderings of squirrels, birds, and cats, it is possible to boost your chances keeping your dog from the particular part of the yard housing the birdbath and the edge of the fence used as the squirrel highway.

EASY (TUG)

Contrary to historical and popular belief, teaching a dog to tug does *not* teach him to be aggressive. Quite the opposite is true. If Tug is taught using a set of rules, it can achieve the following:

- **JAW PRUDENCE:** This teaches a dog to be aware of where he puts his teeth.
- **DROP:** This teaches a dog how to release an item from his mouth on cue
- **DRIVE CONTROL:** This is the most valuable of the elements of a well-designed game of Tug. Unless a dog has been taught to get into and settle out of a prey interaction, it is impossible to expect him to do so in a real-life context.

Begin by teaching your dog the correct way to play Tug. For instructions on doing so, please see **TUG ON PAGE 99.**

INTERMEDIATE/DIFFICULT (LEAVE-IT)

At the same time you teach Tug, it is also necessary to teach your dog a very strong Leave-it. The key to teaching this invaluable skill is to increase the difficulty slowly.

Begin by holding a yummy food treat in your hand, with your palm closed, and allow your dog to nudge it just as you say "Leave it."

Do *not* move your hand. Your dog must learn to leave the item on his own without you pulling it away from him.

1. The *moment* he abandons his effort to pry the food out of your hand, open your hand, mark the behavior with a "yes" or "take it" and allow him to take the treat.

    "Yes" or another release cue is necessary to teach a balanced Leave-it.

    Repeat this ten times.

2. Next, hold out your hand again as in step 1 and say "Leave it," but this time open your hand when it's next to your dog's head so that he can see the food. Each time he heads for it, close your fingers over the food and only allow him to see it when he abandons it. When he actively abandons it for a second or two, say your release cue and allow him to take the food.

3. Next, hold your hand cupped over yummy food on the floor and say "Leave it" just as you did in step 1. However, this time, when he abandons it, you'll mark his correct behavior and treat from the *other* hand.

4. Lastly, set yummy food on the floor with your hand next to it, poised and ready to cover it should your dog begin to head for it. Say "Leave it" just as you uncover it, and the *moment* he abandons it, mark his correct behavior and, again, treat from the *other* hand.

To increase the difficulty of Leave-it, begin at home by increasing the value of the item your dog must leave. Then move to easy items outside of your home such as sniffs on the ground. Then move on to stinky things on the ground, and so forth.

Eventually it's reasonable to begin to ask your dog to abandon his urge to chase things, but *only* train at this level when your dog is achieving 100 percent success at all other levels. Depending on your dog, this may take weeks, months, or even longer.

Tip: Getting control over your dog's predatory drive is all about teaching him the skill of getting into and settling out of a drive behavior. Other helpful games to strengthen this skill are:

Fetch: When playing fetch, be sure to get your dog to sit still near you until you give the cue for him to fetch. When he returns with the item he's retrieved, require him to drop it in your hand or at your feet before you bend to pick it up and toss it again.

Hide-and-Seek: This version of hide-and-seek is one in which you hide a favorite toy or puzzle in a room without your dog seeing you hide it. Once you've hidden the toy, invite him back into the room in which it's hidden. Require him to sit before you issue your cue ("find it").

To teach this game, begin with the item in visible range. When your dog learns the cue "find it" means to seize the item, you may hide the item in more and more hidden locations.

If at any time your dog breaks from his Sit and goes after the item before you have given him permission, retrieve him and start over.

At this stage, you may begin to ask him to leave his urges to lunge after small prey. Be prepared to reward him big time when he does. Remember, this is a *very* advanced level of training so be patient.

Lunging on Leash After Bikers, Boarders, Skaters, Strollers, Cars, Trucks, and/or Motorcycles

While it's expected for dogs to chase after prey-like targets such as squirrels, cats, and birds, it can be shocking when a dog suddenly lunges after a bicycle, motorcycle, scooter, truck, skateboarder, skater, or jogger. This aggressive-looking lunge is a full-force effort aimed at the person or thing as it whizzes by and can be accompanied by barking, growling, panting, and behaviors otherwise classified as crazed-animal-looking. Especially interesting is that this dog won't behave the same way towards these things when they're moving as he does when they're standing still.

Why

The predatory sequence seen in domesticated dogs is made up of eight primary steps: search, stalk, rush, chase, grab, kill, dissect, consume. Every dog is born with some level of predatory drive and many of the most popular breeds are even bred to exaggerate certain steps of the sequence and suppress others. The earliest Labrador Retrievers, for example, were selectively bred to accompany hunters in the field. The ideal companion exhibited strong search, stalk, chase, and grab behaviors. Those with kill (shake), dissect, and consume behaviors were undesirable and were, therefore, culled from the stock.

Today's Labrador Retriever still retains much of the predatory sequence of his ancestors. However, because of great variation in the breeding pool, the range of intensity and presence of these steps is great and some exhibit more or less of the sequence than the original breeding stock.

Many dogs direct their predatory urges at inanimate objects such as balls, stuffed toys, and tug tools. However, those who lunge after moving vehicles can put themselves and others in very dangerous circumstances. Their predatory tendencies should be taken seriously.

Remedy

The predatory sequence in all dogs is a very strong biological drive and, as such, it cannot be eliminated without serious collateral damage. However, you can control and redirect it to avoid injury while maintaining your dog's mental and physical health. Following are methods to manage his behavior and to curb his predatory drive with games of Tug and Leave-it.

MANAGEMENT

Before proceeding with these easy lessons, end the cycle of reinforcement by ceasing all activities that are likely to put your dog in a situation where he may display in this way. If you know he lunges at joggers, do not walk him at the track around the lake. If he likes to target large trucks or cars, stick to side streets for walks, for example.

EASY (TUG)

Contrary to historical and popular belief, teaching a dog to tug does *not* teach him to be aggressive. Quite the opposite is true. If Tug is taught using a set of rules, it can achieve the following:

- **JAW PRUDENCE:** This teaches a dog to keep his teeth off humans entirely.

- **DROP:** This teaches a dog how to release an item from his mouth on cue.

- **DRIVE CONTROL:** This is the most valuable of the elements of a well-designed game of Tug. Unless a dog has been taught to get into and settle out of a prey interaction, it is impossible to expect him to do so in a real-life context.

Begin by teaching your dog the correct way to play Tug. For instructions on doing so, please see TUG ON PAGE 99.

INTERMEDIATE/DIFFICULT (LEAVE-IT)

At the same time you teach Tug, it is also necessary to teach your dog a very strong Leave-it. The key to teaching this invaluable skill is to increase the difficulty slowly.

1. Begin by holding a yummy food treat in your hand, with your palm closed, and allow your dog to nudge it just as you say "Leave it."

   Do *not* move your hand. Your dog must learn to leave the item on his own without you pulling it away from him.

2. The *moment* he abandons his effort to pry the food out of your hand, open your hand, mark the behavior with a "yes" or "take it" and allow him to take the treat.

   "Yes" or another release cue is necessary to teach a balanced Leave-it.

   Repeat this ten times.

3. Next, hold out your hand again as in step 1 and say "Leave it," but this time open your hand when it's next to your dog's head so that he can see the food. Each time he heads for it, close your fingers over the food and only allow him to see it when he abandons it. When he actively abandons it for a second or two, say your release cue ("leave it") and allow him to take the food.

4. Next, hold your hand cupped over yummy food on the floor, say "Leave it" just as you did in step 1. However, this time, when he abandons it, you'll mark his correct behavior and treat from the *other* hand.

5. Lastly, set yummy food on the floor with your hand next to it poised and ready to cover it should your dog begin to head for it. Say "Leave it" just as you uncover it, and the *moment* he abandons it, mark his correct behavior and, again, treat from the *other* hand.

To increase the difficulty of Leave-it, begin at home by increasing the value of the item your dog must leave. Then move to easy items outside your home such as sniffs on the ground. Then move on to stinky things on the ground, and so on.

Eventually it's reasonable to begin to ask your dog to abandon his urge to chase things, but *only* train at this level when your dog is achieving 100 percent success at all other levels. Depending on your dog, this may take weeks, months, or even longer.

At this stage, you may begin to ask him to leave his urges to lunge at motorcycles, scooters, cars, and so on. Be prepared to reward him big time when he does. Remember, this is a *very* advanced level of training, so be patient.

Tip: Getting control over you dog's predatory drive is all about teaching him the skill of getting into and settling out of a drive behavior. Other helpful games to strengthen this skill are:

Fetch: When playing fetch, be sure to get your dog to sit still near you until you give the cue for him to fetch. When he returns with the item he's retrieved, require him to drop it in your hand or at your feet before you bend to pick it up and toss it again.

Hide-and-Seek: This version of hide-and-seek is one in which you hide a favorite toy or puzzle in a room without your dog seeing you hide it. Once you've hidden the toy, invite him back into the room in which it's hidden. Require him to sit before you issue your cue ("find it").

To teach this game, begin with the item in visible range. When your dog learns the cue "find it" means to seize the item, you may hide the item in more and more hidden locations.

If at any time your dog breaks from his Sit and goes after the item before you have given him permission, retrieve him, and start over.

Lunging on Leash After Strangers

One of the scariest dog behaviors an owner can face is having his dog lunge after a stranger while on leash. Not only is this behavior frightening, but it can be very dangerous and can cause psychological damage to both the owner and target. When targeting strangers on leash, this dog will show a strong lunge, persistent loud barking, growling, raised hackles, stiff tail (wagging or otherwise), and tense posture. Even more upsetting for all parties involved is when the stranger is a child.

Why

Dogs are highly social and rely on their investigatory senses to quickly assess novel situations and other dogs and people. Their preferred method of doing so is up close as their eyesight is one of their weaker senses.

If an undersocialized* dog is repeatedly presented with a type of person he is unfamiliar with and is regularly denied the opportunity to investigate him up close, it is highly likely he will begin to develop anxiety associated with seeing these types of strangers. With repeated exposure, his reactivity threshold will lower and his anxiety will increase. At this point, the dog will react aggressively to all strangers he is undersocialized to, and allowing him to greet a person to whom he is displaying aggressively is very dangerous.

The leash complicates this association even further by limiting a dog's usual fight or flight options to just fight. Even if this dog wanted to flee, the leash does not allow it. The leash is literally a catalyst for the undersocialized dog in an on-leash dog-stranger sighting.

---

* The term "undersocialization" is a very individualized measure of socialization. Every dog requires a different level of exposure to novel things in order to become comfortable with them. A dog who is considered undersocialized simply hasn't had enough pleasant exposure with something (this can be anything, really) for him to be relaxed and calm in its presence.

Remedy

The most appropriate remedy for treating on-leash aggression involves a comprehensive behavior modification plan comprised of both desensitization and counterconditiong components. The fix for on-leash aggression is very achievable, but because of its emotional nature and the liability and complexity of the remedy, I recommend that you get in touch with a Certificate in Training and Counseling (CTC) professional trainer (www.sfspca.org/academy/referral .shtml) or a Certified Applied Animal Behaviorist (www.animalbehavior.org) rather than attempt modification on your own.

Note: Beware of the behavior modification plan that uses positive punishment methods to fix on-leash aggression. These methods include scare, dominance, or startle techniques such as yelling, scruff grabs, holding a dog in place, snout swats, chain throws, choke/pinch/prong collars, shaker cans, ear pinches, and electric collars. These tools will only make this serious behavior worse, and in many cases, they are considered inhumane.

CHAPTER 15

Aggression

Few phrases incite more reaction in people than "dog aggression." It is common and normal for every dog to exhibit some level of aggression at some time in his life. However, because of its negative connotation and hot-button nature, aggression is greatly misunderstood by most people, and dogs are regularly treated improperly as a result of well-meaning owners attempting to diminish aggressive behaviors.

Buy understanding the root of behaviors identified as aggressive, you and your dog can benefit from the best course of action to diminish aggressive displays.

Aggressive Display During Handling

Some dogs don't mind if they're moved from a comfy couch, pulled from the car by a collar, or if their toenails are trimmed, knots are brushed out, or tails are pulled. However, the vast majority of dogs will protest certain types of body-forcing movement by their owner or other human friends. The range of behaviors they use to express their discomfort with being handled may be as innocuous as freezing up or may be as severe as putting teeth to skin.

The most common situations in which these displays occur are:

- Moving a dog from a family member's bed
- Moving a dog from his own bed
- Moving a dog from his favorite snoozing spot
- Pulling a dog by the collar
- Holding a dog down on the ground
- Brushing or grooming the dog
- Trimming a dog's toenails
- Lifting a dog into or out of a car
- Petting or jostling a dog while he is resting

Why

Dogs learn very early in life that having their body manipulated by a human can lead to discomfort in certain situations. They also learn that their warnings—freeze, growl, hard eye, snarl, snap, and eventually bite—cause the human to go away. This set of behaviors is collectively called a dog's *protracted warning signs*.

Every dog is born with a genetic envelope that is hardwired into his behavioral repertoire. Every single one of these envelopes houses a set of protracted warning signs that are expressed when the dog wishes to drive away a threat in his environment. This threat does not just have to be to his life; it can also be to his things, favorite locations, and his comfort.

Remedy

It's very important to note that these behaviors are very, very normal and they do *not* indicate a dog with abnormal aggression. Even more important, it's absolutely crucial that a dog never be punished for showing a protracted warning sign.

While it's still the most common approach in the United States, punishing a dog for showing a warning sign is considered very dangerous and is strictly discouraged by leaders in the field. The warning signs listed here are symptoms of underlying discomfort. When a dog is punished for any one of his protracted warning signs, he will *not* learn *not* to bite. Instead, the signals warning a bite will be punished away and he will learn to bite without warning. The prevalence of this problem in adult dogs is alarming.

If their behavior in these circumstances becomes a problem, the most appropriate remedy for treating this challenge involves a comprehensive behavior modification plan. Because of its potential liability and the complexity of identifying triggers, I recommend that you get in touch with a Certificate in Training and Counseling (CTC) professional trainer (www.sfspca.org/academy/referral.shtml) or a Certified Applied Animal Behaviorist (www.animalbehavior.org) rather than attempt modification on your own.

__Note:__ Beware of the behavior modification plan that uses positive punishment methods to fix this behavior. These methods include scare, dominance, or startle techniques such as yelling, scruff grabs, holding a dog in place, snout swats, chain throws, choke/pinch/prong collars, shaker cans, ear pinches, and electric collars. These tools will only make this serious behavior worse, and in many cases, they are considered inhumane.

Aggressive Behavior Around Resources

While the very rare canine specimen will unobjectionably accept sharing his resources with humans, most dogs are protective of their things and will show their unwillingness to share in a variety of ways. The dog who guards his things will display any number of aggressive-looking behaviors including a freeze, hard eye, hunker, snarl, snap, muzzle punch, growl, and eventually bite.

Common things a dog may guard are:

- Empty food bowl
- Food bowl containing food
- Any type of food on its own
- Closet, cupboard, or area in which dog food is kept
- Toys
- Stolen items
- Crate
- Bed
- Back of car
- Area in which food or resources are usually delivered

Why

Every dog is born with a genetic envelope that is hardwired into his behavioral repertoire. Every single one of these envelopes houses a set of protracted warning signs that are expressed when the dog wishes to drive away a threat in his environment. This threat does not just have to be to his life; it can also be to his things, favorite locations, and his comfort. Once a dog learns that a human is a threat to his things, he will use these protracted warning signs to drive the human away.

Remedy

It's very important to note that these behaviors are very, very normal and they do *not* indicate a dog with abnormal aggression. Even more important, it's absolutely crucial that a dog never be punished for showing a protracted warning sign.

While it's still the most common approach in the United States, punishing a dog for showing a warning sign is considered very dangerous and is strictly discouraged by leaders in the field. The warning signs listed here are symptoms of underlying discomfort. When a dog is punished for any one of his protracted warning signs, he will *not* learn *not* to bite. Instead, the signals warning a bite will be punished away and he will learn to bite without warning. The prevalence of this problem in adult dogs is alarming.

If their behavior in these circumstances becomes a problem, the most appropriate remedy for treating this challenge involves a comprehensive behavior modification plan. Because of its potential liability and the complexity of identifying triggers, I recommend that you get in touch with a Certificate in Training and Counseling (CTC) professional trainer (www.sfspca.org/academy/referral .shtml) or a Certified Applied Animal Behaviorist (www.animalbehavior.org) rather than attempt modification on your own.

> **Note:** *Beware of the behavior modification plan that uses positive punishment methods to fix this behavior. These methods include scare, dominance, or startle techniques such as yelling, scruff grabs, holding a dog in place, snout swats, chain throws, choke/pinch/prong collars, shaker cans, ear pinches, and electric collars. These tools will only make this serious behavior worse, and in many cases, they are considered inhumane.*

Mouthing and Nipping During Play

One of the greatest joys of dog ownership is play. Wrestling, fetch, chase, and Tug are some of the greatest games a dog and his owner can enjoy together, and engaging in these activities can actually strengthen the relationship between human and canine. However, it only takes one teeth-on-human-skin infraction to cause significant pain and apprehension and to pull the plug on future games of the same nature.

Why

Dogs who put their teeth on people during play simply have never learned not to. Most have been allowed to play-bite, nip, and mouth often during play, and if the lesson was never taught in puppyhood, it persists into adulthood. Unfortunately, the adult dog who uses his teeth during play is a liability, and although the meaning of his behavior is not aggressive, it can inflict serious damage, especially to children.

Remedy

1. Begin by teaching your dog the correct way to play Tug. For instructions on doing so, please see TUG ON PAGE 99. Contrary to historical and popular belief, teaching a dog to tug does *not* teach him to be aggressive. Quite the opposite is true. If Tug is taught using a set of rules, it can achieve the following:

   - JAW PRUDENCE: This teaches a dog be aware of where he puts his teeth.

   - DROP: This teaches a dog how to release an item from his mouth on cue.

   - DRIVE CONTROL: This is the most valuable of the elements of a well-designed game of Tug. Unless a dog has been taught to get into and settle out of a prey interaction, it is impossible to expect him to do so in a real-life context.

2. Instate a "no-teeth-on-humans" rule. From now on, when your dog so much as brushes a tooth against your skin, quickly say a no-reward marker ("Oops" or "Ouch!") and cease play.

   You may end play temporarily for a few minutes or permanently for the day.

3. It is equally important to give extra praise while your dog is playing without using his teeth.

   Important: Make sure your dog is rock solid with his jaw prudence training before ever playing with children.

 # The Puppy

The professional fields of animal behavior and canine development have progressed at an impressive rate over the last decade or so. Because of the knowledge specific to puppy behavioral development that is now available, owners and professionals are better prepared to make significant behavioral progress before a puppy is even six months old.

Puppies are brilliant little sponges, set up to receive and digest a tremendous amount of information in their first few months. The foundation built now is essential to a puppy's well-balanced mental development and will ensure an adult life free from serious behavioral issues. The relatively small amount of time dogs spend in puppyhood is truly the most important time of their lives. Steps to install proper socialization, rock solid housetraining, good bite inhibition, sturdy confidence, basic manners, and so forth must be taken at key critical periods before this golden window of puppyhood closes.

The following lessons address these key components to a well-planned puppy development plan: socialization, bite inhibition, housetraining, chew training, body handling, resource/location guarding prevention, alone training, and play.

Socialization

Puppies pass through a number of critical periods in the first weeks of their lives, one of which is marked at twelve weeks of age: socialization. Keeping in mind the *somewhat* flexible nature of this calendar marker, twelve weeks is considered the end of this critical period. Maximum benefits of socialization occur from birth up to twelve weeks.

Undersocialized dogs with incomplete socialization histories account for those exhibiting the most serious of all behavioral problems. The undersocialized dog may display any of the following undesirable behaviors:

- Aggression to strangers
- Aggression to dogs
- On-leash aggression
- Barrier frustration
- Redirection aggression directed at owner
- Aggression to children and/or elderly
- Severe anxiety and/or fear from exposure to normal and common stimuli

It's important to note that these are not isolated or uncommon behavior problems. To the contrary, the majority of dogs in today's family homes have at least one of these conditions. And all are very serious behavioral problems in adult dogs that likely could have been avoided or significantly diminished if the correct socialization steps had taken place in puppyhood.

This section is not meant to admonish owners of older dogs who may be exhibiting these problems; instead, it is meant to encourage a revolution for future puppy generations.

Background

Up to twelve weeks, puppies are blank canvases with respect to the people, other animals, and novel situations they encounter. Before twelve weeks, they have not yet formed "opinions," if you will, about how scary or how wonderful any one thing is. Because of this, up to twelve weeks old is the perfect time to convince them that all people, other animals, and novel situations are wonderful. In my opinion, this stage is the absolute most important of all of them, as it will ward off the most unpleasant and serious behavioral issues, listed previously, that your pup could potentially face as an adult without socialization during this time.

The Plan

Up until twelve weeks (and thereafter, although the impact will be lesser) puppies should meet as many people and animals as they can, in as many different situations as you can imagine. They may accompany you to the store to greet people and to the coffee shop; they should be riding in the car watching other cars, motorcycles, and strollers; and they should be hearing trucks and road construction. The people they meet should be of all types: tall, short, large, small, with hats, wearing uniforms, bald, in wheelchairs, or on skateboards.

Be sure during this time that your puppy is meeting a generous number of men and children, as they tend to be the most difficult to socialize to. Socialization is not limited to living things; it is equally important to expose your puppy to novel stimuli in his environment.

Remember not to shelter your puppy from these experiences; encourage him to investigate as you add praise and puppy talk with each novel encounter. If you do notice *extreme* discomfort with any situation, contact a qualified a Certificate in Training and Counseling (CTC) professional trainer (www.sfspca.org/academy/referral .shtml) or a Certified Applied Animal Behaviorist (www.animalbehavior.org).

Biting

Every normal puppy is born with a very strong tendency to use his teeth while playing and investigating. Just observing normal dog/dog play emphasizes the central role mouthing takes in social exchanges. Most puppies seem almost obsessed with teething on humans as well, and the experience can be very uncomfortable due to the jaw pressure and their sharp, needlelike puppy teeth.

There are a number of critical periods puppies pass through in the first weeks of their lives, one of which is marked at eighteen weeks of age: acquired bite inhibition. While this marker is somewhat flexible, it is actually signified by the loss of puppy teeth, which usually happens around eighteen weeks.

Background

As adults, all dogs bite with different jaw pressure and patterns from one another. The pressure with which they bite (their "bite inhibition") is obtained before they lose their puppy teeth.

The reasoning for this amazing phenomenon is better understood today than ever before. Where as in the past we considered the purpose of extreme puppy mouthing teething, we now know that this all-important activity teaches dogs the invaluable skill of ritualization.

Dogs are not born with the understanding of how damaging their jaws can be. They do not understand the concept of pain in another animal as a result of simply putting their teeth on them unless they are given feedback. If an adult dog has not learned to ritualize his jaw (use his jaw in a restrained way to avoid injury to other dogs), he is highly likely to deliver very serious damage when attempting to use his jaw in a normal fashion, simply to communicate by using his mouth. On the contrary, if he has learned to ritualize his jaw, he can live a happy life of communicating normally without delivering serious damage to those he wishes to communicate with.

The truth of the matter is that most dogs will bite someone or something at some time during their lives. Because the likelihood of this happening is so great, the value of installing bite inhibition is immeasurable. Saving the victim of a bite serious injury while greatly increasing the likelihood of sparing your dog the fate of euthanasia is not to be underestimated.

After this age, and after a dog's puppy teeth are replaced by adult teeth, bite inhibition *cannot be changed*; a dog with poor bite inhibition will always have poor bite inhibition, and, likewise, a dog with good bite inhibition will always have good bite inhibition.

> **Note:** *The thought of a biting dog usually incites visions of aggressive, "mean," and dangerous dogs, especially of specific lineage and breed. However, even the loveliest dog will bite if pushed when he's in some very common situations; for example, if his foot is stepped on or his tail is accidentally shut in a door, if he is otherwise in pain, and even in normal behavior exchanges such as resource, location, or body guarding. It is naïve and irresponsible for an owner to believe that his dog will not bite. Given the right circumstances, every dog will bite.*

The Plan

While it's still the most common approach in the United States, punishing a puppy for biting is considered very dangerous and is strictly discouraged by leaders in the field. Turning puppy biting off without giving proper feedback ensures unknown bite inhibition and the potential for this dog to develop a very heavy bite is extremely good.

Teaching your puppy how to have a soft mouth should be a required task for all puppy owners. Up to this age, a puppy must count on you and other dogs to give him appropriate feedback about the pressure and whereabouts of his mouth.

The most effective preventative plan consists of two components: dog/dog training and human/dog training.

DOG/DOG TRAINING

Simply allowing your dog to have lots of puppy and dog exposure before eighteen weeks of age will do wonders for installing a soft mouth. Look for off-leash play groups in your area that do not punish for mouthing. Three to four visits a week is usually sufficient, although more exposure is recommended.

HUMAN/DOG TRAINING

Teaching your puppy to use his mouth softly with humans is slightly more involved.

1. Begin by deciding on how hard a bite is acceptable. It is reasonable to allow just a gentle brush against your skin as a measure of this.

2. Encourage your dog to play with you with his mouth. You may involve toys in this play or not.

3. The *moment* your puppy delivers a bite harder than that which you'll allow, say a loud, firm, but controlled "Ouch!" and cease play immediately.

You may remain in the area if you wish or you may get up and leave altogether.

Tips: Leave the bite inhibition training to adults. Children should not endure sharp puppy teeth until this task is complete.

If your puppy is too excited and your feedback does not seem to phase him, consider one of two things:

1. Remove yourself and allow him to calm down. You may also put him in his confinement area while his excitement subsides.

2. Refine your "ouch!" Often, your verbal feedback alone, especially if delivered in a high pitch, can actually incite more biting. Instead, aim for a low, firm, direct, controlled tone.

4. With just a few trials, you should notice your puppy biting softer and with less frequency.

   Don't forget to give jolly praise when he's playing softly.

5. After eighteen weeks, you may *then* begin to teach your puppy not to put his teeth on humans, but not before then.

Note: The pressure with which your dog takes treats from your hand is not an acceptable measure of bite inhibition. Acquired bite inhibition, while very reliable in most situations, is known to fail in a food-acquisition behavior such as chasing prey with the intention of consuming it.

If you notice that your puppy is not biting at all, or if he is still biting hard after working on this skill consistently for a week, contact a qualified a Certificate in Training and Counseling (CTC) professional trainer (www.sfspca.org/academy/referral.shtml) or a Certified Applied Animal Behaviorist (www.animalbehavior.org).

Housetraining

You've just brought your new puppy home and have shown him where to potty outside. However, the *moment* his toes touch your floor, he squats to relieve himself on one of your area rugs. Even after praising him on the rare occasion that he does hit the right spot outside or on his indoor potty substrate, he can't seem to get it right and he has littered your home with pee spots and poop deposits. Even more frustrating with this new family member is his inability to tell you when he has to go.

Why

There is more to potty training than just showing a puppy where to go. He is struggling to learn where, how, when, and why he should go where you've told him to go as opposed to where he feels like going any time he wants. He's also struggling with immature bladder and bowel structures that don't allow him the control to know he has to eliminate let alone the control over how to do it the way you want. Because of this, it's imperative you effectively teach him correct habits while encouraging control.

Remedy

The key for successful housetraining is 100 percent management. With 100 percent management, and the consistency that goes along with it, you'll avoid costly "accidents" that can hinder successful potty training. Jumping into a solid housetraining program from the very first day you have your puppy will increase the chances of good success.

1. Begin by setting up two types of confinement areas in your home:

   • **A SHORT-TERM CONFINEMENT AREA:** His crate, fitted with a snuggly blanket, some chewies, and a favorite toy. The crate may hold your puppy for periods no longer than the amount of time he can physically hold his bladder. It may also be his nighttime sleeping area.

   • **A LONG-TERM CONFINEMENT AREA:** This area should be no bigger than ten by ten square feet and may be set up using an expen or small room. In it, place your puppy's crate, food and water, and, if your puppy will be required to be confined longer than he is capable of holding his bladder, an indoor bathroom substrate.* This confinement area will hold your puppy for times you cannot be watching him 100 percent of the time. It is analogous to a baby playpen.

   Note: If your puppy is not in his confinement area or his crate, he cannot be left alone to wander through the house unsupervised.

---

* If you choose to leave your puppy for periods longer than he can physically hold his bladder and bowels and you wish not to use an indoor substrate, you must make arrangements for someone to allow him access to his potty area at various scheduled times throughout the day. This can be a neighbor, dog walker, or friend.

This is a recipe for disaster and it will, without exception, result in potty accidents and failed potty training. Do not open your house to your puppy upon his arrival. Instead, systematically open your home to him upon potty training success.

2. Next, determine about how long is reasonable for your puppy to hold his bladder and bowels. A good guideline is one hour for every month old he is. Please note that this measurement is only valid during the day. (Puppies can hold their bladders for a very long time overnight because of a hormone called ADH [antidiuretic hormone].)

3. Write that amount of time here: _____ .

   After you've erected these confinement areas and determined his starting point for the amount of time he can hold his potty, proceed to the next two lessons (see **CRATE POTTY TRAINING, BELOW,** and **INDOOR POTTY TRAINING ON PAGE 245**) depending on your preferred method of training.

Crate Potty Training

Please review **HOUSETRAINING ON PAGE 241** before proceeding with this lesson.

Why

Crate training is one of the easiest, most fail-safe methods of potty training available. Contrary to popular and lasting belief that the crate is cruel and robs your puppy of the rights to freedom he so desires, many animal welfare organizations including the Society for the Prevention of Cruelty to Animals (SPCA) consider crate training more humane than any other method as it avoids the training mistakes that can cause the puppy to receive unnecessary punishments. It also helps to diminish the confusion that can accompany housetraining, thus strengthening the puppy/human relationship. Puppies learn quickly to love the crate and it can become a safe place for them to retreat to when they need security and when they sleep, travel, and relax.

Remedy

It's best to start a crate training plan with your puppy first thing in the morning on a weekend. Choose a small area that will be his potty area: a small patch of grass, a gravel potty pit, a dirt bed, and so on. You will need a kitchen timer for this lesson.

1. Begin by letting your pup out of his crate, avoiding any fanfare, and leading him outside *on leash* to a predetermined elimination area. *Bring treats.* Don't say a word or make any acknowledgement of him until he eliminates. Stand completely still for up to five minutes without saying a word or moving. When he pees, throw a huge party and feed treats, shower him with loves, kisses, and so on.

   If he does not eliminate during this five-minute allowance, return him to the crate for ten minutes and then repeat this step. Continue this pattern until he eliminates.

   Note: *It's imperative that you remain still with him on leash so that he learns that his first order of business outside is to go potty. He will get bored with the small area to which he has access, leaving him little choice but to eliminate. Because of this, you will notice the amount of time you will need to wait for him to eliminate will get shorter with each day.*

2. At this point, you may let him off the leash to play or lead him back inside to his long-term or short-term confinement area. Start your timer with the amount of time he can hold his bladder and bowels: _____.

3. Thirty minutes before the timer goes off, return your pup to his crate. When the timer goes off signaling the completion of the time he can reasonably hold his bladder and bowels, repeat step 1.

4. Repeat this sequence for seven days.

5. After seven days without accidents, slowly increase the amount of time you set your timer in fifteen-minute increments every seven days.

With each successful week of training you'll notice the amount of time between eliminations getting longer and longer. Before long, you'll be amazed at the progress you and your puppy have made!

Indoor Potty Training

Please review HOUSETRAINING ON PAGE 241 before proceeding with this lesson.

Why

Many owners choose to have their puppy eliminate on an indoor substrate. There are a number of great new products on the market making this lifestyle much more pleasant than it used to be, including the PETaPOTTY, Potty Park, Wizdog, Pup-Head, and litter systems.

Remedy

Training your puppy to use an indoor substrate is most effective when you're using a crate.

1. First thing in the morning, let your pup out of his crate, avoiding any fanfare, and lead him *on leash* to his indoor potty substrate. You may wish to encircle the substrate with an expen or a gate while your puppy is learning to target it. Don't make any acknowledgement of him until he eliminates. Stand completely still for up to five minutes without saying a word or moving. When he pees, throw a huge party and feed treats, shower him with loves, kisses, and so on.

   If he does not eliminate during this five-minute allowance, return him to the crate for ten minutes and then repeat this step. Continue this pattern until he eliminates.

> ***Note:*** *It's imperative that you remain still with him on leash so that he learns that his first order of business when he leaves his crate is to go potty. He will get bored with the small area to which he has access, leaving him little choice but to eliminate. Because of this, you will notice the amount of time you will need to wait for him to eliminate will get shorter with each day.*

2. At this point, you may let him off the leash to play or lead him back inside to his long-term or short-term confinement area. Start your timer with the amount of time he can hold his bladder and bowels: _____.

3. Thirty minutes before the timer goes off, return your pup to his crate. When the timer goes off, signaling the completion of the time he can reasonably hold his bladder and bowels, repeat step 1.

4. Repeat this sequence for seven days.

5. After seven days without accidents, slowly increase the amount of time you set your timer in fifteen-minute increments every seven days.

With each successful week of training, you'll notice the amount of time between eliminations getting longer and longer. Before long, you'll be amazed at the progress you and your puppy have made!

Puppy Potty Training Tips

Do not punish your puppy for going in the wrong place. That will only teach him not to go in your presence. Instead, you must always give him feedback about where and when to go:

- If he begins to squat and go in an inappropriate place, gently but firmly interrupt him with an "Ah-ah" and then shuttle him off to where he is supposed to go. When he completes the deed, reward him.

- If he goes in the wrong place and you didn't see it, there was a failure in management. Chalk it up as a missed learning opportunity. If you punish a dog for going potty after the fact, he will not learn the intended lesson. Instead, he'll learn to hide his urine and feces where you cannot find them—a *very* difficult lesson to undo.

Once your puppy is going potty on a schedule, you'll begin to notice his pre-elimination behavior. This is usually circling and sniffing just before he squats. Once you can predict his potty behavior with 90 percent reliability, you may say a verbal potty cue such as "go potty," "hurry up," or "go woods." Do not insert a verbal cue before this level of reliability as it will lose meaning and your puppy will not associate it with the act of going potty.

If your puppy continues to have accidents as you are training him, review the previous lessons to get him back on track. It's not unreasonable to back up a few weeks in the program to make sure the plan is solid and to ensure success. The usual suspects in a potty training program that's not progressing as desired are:

- **THE PUPPY HAS TOO MUCH ACCESS TO TOO MUCH SPACE:** Remember, it's unreasonable for a non–potty trained puppy to have access to an area much bigger than ten by ten.

- **MANAGEMENT FAILURE:** If your puppy goes potty somewhere and you didn't catch him, there was a failure in the 100 percent management plan. Really rely on that long-term confinement area, his crate, and your eagle-eye supervision for success.

- **BREED, AGE, AND INDIVIDUAL CONSTRAINTS:** Just like people, some dogs will potty train faster than others and some, slower. One of the biggest errors owners make during potty training is moving along the training plan too quickly for their particular dog. Stick closely to the "build on success" rule and you'll be in great shape.

Chew Training

Even more than adult dogs, puppies seem to have an insatiable appetite for chewing. Their preferred chew substrates range from wood to cloth and run the range of almost every material in between. Attempts to deter the chewing puppy usually result in redirection to yet another illegal chew item or a lack of response altogether.

Why

Chewing is a strong drive behavior very similar to one of your favorite rituals: perhaps it's having your morning cup of coffee, doing yoga, or relaxing in the evening with a glass of wine and a good book. Just as you are rewarded by these calming and repetitive activities, your dog is rewarded by the soothing nature of chewing. Shoes are attractive because they contain smells from your whereabouts, provide fabulous chewing surfaces, and are portable.

Because chewing is a drive behavior born into every dog, you cannot stop it without undesirable side effects. But you can modify it so that you and your puppy remain the best of friends while he exercises his all-important chompers.

Remedy

1. You must first manage his environment to prevent him from exercising his urges on your favorite pair of running shoes. To do this, limit his exposure to things he's not allowed to chew on. You may choose to erect an expen, baby gates, or other temporary structures to help with this.

   Be sure you *never* leave your puppy unsupervised in an area in which he may chew on something he's not supposed to. Not only is it a sure recipe for disaster, but also it is actually considered unkind to then punish this puppy for breaking a rule he never knew existed.

2. During this management period, inundate him with items that are even more interesting than your shoes. Populate his environment with an array of legal chew items to satiate every chewing urge: tasty items, chewy items, hard items, squishy items, squeaky items, furry items, and the like. Don't forget to praise him with jolly talk when he settles in with one of these things.

3. As your puppy matures, you may begin to allow him more and more access to your home, making sure to open these areas slowly and on his success exercising chewing restraint.

   When you begin to open your home, supervise, supervise, and supervise. This is the all-important teaching portion of this lesson.

   When you open your home to your puppy, he will be presented with dozens of new chew items such as furniture, clothing, and fixtures. It is very normal for him to attempt to chew on one or more of these illegal items. But now that he has a history of chewing on appropriate things and you've worked with him to interrupt and redirect him, you can apply these great lessons in their new context. Keep an ample number of chew items on hand and use the "ah-ah" interruption and redirection to continue to teach him until your entire home is open to him and he is coexisting with all your things without destroying them.

   Note: Dogs discriminate your presence from absence when learning what to chew and what not to chew. To make sure your puppy doesn't chew illegally in your absence, make sure he's confined in your absence until he's older.

4. Only when your puppy is 100 percent trustworthy in your presence may you grant him limited exposure to larger areas in your absence. If he makes any mistakes during this time, it's an indication he needs to be confined in your absence.

   This is a very personalized measure; every dog is different. Do not measure your dog's success by other dogs' successes. Instead, focus and build on the success your own dog achieves.

   Because it is unpleasant to your puppy to be interrupted by you in the middle of a chewing episode, with your guidance and consistency he will learn to direct himself to legal chew items instead of illegal ones.

Body Handling

While being touched and handled is readily accepted by some puppies, most puppies show at least a little resistance to it. This protest may be as subtle as pulling a paw away when it's held to putting teeth on you. Attempts to overpower the puppy showing these symptoms most often result in an escalated interaction of pulling and pushing and in a starling number of cases can actually push a puppy to bite.

Why

Though it's hard to believe, puppies are not born being comfortable with the human touch. However, they will face a lifetime of people handling them in all kinds of situations, from loves at home to vet procedures to grooming, and so on. It is essential that they be taught to accept and enjoy these handlings so that as adults they won't fear being handled or have the potential of causing harm to someone attempting to touch and/or restrain them. It's easiest to teach puppies to be comfortable when they're handled when they're very young.

The behaviors a puppy shows to indicate his discomfort with being handled are collectively called *protracted warning signs*. They include but are not limited to, tensing, pulling away, struggling, raising hackles, growling, whining or grumbling, vocalizing, snarling, snapping, and biting.

Remedy

While it's still the most common approach in the United States, punishing a puppy for showing a warning sign is considered very dangerous and is strictly discouraged by leaders in the field. Biting is a symptom of discomfort with being handled, as are the escalating signals and warnings listed earlier. When a puppy is punished for any one of his protracted warning signs, he will *not* learn *not* to bite. Instead, the signals warning a bite will be eliminated, resulting in an adult dog who bites without warning. The number of adult dogs who bite without warning because their protracted warning signs were punished out of their behavioral repertoire is alarming.

The more appropriate, effective, and kind approach is to change the association with being touched from being a bad experience to being a good one, instead of punishing the puppy for expressing his discomfort.

It's best to start the following exercises with your puppy when he's very young.

1. Begin by taking every reasonable opportunity to snuggle with your puppy. Rather than attempting to grab him when he's in the throes of play or another exciting activity, capitalize on his quiet times such as when he's snoozing on your lap, with you during a movie, or settled in a quiet chewing episode.

   Be sure to pay attention to these areas: head, jaw, mouth and muzzle, collar, scruff, ears, feet, toes, excess skin, hindquarters, and tail. These are the areas most likely to cause an uncomfortable reaction in your puppy.

   Consider an escalating level of touch: reach towards, touch, cover, gently hold, squeeze, manipulate, restrain, and so on.

   Only move forward to more and more intense handling activities when your puppy shows no discomfort with the current level.

2. If your puppy shows a high-tented level of discomfort with an area of his body being handled, consider one or both of the following:

   • Lessen the intensity of the touch.

   • Pair the touch with a yummy treat.

   The order in which you execute this is very important. The correct sequence is: *touch, present treat, stop touching, stop treating*.

If you notice that your puppy is not responding to your attempts to get him used to handling, immediately contact a qualified Certificate in Training and Counseling (CTC) professional trainer (www

.sfspca.org/academy/referral.shtml) or a Certified Applied Animal Behaviorist (www.animalbehavior.org). Young dogs in puppyhood may greatly benefit from professional intervention, whereas the older a dog is, the more difficult a behavior can be to fix. Time is on your side if you have a puppy with a behavior problem.

Resource Guarding

Few things are more shocking to owners than to be on the receiving end of a growl, snarl, snap, or even a bite when trying to take a favorite item or piece of food from their puppy. This protest may be as subtle as picking up the item and walking away with it or it may be as obvious as snapping. The things a dog chooses to guard need not be of extreme value; they need only be of value to your dog. While pigs ears and bones are likely treasures, your puppy may also guard facial tissues, socks, and toilet paper tubes. Attempts to overpower the puppy showing this behavior most often results in an escalated power struggle, and a startling number of cases actually push a puppy to bite.

Why

Every single dog is born with a tendency to guard his things and/or his favorite locations. The adaptive significance is great. The dog who can protect his resources has a much better chance of having his genes continue on to the next generation and as such, the behaviors associated with protecting these valuables are deeply ingrained.

Just as it would be rude to walk up to another person and pull food from his or her mouth, it is also considered inappropriate for you to remove a piece of food from your puppy's mouth without first teaching him to tolerate it. Aside from being rude, it can be very dangerous.

Guarding tendencies naturally increase with maturation, and the adult dog who guards his things is a serious liability. Unless a puppy is taught to accept sharing, resource guarding marches progressively on into adulthood.

The behaviors a puppy shows when guarding resources and locations are collectively called *protracted warning signs*. The very first indicator that a dog is guarding is a change in behavior. The rest of the indicators include but are not limited to, a freeze, hunker, hard eye, snarl, snap, growl, muzzle punch, and bite.

Remember, this is very normal behavior and should not be considered anything but.

Remedy

While it's still the most common approach in the United States, punishing a puppy for showing a warning sign is considered very dangerous and is strictly discouraged by leaders in the field. The warning signs listed previously are symptoms of underlying discomfort. When a puppy is punished for any one of his protracted warning signs, he will *not* learn *not* to bite. Instead, the signals warning a bite will be eliminated and he will learn to bite without warning. The number of adult dogs who bite without warning because their protracted warning signs were punished out of their behavioral repertoire is alarming.

The most appropriate, effective, and kind approach is to change the association your puppy has with you (or another person) being present while he has a resource. It's best to start these exercises with your puppy when he's very young.

A comprehensive preventative plan consists of two parts: chew toy and bone exchanges, and food bowl additions. These exercises teach your puppy that it's good when you approach him while he is eating or engaged in a high-value activity, and he does not have reason to guard his things from your reach.

CHEW TOY AND BONE EXCHANGES

At various random times, when you see your puppy chewing on his food items and other toys, approach him and pick up the his highly valued treasure with one hand while laying down a small pile of high-value food treats. Once he's consumed the food, immediately return his chew toy/bone. Repeat this randomly several times a day.

FOOD BOWL ADDITIONS

While your puppy is actively eating, approach him and alternate between these activities, without giving him any verbal cue or warning:

- Dump tasty treats near his food bowl while it is on the floor, making sure your addition is something of higher value than his food.
- Pick up his bowl, add a higher-value food to it, and then replace it on the floor. Do these additions and exchanges during every meal.

Tips: Go slowly. Progress through increasingly valuable items only after several days have passed. If your puppy shows any guarding tendencies at any time during these exercises, go back a step or two.

Children should not be involved in these exercises. Not only are children more prone to injury, but their relative incoordination can actually increase the likelihood of guarding. Only after adults in the household have worked through all levels of guarding may children participate in low-level exchanges and additions.

Note: If your puppy is already aggressively lunging or biting, do not attempt these exercises on your own. Contact a qualified Certificate in Training and Counseling (CTC) professional trainer (www.sfspca.org/academy/referral.shtml) or a Certified Applied Animal Behaviorist (www.animalbehavior.org).

Alone Training

The heart-wrenching whines and cries from a puppy who's just been left alone can make even the most hard-hearted of humans melt into a puddle of goo. The puppy may simply just cry or also paw at the crate, chew at exit doors, or even thrash. This protest to being left alone is very normal in puppies, and it's not cause for alarm. However, alone anxiety that goes untreated in puppies leads to very serious separation anxiety in the adult dog. The adult dog with separation anxiety exhibits extreme vocalizing, destruction at exit points, vomiting, self-mutilation, and anorexia. For more on separation anxiety, **SEE SEPARATION ANXIETY: BARKING INCESSANTLY IN OWNER ABSENCE ON PAGE 147.**

Why

Puppies are babies, and just like human babies, they can go through anxiety when they're separated from the humans they live with. Often, the contrast between times with the family and times away from the family is just too great. In other words, puppies learn quickly that being out with the gang is fun, exciting, playful, interesting, and, overall, super-rewarding. In contrast, alone times are void of almost all stimulation and the anxiety associated with being alone can escalate fast.

Remedy

A comprehensive program of simultaneous efforts is most effective.

1. First, make sure your puppy's confinement areas, both short-term and long-term, are filled with great things: bones, toys, a Comfort Pup, a warming disk, and the like, to make his time in the crate enjoyable. For product suggestions, **SEE PART III, RECOMMENDED TOYS AND PRODUCTS, ON PAGE 265.**

   Make things available to your puppy during alone times that he doesn't get any other time. Try as you may, you will never be able to trump time with you as a reward, but you can make it easier on him.

Turn on a radio or TV to a soothing channel in your puppy's alone area.

2. Next, avoid any fuss upon your departure and arrival. This is hard because your puppy is so cute and irresistible, but making an extreme fuss during these times actually increases the contrast between times when your puppy is with you and times when he's alone.

When you return home to your pup, nonchalantly head to his crate or confinement area and let him out. After a few minutes he will calm down; then you can shower him with all kinds of loves.

When you leave, don't trick him into his crate but do remain calm and make the experience as uneventful as possible. Toss a yummy Kong into the crate before him, or require him to step in before presenting him with his prize. With consistency, your pup will learn to take alone times as a relaxing time to enjoy some of his favorite activities.

Tips: Your puppy may whine during the first few days of this training. Consider bringing the crate into a room in which you spend a lot of time such as the TV room or your office. Systematically move the crate into another room until he settles quietly away from you.

At first, feel free to verbally soothe your pup with a few words here and there. However, as training goes on, do this less and less.

Make sure you train for absences both when you leave the premises entirely and for when you simply leave the room in which your dog is.

Do not allow your puppy to shadow you excessively. An interested and attentive puppy is good, but when he cannot lose site of you without getting upset, you need to address this behavior.

Play

Today's new puppy is lucky to have been born into a world offering more options for dog activity than ever before. The dog park, dog daycare, walkers, breed parties, play groups, and other social gatherings provide even the most finicky of dogs with a place to enjoy time with his friends. These dog-heaven-on-earth places are also breeding grounds for hysterical owners, poor social manners, bullies, and even fights. The dog park itself can cause owners such a raise in blood pressure that it can become a "members-only" clique that admonishes and drives away owners of dogs exhibiting perfectly normal but misunderstood behavior.

Why

Normal puppy play involves any number of these things:

* Bouncy inefficient movements
* Play face
* Role reversals
* Extreme mouthing
* Barking
* Vocalizing
* Hip checks
* Elbow bends
* Tug
* Chase
* Humping
* Wrestling

Undersocialization is at the root of many of the most serious adult behavior problems. Thus, play between puppies is essential for normal social development. It is not unusual for normal play to escalate to a point that causes alarm for observers. Play is meant to ritualize and practice behavior; therefore, it features a range of expressions. The truth is, humans are uncomfortable with much of the play behavior they see, no matter how normal is it; this can lead to dogs developing poor skills, being punished for perfectly courteous decorum, and angry run-ins at the dog park.

Remedy

1. Before anything, commit the preceding list of normal behaviors to memory. Be prepared to see these things and advocate for your dog when he's playing nicely.

2. Find a park, daycare, playgroup, or other social setting that will allow your puppy to exhibit a full range of normal behaviors.

    If your puppy attends daycare, sees a dog walker, or will be attending playgroups, interview the owners and staff of the facility where your little one will be playing. If the facility doesn't recognize the behavior listed previously as normal, move on and find a place that does.

    Never push a shy puppy to play. He will join in the fun when he's ready, but forcing him will push him over his threshold and result in fear and potential dog aggression.

3. Help your puppy learn the difference between polite and impolite play.

    The most common impolite behavior seen in puppies is a lack of role reversals. Puppy interactions should look like "I chase you, now you chase me," "I wrestle on top, then let you up so you can," and the like. If any interaction goes on for more than a couple of seconds, it's appropriate to gently interrupt your puppy and head him in another direction.

    Praise your puppy for good play. This is key to making sure he not only learns the behaviors to avoid but also learns the ones that are good.

If your puppy's impolite play or shy demeanor continues, after he's been given many chances to change his behavior, consult a qualified Certificate in Training and Counseling (CTC) professional trainer (www.sfspca.org/academy/referral.shtml) or a Certified Applied Animal Behaviorist (www.animalbehavior.org) for help modifying it.

Puppies Mouthing People

After bringing home a puppy, it may only be a matter of time before an owner wonders if he brought home a snapping turtle or alligator instead of a baby dog. Although a puppy is wrapped in the most adorable package of fur and doe eyes, even the tiniest ones can deliver an astonishingly strong bite made ever-so-much worse by needle-like teeth.

Why

Puppy mouthing is very, very normal and can occur for a number of different reasons. Please refer to the following sections, found previously in this chapter, for specific information and lessons:

- BITING ON PAGE 238
- BODY HANDLING ON PAGE 250
- RESOURCE GUARDING ON PAGE 252

 The Geriatric Dog

J ust as puppies have special behavioral needs and challenges, the geriatric dog has his own set of behavioral issues. Because of ongoing progress being made in the field of companion animal research and behavioral modification, professionals are better prepared to make older dogs more comfortable and healthier, and the aging process easier to manage.

This special section addresses common situations unique to the older dog.

Physical and Mental Changes

Similar to humans, dogs face several progressive conditions associated with aging, such as arthritis, joint pain, decreased stamina and muscle density, increased frailty, hearing and vision impairment, dementia, confusion, and anxiety. While these changes went greatly unnoticed for decades, today we know that keeping a dog comfortable as he grows older and facing advanced-age-onset behavioral issues with special consideration for the older dog can ensure a relaxed and comfortable aging experience for both a dog and his family.

General Environment

It's key to keep a warm, safe, and comfortable environment for your dog as he lives out his twilight years. Take a critical look at your dog's environment to make sure he can get around easily.

- Make sure your dog has a place that's out of the way when he's resting so he won't be inadvertently stepped on or roused by other dogs in the house. Move his bed or other comfy area if needed to accomplish this.

- Consider the route he must take to go to his potty area. If stairs or long distances are part of the current terrain, try to find an easier, flatter path.

- For those dogs with back-end weakness, think about a telescoping ramp for the car and a hip ComfortLift Carrier for help moving about.

- Dropping temperatures and damp drafts should be avoided. Keep his living and resting quarters free of both.

- As he may begin to lose his eyesight, try to avoid moving furniture or cluttering his environment with obstacles over which he may trip.

- Take your cues from him about how much exercise he can tolerate. If your walk-happy pup begins to lose his enthusiasm for a walk or he's in bed for a day after an outing, take it down a notch.

- Bending or stretching his neck to eat may be uncomfortable for the older dog. Replace short or tall bowls or eating trays with an adjustable double diner.

Alone and Resting Times

One of the most common times an aging dog will begin to exhibit behavioral problems is when he's alone. His discomfort during alone times may be expressed by whining, howling, barking, pacing, frequent waking, and/or general unrest.

To keep alone times free of anxiety, focus on comfort:

- Cushion your dog's bones and joints with an orthopedic bed. Models are available with and without heat options.
- Consider placing a Comfort Pup, Snuggle Pup, or warming disk in his bed with him to keep him warm and relaxed.

Hearing and Sight Impairment

As a dog's hearing and sight begin to fail, you will likely notice that he may fail to respond to cues, take longer to respond to cues, seem to lose his way in familiar territory, or be less likely to venture beyond his home or even a specific room. He may also develop skittish or fearful behavior in odd situations in which he was very comfortable in the past. This is all very normal but you should consider it when adjusting your behavioral expectations.

Potty Accidents

It's very normal for the older dog to begin to lose some control of his bladder and bowels.

- When this first happens, consult your veterinarian. Tremendous progress has been made in the area of incontinence and your vet may be able to prescribe a medication to greatly decrease or completely alleviate incontinence altogether.
- Do *not* punish the older dog who suddenly begins having accidents in the house. In most cases, he is not able to control his urges and punishing him is considered unkind.

- Allow your dog more frequent potty breaks. Incontinence is usually a progressive condition that worsens with time. Your dog may not be able to hold his need to go to the bathroom as long as he used to be able to, but he still may retain some control.

- If medication and management don't cover all accidents, consider a diaperlike product to keep his bedding and your home dry.

Tips: Geriatric dogs are especially sensitive to losing a family member to divorce, a move, or death, or the loss of another dog or other animal companion in the home. Consider these things when determining the best way to tackle anxiety.

Dogs are biologically designed not to show symptoms of distress until the level of discomfort is great. Keep up with your dog's regular vet visits and be sensitive to subtle changes in appetite, sleeping patterns, weight, and behavior.

Note: *The sudden onset of any behavioral change warrants a trip to the veterinarian. While many symptoms of aging are very normal, a significant number have a physiological cause. It is necessary to rule out any physical explanation for a behavioral change before it is reasonable to instate a behavior modification plan.*

PART III

Recommended

Toys and

Products

The dog supply market today is filled with thousands of toys and tools for your dog. While many are wonderful, this list of products stands out from the others. These tools are beneficial because of their usefulness, ingenuity, practicality, and brilliance. They are meant to enrich the life of the companion dog and owner, helping to relieve anxiety, stress, boredom, discomfort, and ultimately, improve behavior problems. My very favorite products are marked with a star. For convenience, an assortment of these products can be found at drugstore.com.

Work-to-Eat Puzzles

AMAZE-A-BALL TREAT BALL: The Amaze-a-Ball offers a soft-sided alternative to the Talk to Me Treatball and a simpler alternative to the Tricky Treat Ball in this list. Large enough to hold lots of kibble, this puzzle comes in three convenient sizes.

★ BUSTER CUBE: One of the original dispenser toys, the Buster Cube comes in two sizes: small and large. Its hard-sided construction makes it almost indestructible, while its clever internal maze delivers kibble as your dog plays.

BUSY BUDDY GROOVE THING: The Groove Thing can be smeared with peanut butter or cream cheese to deliver a high-value, immediate gratification work-to-eat experience. Also is great for teeth and is dishwasher safe.

BUSY BUDDY SQUIRREL DUDE: Very similar to the Kong, this puzzle is more difficult as it features small, soft, inward-facing tabs near the opening to make getting food out especially challenging.

BUSY BUDDY TWIST 'N TREAT: This clever tool screws apart to load the disc with yummy treasures. It is dishwasher safe and can be an excellent choice for those who are not aggressive chewers.

★ BUSY BUDDY WAGGLE: Another favorite product I like to recommend, the Busy Buddy Waggle, is made of soft rubber and has the added benefit of small inward-facing tabs on its openings to hold kibble and increase the challenge of the game.

CANINE GENIUS LEO: This truly revolutionary puzzle system is unlike any other on the market. Leo's soft plastic pins can be filled with kibble and joined together in challenging arrangements with tons of brain-teasing possibilities.

HAVABALL: This hard rubber contraption is a close relative of the Kong. It's an excellent puzzle for a small handful of kibble or a few hard cookies. Stuffing a bully stick through its center can make it especially enticing.

HOLEE ROLLER: Long, hard cookies inserted into the Holee Roller create a challenging work-to-eat puzzle for dogs who like to see what they're after. Not suitable for the aggressive chewer.

KONG: Considered the original work-to-eat puzzle, the Kong can be stuffed with soft or hard food; can be frozen, creating a long-lasting "Kongsicle"; and is dishwasher safe.

KONGTIME: Created by Sandi Thompson and Dave Rucker, this ingenious tool delivers tasty Kongs to your dog in your absence to keep him busy and his drives satiated.

MOLECUBALL: The Molecuball is perfect for dogs just learning to work to eat. Its simple design, hard plastic exterior, and large opening allow food to spill out readily with little effort.

PAW-ZZLE BALL: With an outer "teaser" ball constructed of hard plastic and the inner kibble-dispenser ball made of soft plastic, its multiple features pair together for an irresistible brain bender.

PETSTAGES ORKA JACK: Although the food compartments on the Orka Jack are somewhat small for accommodating a full meal, this soft plastic puzzle is great for keeping dogs busy as it bounces and rolls around.

TALK TO ME TREATBALL: This hard-sided plastic ball can be filled with kibble that pours out as your dog rolls the ball around. As an added benefit, owners can record a short verbal saying into a small microphone that's played back when the ball is moved.

TREAT STICK: This unusually shaped stick is constructed of heavy-duty plastic meant to challenge even the most skilled work-to-eat master. Kibble is loaded through the twist top and then secured for a multidimensional puzzle.

★ **TRICKY TREAT BALL:** A personal favorite, the Omega Paw Tricky Treat Ball is made of soft plastic and features a compartment to accommodate a good amount of kibble. As an added benefit, this tool is designed to pay off fast when it is full and less frequently the closer to empty it becomes. Very addicting!

ZANIES PEEK-A-TREAT: The Peek-a-Treat features a see-through window between two large, soft plastic hollow ends. Its unique dial lid allows for a variable reward size and delivery rate.

Activity Toys

BABBLE BALL: These hysterical plastic balls each come with a pre-recorded series of sayings and sounds—like "Rock 'n Roll, Big Doggy" and "Sweet Puppy"—to keep dogs interested as they chew, roll, and scoot them along.

★ **CHUCKIT! BALL LAUNCHER:** A classic, the Chuckit! Ball Launcher is a must-have for anyone with a retriever or other fetch-aholic. The long arm design will spare your shoulder muscles while launching the ball dozens of yards further than you could with plain throwing alone. It even allows you to pick up the ball without bending over!

CHUCKIT! FLYING SQUIRREL: An alternative to the tennis ball, this far-flying, easy-to-launch canvas squirrel is great for hours of fetch and retrieve.

KONG TUG TOY: Essential for a good game of Tug is a toy that is rugged and fun enough to entice even the most finicky of dogs. While sticking to this particular model is not necessary, every dog should have a tug toy that is long in design, features something for you and your dog to hold onto, and will stand up to abuse.

★ **SQUIRREL TENNIS TAIL:** These adorable toys are especially attractive to dogs because of their sailing tail. Excellent for improving drive control and ball manners, they're a must-have for a well-behaved dog.

WIGGLY GIGGLY BALL: Inside this clever ball is an unusual sound maker that sighs and giggles as your dog rolls it around. The sound and movement alone are enough to keep dogs busy without ever involving food.

Puzzle Toys and Brain Teasers (Non-Food)

ALLIGATOR EGG BABY BY PLUSH PUPPIES: A variation on the IQube featuring a mama alligator and two plush eggs.

HIDE-A-BEE BY PLUSH PUPPIES: A variation on the IQube featuring a beehive stuffed with plush bees.

HIDE-A-BIRD BY PLUSH PUPPIES: A variation on the IQube featuring a birdhouse and colorful birds.

HIDE-A-SQUIRREL BY PLUSH PUPPIES: A variation on the IQube featuring a hollow plush stump and adorable little squirrels.

IQUBE BY PLUSH PUPPIES: This soft-sided box contains several small plush balls. Great for small breeds and those entertained by a moderately easy tool. Not recommended for aggressive chewers.

POOCH BALL: Maddeningly addictive to any tennis-ball fanatic, this brilliant puzzle features a traditional tennis ball fitted into a hard plastic pipe.

PULL-A-PARTS BY PLUSH PUPPIES: These novel toys are designed to pull apart without being destroyed. Once your dog separates these figures from their arms and clothes, owners can reconstitute them for more play.

PUZZLE PUP: A variation on the IQube, soft rings are stacked around a plush dachshund. Dogs have a great time pulling the rings off one by one and owners can easily place them back on for continued play. Not recommended for aggressive chewers.

Long-Term Chew Items

BULLY STICK: Made from bull unmentionables, these incredible long-lasting consumables are an all-time dog favorite. Super tasty and 100 percent protein.

NATURAL BONES: Sectioned bones from various livestock, these bones are a necessity for any chewer. Stuffed or empty, dogs love 'em.

NYLABONE BIG CHEWS FOR BIG DOGS: Especially great for large dogs, these classic Nylabones come in various scents to keep your dog interested for hours.

NYLABONE DENTAL DINOSAUR: Good for teeth and your dog's chewing drive, the dental dinosaur stands up to even the most voracious chewers.

NYLABONE DOUBLE CHEW: This great chew combines the dental health benefits of a ridged rubber center with traditional Nylabone ends to promote healthy teeth and create a relaxed pup.

NYLABONE FLEXIBLE CHEW: A variation on the Dental Dinosaur, this chew is more flexible but still stands up to rough chewing.

For Puppies

★ **COMFORT PUP:** Made to ease alone times and training for puppies, this brilliant bed has a secured plush dog and an internal heartbeat to lull pups into a deep sleep. Also can be used for the geriatric dog.

COOL PUPPY TEETHING STICK: Similar to human teething rings, this colorful stick is made of crinkly fabrics and soft materials. Can be frozen for extra teething relief.

KONG PUPPY TEETHING STICK: This rubber stick from Kong is designed with dental ridges and soft rubber to soothe teething puppies. Doubles as a work-to-eat puzzle with a central cavity for soft foods.

NYLABONE PUPPY TEETHING KEYS: This set of keys is made of a soft plastic formulated especially for little puppy teeth.

NYLABONE PUPPYFISH TEETHING TOYS: Cute and useful, these hard gel toys are designed with a colorful skeleton surrounded by a glow-in-the dark body. Specially formulated for oral health, they help promote the correct development for a puppy's all-important choppers.

PETSTAGES CHEW TOYS: Petstages, an innovative and revolutionary toy company, has thought of everything when it comes to puppy's young development. Each of these toys has a developmental purpose such as teething, chewing, brain development, and puzzle solving skills.

SNUGGLE PUPPY: Snuggle Puppy is a stand-alone plush puppy designed to bed down or cuddle with your young puppy. Complete with a heartbeat and warming component, its creative design makes snuggling easy. Great for geriatric and anxious dogs, too.

★ **SNUGGLE SAFE WARMING DISK:** A few minutes in the microwave warms this disk for hours. Slip it in your puppy's bed or in its included fleeced pouch for a relaxation-inducing experience. Also great for older and anxious dogs.

For Geriatric and Special Needs Dogs

★ **ADJUSTABLE DOUBLE DINER:** Sometimes just dipping his head or reaching his neck can be painful for the geriatric dog. This sliding mount enables you to adjust his food bowls to a position he can eat comfortably in.

COMFORT LIFT CARRIER: Whether your dog is recovering from surgery or suffers from arthritis or joint pain, this sling slides under your dog's hindquarters for an ergonomic lift for both human and canine.

GUARDIAN GEAR ALL-PURPOSE PET TRAVELER: Just because your dog no longer enjoys walks due to painful bones and joints doesn't mean he can't accompany you on your regular outings. Treat him to a stylish stroller that doubles as an under-arm carrier.

ORTHOPEDIC DOG BED: This bed is made of several layers of orthopedic padding. Meant to keep sore bones and joints warm and comfy, it does wonders for the dog experiencing discomfort.

★ **PET RAMP FOR CAR:** The pup who could jump enthusiastically into the back of the car as a babe is unlikely to be able to continue to do so in his older years. This handy telescoping ramp fits into the back of your car and folds for low-profile storage.

PET STEPS: Perfect for the arthritic or sore pet, these steps are both attractive and functional. Ideal for the aging canine.

PETSAFE WELLNESS SLEEPER (HEATED): This specialized bed is equipped with an internal warmer. Great for older and/or arthritic dogs.

POOCH PANTS: Just like older people, older dogs have a higher occurrence of incontinence. These potty pants come with disposable or washable liners and feature rubber construction to avoid accidents.

Potty Tools

★ **DOGGY LOO FIRE HYDRANT:** This attractive fire hydrant is just the thing to help teach male dogs where to go. Especially wonderful for the inside "marker," the Doggy Loo Fire Hydrant can be placed outdoors in your pet's potty area.

PETAPOTTY INDOOR PET POTTY: Attractive and very user-friendly, the PETaPOTTY is a clean, hassle-free option for dogs trained to potty inside. Synthetic lawn and a pull-out urine tray make cleaning a cinch.

PUP HEAD: This low-profile potty substrate combines the beauty of grass with a clean, low-odor, antimicrobial design that dogs are quickly drawn to. The easy-to-drain inner tray is fitted with a sturdy internal grate.

PURINA DOG LITTER BOX AND LITTER: Dog litter and boxes have become a popular alternative to messy pads and papers. The specially designed box allows dogs to walk in easily, and absorbent litter keeps odors down and makes cleanup easy.

WIZDOG INDOOR POTTY: A more economic alternative to the PETaPOTTY, the Wizdog features a sturdy plastic tray fitted with permeable plastic mesh. Absorbent disposable material used to collect urine and feces is removed from the surface for disposal.

Basic Training Necessities

CLIP-ON BAIT POUCH: A bait pouch is required to keep pockets clean while training with bait. Clip-on models are easy to use and can be snapped on a belt on the way out the door.

COTTON LONG LINE: Although not necessary, a light cotton training lead of fifteen to thirty feet can be invaluable in training a long-distance recall, retrieving, and other distance cues.

FLAT LEASH WITH SAFETY SNAP: A flat leash is a training necessity as retractable leashes do not offer control or safety. While the common trigger snap on most leashes can come loose and release your dog unexpectedly, the safety snap is almost foolproof.

★ **GENTLE LEADER® EASY WALK™ HARNESS:** An absolute essential for the puller, this innovative harness latches at the front of your dog's body instead of his back. By diffusing the power of his weight at the end of the leash, this is a magnificent tool and is approved by numerous animal welfare organizations.

★ **GENTLE LEADER HEAD COLLAR:** A favorite of animal welfare organizations across the nation, the Gentle Leader is a kind alternative to prong and pinch collars, choke chains, and the like to manage the enthusiastic leash puller. While the tool is highly effective once your dog is used to it, it does require desensitization before use.

I-CLICK (FOR SOUND-SENSITIVE DOGS): Designed especially for dogs who are afraid of the original clicker because of its volume and pitch, the i-Click is not only softer on dog's ears but is also comfortable in your hand.

★ **MARTINGALE NO-SLIP COLLAR:** One of the safest collars on the market, the Martingale No-Slip Collar hangs loosely around your dog's neck but pulls shut if he attempts to back his head through it.

NATURAL BALANCE TRAINING BAIT: This training essential is formulated like a dog food rather than a treat. As such, it is lower in calories, higher in protein, and is more palatable than kibble and cookies. Affordable and easy to prepare and store, it's a favorite of trainers.

ORIGINAL CLICKER: A behavior "marker," the original clicker emits a loud succinct chirping sound that is salient to the canine ear.

PREMIER BREAKAWAY COLLAR: The breakaway collar is essential for dogs in play with other dogs or those left alone while wearing their collar. The breakaway stays firmly latched while your dog is leashed but will break loose if he gets caught in a situation where enough pressure is put on his collar to inflict harm.

QUICK DRAW PROFESSIONAL BAIT POUCH: For the more serious trainer, a professional bait pouch is a staple. With a durable canvas exterior, a breathable rubber interior, and adjustable belt, and a quick draw mouth, it's the perfect tool.

QUIET SPOT PET TAG SILENCER: It is necessary to keep your dog's tags on him at all times, but that doesn't mean they must jangle and cause an annoying cacophony. The neoprene pocket-like Quiet Spot Pet Tag Silencer slips over your dog's tags and Velcros in place.

TRADITIONAL HARNESS: The traditional harness, one that latches in the back, is a perfectly good collar alternative. Also great for dogs with tracheal problems and back/neck soreness.

Noteworthy Specialty Products

★ ANXIETY WRAP: This very clever garment uses the phenomenon of "maintained pressure" to calm a dog. Similar to bundling an infant, the anxiety wrap can be used for dogs exhibiting anxiety in any situation.

GLOBAL GPS PET FINDER: Use your cell phone or the Web to monitor the whereabouts of your dog with Global Positioning System (GPS) precision. Great to help relocate an escapee.

PREMIER CALMING CAP: This product is designed to help soothe dogs who are overly stimulated by visual cues. Made of a somewhat transparent sheer fabric panel, the cap makes a dog's vision indistinct. Useful for car rides, vet visits, desensitization, and anxiety.

★ **ROADIE SEAT BELT:** Not only does a good seat belt keep your dog safe when traveling in the car, but also it can actually help him learn to stay still and calm.

SPORN ANTI-PULL HARNESS: The Sporn training harness is an alternative to the Gentle Leaders and Sensation Harness. Also kind and gentle, this tool is very effective for the avid on-leash puller.

Confinement and Management Necessities

BOW HAUS DOG CRATE: An attractive alternative to traditional crates, the Bow Haus proves that even crates can be an attractive home furnishing. This clever tool moonlights as an occasional table.

★ **EXERCISE PEN (EXPEN):** A must-have for any dog owner, this vital tool comes in handy from the first day you bring your new pup home. As a stand-alone or bent around a large opening, the expen is sturdy, safe, and can fold away to fit under a bed or behind a door.

PRESSURE GATE: Less sturdy than other gates but still very useful, the pressure gate goes up quickly and preserves doorways from screw holes or other damage.

SEMI-PERMANENT CONFINEMENT GATE: An attractive barrier for your home, the semi-permanent gate uses pressure to fix in place but features a swinging gate for easy pass-through.

★ **TRADITIONAL METAL CRATE:** A crate is a necessity and a metal option may be just the thing. Especially great for hot climates because it allows for good circulation, the metal crate is sturdy, extremely useful, and many models fold for easy transport.

★ **TRADITIONAL PLASTIC CRATE:** A common confinement option, the plastic crate is a cozy and useful must-have.

Index

About the Author

Cristine Dahl is the founder and owner of the Seattle Dogworks Training & Education Studio in Seattle (www.seattledogworks.com). She holds a Certificate in Training and Counseling from the San Francisco SPCA Academy and a BS in Biological Science with a focus on mammalian mind and brain matters. She has worked professionally with horses and dogs for fifteen years. Cristine is also the founder and director of the acclaimed Canine Studies Program designed for those seeking an intense education in companion canine behavior.

Identified as a distinguished graduate of the SPCA Academy, Cristine has been a featured speaker at the Seattle Pet Expo, has written for various publications (including *Our Animals*, *CityDog Magazine*, and *The Chronicle*), and has been recognized by the American Medical Association for her work helping doctors better understand the circumstances surrounding dogs biting children. She writes regularly as drugstore.com's in-house dog expert and as *Seattle Dog Magazine*'s training and behavior expert.

Cristine and her husband, Anders, reside in Seattle with their two dogs, Maddison and Ollie.

Jean Donaldson is the founder and director of the San Francisco SPCA Academy for Dog Trainers. The award-winning author of *The Culture Clash*, *MINE!*, and *FIGHT!*, she lives in San Francisco, CA.